PRISONERS IN PARADISE

PRISONERS IN PARADISE

*American Women in
the Wartime South Pacific*

THERESA KAMINSKI

UNIVERSITY PRESS OF KANSAS

Published by the University Press of Kansas (Lawrence, Kansas 66049), which was
organized by the Kansas Board of Regents and is operated and funded by Emporia
State University, Fort Hays State University, Kansas State University, Pittsburg
State University, the University of Kansas, and Wichita State University.

Library of Congress Cataloging-in-Publication Data

Kaminski, Theresa, 1958–
Prisoners in paradise : American women in the wartime South Pacific /
Theresa Kaminski.
p.   cm.
Includes bibliographical references and index.
ISBN 0-7006-1003-0 (cloth : alk. paper)
1. World War, 1939–1945—Prisoners and prisons, Japanese.   2. Women
prisoners—Philippines—History—20th century.   3. Prisoners of war—United
States—History—20th century.   I. Title.
D805.P6 K36 2000
940.54'7252'09599—dc21   99-047059

British Library Cataloguing in Publication Data is available.

Printed in the United States of America
10 9 8 7 6 5 4 3 2 1

The paper used in this publication meets the minimum requirements of the
American National Standard for Permanence of Paper for Printed Library Materials
Z39.48-1984.

For my parents, Michael and Irene Kaminski,
who got me started.

For my husband, Charles Clark,
and my son, Samuel Kaminski Clark,
who keep me going.

And in loving memory of my grandmothers,
Martha Lewis and Lillian Kaminski Bacchiere,
both of whom gave me so much.

CONTENTS

ACKNOWLEDGMENTS

I have incurred many debts along this road to publication and gratefully acknowledge them here. The American Association of University Women awarded funding, through its American Fellows Summer Faculty Leave Fellowships, for a crucial summer of research. The University of Wisconsin–Stevens Point provided support in a variety of ways: the University Personnel Development Committee granted additional funding; Christine Neidlein and her staff of the Interlibrary Loan Department kept my traveling to a minimum; John Smith in Art and Design and his student Rebecca Hedtke fine-tuned the maps. The Institute for Research in the Humanities at the University of Wisconsin–Madison allowed me a productive writing year, and Paul Boyer, its director, provided a stimulating intellectual environment.

Douglas E. Clanin of the Indiana Historical Society launched me on the long road of important contacts. Jan K. Herman of the Navy Medical Department and Major Constance J. Moore, Army Nurse Corps historian, gave invaluable assistance with information about the military nurses. Former internees and evaders copiously and patiently discussed their experiences and their perceptions of those experiences. I especially thank Nora Ream Kuttner, Betsy Herold Heimke, Dorothy Dore Dowlen, James R. Halsema, Dorothy Janson, Peter Wygle, Margaret Sams, Betty Foley, and Charlotte Brussolo. Many others shared additional insights; I regret I could not name all of them in this book.

Scholarly advice came from Frances Cogan, Carol Petillo, Beth Bailey, Sonya Michel, Gretchen Kreuter, and Elizabeth Norman. Susan Brewer and Leslie Midkiff DeBauche, elegantly eloquent scholars, forced me to face tough questions, while William B. Skelton prompted me to reevaluate some military issues. Elizabeth Dunn, a superior friend and colleague, patiently followed the fortunes of this book and offered great suggestions. Meaghan Pack helped me live through the writing of an early draft when we shared Hamilton House in Madison, both of us separated from our families in order to pursue necessary scholarly work but unfailingly drawn home each weekend by radar love.

My family, large and boisterous, has cheered me on since the beginning of this project; that enthusiasm has kept my spirits up. Michael Kaminski, who provided the original map designs, came to know the Philippines because of a different war, and somehow I picked up on the belief that those islands are wonderful. He and our cousin, Tony Martin, brought back some very helpful books, photographs, and videos from their trip there in 1997. I still owe them a case of San Miguel. Irene Kaminski, thinking like a mother, posed the provocative question of whether or not American women today would fare so well under similar circumstances.

Nancy Scott Jackson at the University Press of Kansas recognized the potential of this manuscript, and she and Kerry Callahan ably guided it through the final revision.

Nothing in my life is possible without my husband, Charles Clark, who patiently took time from his own pressing scholarly pursuits to read and comment on a draft of this book. He also helped with computer and other intellectual snafus. Our son, Sam, the very best part of my life, loved this book from the beginning, especially the rough drafts, which made such good drawing paper. He believes that all of this attention to books is quite normal, and he already shares his parents' passion for reading, writing, and thinking about history. To paraphrase Agnes Newton Keith, we face everything together, all three.

Finally, this book is for all of the women of the South Pacific who endured and survived World War II. It is so everyone will know.

INTRODUCTION

"We are waiting for America."

Natalie Crouter, a forty-six-year-old American wife and mother living in the Philippine Islands, sat down at the end of an evening in late October 1942 to write in her diary, a daily exercise for her since the previous November. She recounted a school pageant, which her two children, Fred and June, participated in, celebrating both Halloween and Thanksgiving. Natalie carefully described the stage setting and the costumes but was especially moved by the Thanksgiving portion of the pageant that retold the familiar story of the first Thanksgiving feast at Plymouth Rock. With the United States almost one year into World War II, the story of the Pilgrims and Native Americans meant something even more to Natalie who, as a prisoner of the Japanese, felt a personal connection to the tale of newcomers in a strange land worrying about food, getting along with an alien population, and just surviving. She ended her entry that evening lamenting that "we are waiting for America."[1]

Contemporaries of Natalie's sneaking a peak at that diary entry may have regarded those five words as an opening phrase that would end with "to win this war." Her counterparts on the home front, as well, waited, hoped, and prayed for the United States to win its arduous battle against the Axis powers of Germany, Japan, and Italy. But American women did not wait in idleness. Just like their foremothers during the Revolution, Civil War, and World War I they expressed their patriotism and understanding of American womanhood through action, showing their support for the Allied cause by taking up a variety of war-related work ranging from riveting in airplane factories to enlisting in the armed forces to serving donuts and lemonade at USO socials.[2] Stretching traditional wife and mother roles was acceptable to most Americans because the changes were only for the duration; victory remained the central concern of Americans. Women worked and waited from December 1941 to August 1945, sometimes patiently and optimistically, other times in anguish and despair, for the war to end.

In many ways, Natalie Crouter waited for victory just like other American wives and mothers. She kept a close eye on the activities of her two children, monitoring their progress in school, keeping track of their friends and leisure-time activities, worrying about their health, and discussing the war and its possible implications for their future. A smart and resourceful woman, Natalie adjusted to doing without materials and foodstuffs, substituting new items into her family's wardrobe and diet to replace the unattainable ones. She generally expressed optimism for a decisive Allied victory, but at times she despaired because it was taking so long. In all of this, Natalie represented a typical middle-class American housewife.

But Natalie, interned since late December 1941, knew that only an Allied victory, spearheaded by American forces, would ensure her liberation and save her life. Coinciding with their attack on Pearl Harbor on December 7, 1941, the Japanese struck at other American territories including Guam and the Philippine Islands, and the trapped American civilians became enemy aliens. To prevent sabotage, humiliate the Allies, and hold on to possible bargaining chips, the Japanese rounded up all Allied citizens including Americans, Canadians, British nationals, and Australians. Natalie, her husband, Jerry, and Fred and June were interned along with about five hundred other civilians in Baguio, a mountain resort city and summer capital north of Manila on the island of Luzon. Altogether, close to fourteen thousand American civilians spent about three years as prisoners of the Japanese.[3] Most of them were concentrated in the Philippines: in Baguio, in Manila on the campus of Santo Tomas University, and at a nearby agricultural college in Los Banos; other Americans abided internment in China, Borneo, and the nearby island of Celebes.

The Crouter family was relatively lucky, since they managed to stay together in the same camp. Natalie carried on her duties as wife and mother as normally as possible, and Jerry, housed in a separate barrack, remained close by to help. Still, internment altered normal family life, as husbands and wives experienced changes in the typical, if ideal, male-female roles of the 1940s, where the husband went off to work and the wife stayed home to mind the housekeeping and the children. Internees struggled to maintain this sense of normality even though their families had been divided, but basic survival in enemy-occupied territory concerned them the most. From the beginning of their conquests, the Japanese proved unwilling to divert their precious resources to the sustenance of captured civilians, so captives spent their own money, arranged loans, relied on outside gifts, and bartered with indigenous civilians to secure food, clothing, and medicine. They also built shelters and furniture, made clothing from scraps of material and string, and, near the end of the war, created food from garbage and insects. Women who prior to the war normally had servants to perform housework and child care pitched in, took on heavier work burdens, and altered and stretched acceptable meanings of "woman" and "mother" to make sure that everyone lived until the Americans liberated them.

In their accounts of the war years, Natalie Crouter and other women used the words "prisoner" and "internee" interchangeably, indicating their ambiguous position in enemy-occupied territory. The Japanese generally ignored the 1929 Geneva Convention Relative to the Treatment of Prisoners of War, a transgression evident in their egregious treatment of military prisoners, but they also claimed that the convention did not apply to civilians. The treatment of civilians in war zones was not specifically addressed until the Geneva Convention IV of 1949, so captured Americans endured a diplomatic limbo, which jeopardized their lives. By insisting that these civilians were "internees," the Japanese claimed to be protecting them from local populations who allegedly hated and distrusted Caucasians; therefore, the internment camps served as "safe havens" for Allied nationals. But the internees understood that they were prisoners, captives, detained because of the war and because of their nationality.[4]

The Japanese did not only intern civilian women, further complicating categorization. When Manila fell to the Japanese at the end of December, eleven navy nurses were forced to give up their duties at the U.S. naval base and were taken to Santo Tomas, where sixty-seven army nurses eventually joined them after the surrender of Corregidor in May 1942. These professional women, without husbands or families, were welcomed by the internees for their health care skills, which were much needed in the camp. The Japanese had no conception of women as members of the military and so treated them as civilians, separating them from the American soldiers; though the Japanese refused to recognize their military status, the nurses considered themselves prisoners of war. Reflecting these ambiguities, I use the words internee, prisoner, and captive interchangeably throughout this book.

For some American women, being "caught" by the Japanese was not a literal reality: while entrapped by the invasion and occupation, they waited for American rescue outside the confines of internment camps. Most who evaded internment for all or part of the war did so by hiding out in the mountains of the Philippines, anticipating that they could stay hidden from Japanese troops for as long as necessary. Several Americans associated with Silliman University, a Presbyterian institution on the island of Negros, chose this option. Teachers, including Jim and Virginia McKinley and Gardner and Viola Winn, packed up their families and fled to the hills in the wake of the Japanese advance. Other women, like Claire Phillips and Margaret Utinsky, stayed out of internment by hiding their nationality, allowing them to spy on the Japanese and aid American and Filipino prisoners in every way possible. These evaders, like the interned women, had to adapt quickly to their new situation if they were going to survive the war.

GENDER, WOMANHOOD, AND FAMILY

This book is a story of survival. It examines the experiences of women whose perseverance during World War II was bolstered by their varying beliefs of what it meant to be an American woman. Whether civilian or military, internee or evader, their perceptions of gender roles and womanhood provided them with the strength to survive their ordeals.

Reflecting on her wartime experiences, Agnes Newton Keith, one of the American captives on Borneo, observed that "in war, we women must fight with all of ourselves." While Agnes certainly referred to what happened to women on that island, she also implied that women in other places and at other times would have to rise to a similar challenge—men are not the only ones who fight in wars. Some forty years after her remarks historians and literary scholars began examining war as a "gendering activity": as boundaries between war zones and the home front blur, war involves and changes women as much as it does men. American women in the South Pacific were captives in a war zone, which put their lives at risk almost as much as if they had been soldiers. Instead of traditional combat, however, women fought to keep their families together and healthy, struggling with changes in their work habits to accomplish this, while Japanese soldiers, armed with guns, controlled their lives. Additionally, as Victoria Bynum argues, war sometimes "upset the boundaries of gender and race," complicating the "gendering activity" of war.[5] American women in the South Pacific lost their privileged colonial lifestyle, which had made their lives a paradise, found themselves at the mercy of people they considered racially inferior, and strove to make sense of this reversal by stubbornly insisting that it was a temporary fluke.

Even in a specific time and place, among a certain group of people, meanings of womanhood will be debated and contested in an attempt to establish and abide by a "norm." Gail Bederman has described gender as a "continual, dynamic process" rife with "contradictory ideas."[6] This process can be found in the internment camps and in places of hiding as American women tried to adjust their perceptions of womanhood to the realities of their wartime situation. Women grappled with, among other things, changes in their work patterns, contributions to camp organization and politics, and perceptions of femininity, and they considered how these changes affected their womanhood. Those who left accounts of their experiences had been among the privileged classes in the South Pacific, so these changes were not simple, since for them womanhood was deeply entangled with race and social standing.

"Womanhood" is used herein as a descriptive term for the shifting roles and actions of the white middle-class woman in the first decades of the twentieth century, the woman most likely to make her way to the South Pacific.[7] By 1900, more of these women had access to higher education and employment in traditionally female fields such as teaching, nursing, and social work, yet the majority believed that employment was temporary, that the fulfillment of their nature was best expressed through marriage and motherhood. Wedding vows contained the pledge to love, honor, and obey; therefore, faithfulness and obedience to or cooperation with a husband made a woman a "good" wife. Additionally, one of the cornerstones of being a "proper" wife also meant being a "good" mother, and the sum of these activities equaled womanhood. Yet in choosing a life outside of the United States, these women demonstrated a bent for the unconventional—even if they did live within Caucasian colonial communities with plenty of hired help—and proved to be the ones most likely to survive an unexpected ordeal.

War and internment put enormous stress on traditional womanhood. "Lucky" women like Natalie Crouter remained both wife and mother, although she had to negotiate slightly altered versions of both during internment, especially since she lived apart from Jerry. "Unlucky" women—Elizabeth Vaughan, for example—endured the war with a fractured family and a new burden of responsibilities. After getting trapped in Manila after the bombing of Pearl Harbor, Elizabeth's husband, Jim, joined the United States Armed Forces Far East, leaving her in sole charge of their two pre–school-age children. Prior to the war Filipino servants cleaned, cooked, and watched the children, so Elizabeth had a lot to learn during internment. She quickly grasped the importance of being a full-time mother and housekeeper, but she became a wife without a husband, something she had never expected. Margaret Sherk found herself in a similar situation, but she stretched the boundaries of acceptable behavior, discarding honor, faithfulness, and obedience to guarantee that she and her son survived internment: she began an adulterous affair. The choices Margaret made appeared satisfactory and rational to her, given the circumstances; other internees labeled her a bad woman and a bad mother.

These women had all become mothers during the overlapping eras of "scientific motherhood" and the "permissive era" of mothering in the 1920s and 1930s. As mothers they relied on the knowledge of experts to help them raise their children but also focused on instinctive motherly love as central to children's development, which they increasingly relied on during the war to keep them from being labeled bad mothers. Although most women did not make the same choice as Margaret Sherk, they worried that people in the United States unfamiliar with their peculiar situation would view them as bad mothers. According to categories later established by historians Molly Ladd-Taylor and Lauri Umansky, women caught by the Japanese fell into one or two general groups of women perceived as bad mothers: "Those who did not live in a 'traditional' nuclear family [and] those who would not or could not protect their children from harm."[8] Though the war forced these alterations, some women were anxious to set the historical record straight by writing autobiographies to show that they had been conducting themselves properly, that the war and the Japanese caused them to do things they normally would not have done so they could preserve their families.

NATIONAL IDENTITY AND PATRIOTISM

To be a good woman was to be a patriotic American, a link made back in the years immediately following the American Revolution when women were encouraged to become staunch "Republican Mothers." They embraced this role to secure their position in the new United States and to prove that they could raise the kind of citizens the young country required. Republican motherhood also provided women with a strong argument in favor of female education, a movement that gained momentum in the early nineteenth century and provided an array of benefits, mostly for white middle-class women.[9] Although kept from complete political involvement until 1920 when they won the universal right to vote, American women long understood their crucial connection to the state, considering their womanhood interwoven with citizenship and loyalty to country.

American women caught by the Japanese during the war demonstrated their patriotism but occasionally despaired over their fate, and at certain times boredom and the struggle for survival superseded patriotic sentiment. Categorized as enemy aliens, these women tried to hold on to and emphasize the positive characteristics that composed their national identity. In one of her studies, Lynn Bloom listed the "quintessentially American" traits the Baguio internees believed in: "education, ingenuity and resourcefulness, democracy and cooperation, family solidarity, and the exercise of religion, free speech (even in the face of strict Japanese censorship), and a sense of humor."[10] Baguio, like the other camps, consisted of Allied nationals in addition to Americans, people likely to take exception to the assumption that the above attributes were *peculiarly* American. What, then, distinguished Americans from the rest of the interned Allies? When thrown together with other Allied nationals during the war, as subjects of countries who had been trounced by the enemy, how did the Americans retain their pride of citizenship and a sense of superiority over the Japanese as well as the other nationals?

Perhaps national pride led Americans to believe that Japanese victories were temporary, that the strength of the U.S. military would bring about their final defeat, a strength indicated in American newspapers and magazines sent to the Pacific in the late 1930s and by the American military personnel stationed there. By early 1942, when Americans had been interned or had gone into hiding in the Philippines and adjacent areas, the Germans had overrun most of Europe, invaded the Soviet Union, and launched the Battle of Britain. The Axis powers appeared invincible. Americans caught in the Pacific drew comfort from their belief that only the United States had the industrial and manpower capabilities to coordinate a sustained war against their enemies.

This hope about American military prowess gained an additional boost from American racial views. John Dower has shown that Americans believed the Japanese to be an inferior race, physically and intellectually incapable of conducting a successful war. Even when the

Japanese clearly dominated the military situation, Americans rationalized that they could not hold it indefinitely.[11] The combination of
these beliefs, about the military and about race, provided the Americans with a great deal of strength to survive their ordeal in the Pacific.
They could, then, recite Natalie Crouter's line "we are waiting for
America" with pride and trust as they glanced at the skies for signs of
their liberation.

SOURCES, APPROACH, AND ORGANIZATION

Most of the over fifty primary sources for this book come from what
Sidonie Smith describes as a broad range of autobiography: women's
letters, journals, diaries, oral histories, and memoirs.[12] Several of these,
written predominantly by middle-class white women, were published
after the war by trade, university, and vanity presses, but few of them
received any serious attention, perpetuating the belief that war is primarily about men and the military. As a historian of American women,
I chose to focus on autobiographies not to analyze their literary merits,
but to mine them for their historical value of reflection on and interpretation of the authors' wartime experiences.

Memory and bias must be acknowledged in any body of sources.
These autobiographies span the decades of the 1940s to the 1990s;
some are diaries written during the war, some are memoirs crafted later
from wartime diaries, and others are memoirs composed from recollections of events that took place decades ago, so accurate memory
can be a problem. Race and class are important as well. These middle-
class white women enjoyed a privileged colonial life in their paradise,
generally assuming a racial superiority over the colonized as well as
their own conquerors. The fact that white middle-class women gen-
erated most of these autobiographies indicates that the story of women's
internment is not complete, since the voices of less privileged women
and women of color are muted. Unable to expand the class and race
categories, I stretched the geographic boundaries to demonstrate how
location and camp commandants and guards affected women's survival. Almost all of the American women were caught in the Philippines, but Agnes Keith and Darlene Deibler, interned on Borneo and
Celebes respectively, endured especially brutal conditions during the
war, while Emily Hahn, trapped in Hong Kong, used deceptions and
acquaintances to evade internment.

These sources, despite memory lapses or biases, serve as reliable corroboration of basic time lines and events. They also, as Lynn Bloom has shown, put the autobiographer in the "star" position, center stage among hundreds or thousands in camp or within various communities of evaders, a position that helps the writer maintain her sense of personal identity amidst a chaotic situation.[13] This focus or self-awareness cannot strictly be construed as selfish, although the autobiographies do function as explanations and defenses of actions taken that outsiders might consider inappropriate or dangerous for women. Maintaining self-identity helped these women cope and survive; it provided them with strength and purpose to endure the war. And clearly the women who wrote autobiographies were "stars": they were survivors, patriotic women, (usually) faithful wives, good mothers, hard workers, and had come to view their wartime experiences in a positive way. Women who failed in more than one of these categories have thus far left no accounts.

Central to the intersection of women's history and autobiography are the subjects of family and motherhood. War changed women's traditional functions; women took it upon themselves to explain how and why—a right they claimed as good American women. In writing (and in some cases publishing) their autobiographies, these women circuitously asserted, even if they expressly denied, that they were in the best position to elucidate the events of the war, to preserve these memories for their children and their descendents. They put themselves in the star position as author and interpreter but insisted on espousing womanly reasons for doing so: they wrote a family story, which, as wife and mother, they were entitled to do.

Available secondary sources only touch tangentially on this aspect of American women in World War II. During the 1980s and 1990s, some scholars turned their attention to the subject of women and war, mostly focusing on the home front or the military, but the women in this book do not turn up in those studies. General works on the relationship between the Philippines and the United States do not dwell on the topic. The scholarship on wartime concentration camps is vast but does not mirror what these women experienced; in Europe, the Nazis targeted Jews for extermination because of racial hatred, not military necessity. Carol Rittner and John K. Roth argue that more Jewish women than men died in Nazi death camps because the Nazis were dedicated to eliminating the childbearers of the Jewish race. The U.S. government set up camps for Japanese Americans, most of whom were citizens, out of a baseless fear that they supported the Japanese war effort. Japanese

Americans experienced complex changes as a result of their internment; some became increasingly Americanized, while others clung even more tightly to their Japanese heritage.[14]

American women in the South Pacific found themselves interned because of their race only insofar as it was connected to their enemy status, so there was no question of a violation of civil liberties; these women were not citizens of the countries in which they resided. The Japanese, while viewing Caucasians as inferiors, had no plans for systematic annihilation, but they worked their military prisoners to death if need be and adopted a laissez-faire attitude toward the civilian internees. American women realized their perilous position from the very beginning of the war. To survive internment or evasion they would have to alter most of what they knew from their prewar life; they would have to organize, compromise, and work just to make it through those years, shifting their perceptions of womanhood to make survival possible.

Organized both chronologically and topically, this book begins with the arrival of American women in the South Pacific (an area today referred to as the Pacific Rim but at the time also called the Orient or the Far East) at the turn of the century, traces their activities during the war, and carries them through liberation and its immediate aftermath.[15] It also explores specific topics such as camp organization, work, family and private lives, and evasion. How American women came to the South Pacific and why they chose to stay despite the growing threat from the Japanese are discussed in Chapter 1. Taking the women into internment and showing how they contributed to camp organization and politics are the topics of Chapter 2. Chapter 3 examines the various types of work that women did in the camps, while Chapter 4 looks at the effects of internment on women's private lives. The motivations and activities of women who managed to evade internment are highlighted in Chapters 5 and 6; how the internees were finally freed is explained in Chapter 7. The common threads running through all of the chapters are perceptions of womanhood and national identity and how they provided the necessary support for women to survive their ordeal. In this book I have attempted to show how these women used womanhood and national identity as their primary weapons in the struggle to survive a totally unexpected chapter in their lives.

1

WOMEN'S DUTY AND THE DECISION TO STAY IN THE PACIFIC

"If we were born to war in our time, then we would face it together."

Agnes Newton Keith, the attractive dark-haired American wife of a British civil servant stationed in Sandakan, North Borneo, sat listening to the European war news on the family radio one day in early 1941. Agnes, a former journalist and the author of the book *Land Below the Wind*, an affectionate account of her first years on Borneo, kept a sharp eye on world events, especially the developments of the Second World War. Her husband Harry's country was already at war with the Axis powers, so Agnes considered herself involved as well. Though it was being fought thousands of miles away on a different continent, the conflict had personal and immediate implications for her. She later wrote: "Homes like ours were being blown to bits, babies like George were being killed, lives like our own were destroyed and loves like ours were torn apart. Thus in the shadow of Europe's destruction, we waited with dreadful certainty for Pearl Harbor."[1]

The main question in the minds of the Keiths was whether Agnes and their toddler son George should leave Borneo and return to the United States. Members of the small Caucasian community in Sandakan strongly believed that the war would widen into the Pacific, drawing the United States into a fight against the Axis powers. The only question was when. The Japanese launched a major attack against China in 1937; by 1941 it was clear that they had designs on all of Southeast Asia, making Malaya, Borneo, Java, New Guinea, and the Philippine Islands likely targets. All contained a "European" or Caucasian population, both civilian and military, including women and children. What would become of them?

The Keiths' decision mirrored one made by thousands of other Allied families in the Pacific theater: they stayed together and they stayed put. For Agnes, her life was with her husband and her son: "If we were born to war in our time, then we would face it together, all three."[2] Given this strong determination, what was the appeal of the South Pacific to American women? What were their reasons for venturing there at the turn of the century? As war drew closer, how did they use concepts of womanly duty and definitions of an American identity as justifications for remaining?

WOMEN MISSIONARIES IN AMERICA'S EMPIRE

Agnes Keith was one of thousands of American women living in the Pacific during the first half of the twentieth century. White middle-class women began arriving in large numbers at the turn of the new century for a variety of reasons, most of which were connected with the United States' first major imperialist ventures and with the broad progressive spirit that swept America. Throughout the 1800s, as American traders sought profitable business enterprises in the Far East, the U.S. government quickly backed up these private actions with formal trade agreements with China, Japan, Hawaii, and other countries in the region. This desire for free trade guaranteed that the United States would be drawn into a power struggle for dominance in the Pacific region.

The United States proceeded to carve out its sphere of influence in the Pacific throughout the nineteenth century by forcing open trade relations with Japan in the 1850s, purchasing Alaska from the Russians in 1867, annexing Hawaii in 1898, going to war with Spain over Cuba that same year, and issuing the first of the "Open Door" notes regarding trade in China in 1899. Winning the war with Spain resulted in the United States launching its first major overseas imperialist venture by purchasing the Spanish possessions of Guam, Puerto Rico, and the Philippine Islands. The Philippines were considered a special prize because of their close proximity to China and Japan; they provided the United States with a strong trading presence in the Pacific area.

However, most Filipinos, expecting self-rule at the conclusion of the Spanish-American War, resented the decision of the Americans to retain direct control over the islands, and in 1899 Filipino nationalist Emilio Aguinaldo launched a bloody three-year rebellion against the Americans. With the insurrectionists subdued, disregarding the Filipinos' readiness or inclination, the United States began a decades-long program of American acculturation designed to prepare the Filipinos for self-rule. The goal, according to President William McKinley, was "benevolent assimilation," with the Filipinos learning how to appreciate American democracy and American capitalism.[3] And while Filipinos might become assimilated or acculturated, they could not technically become "American" because even though Filipinos were made nationals of the United States, they were not entitled to all the privileges of full citizenship. Despite any good intentions on the part of the Americans, the Filipinos were generally treated as second-class citizens in their own country.

Trade was not the only thing that attracted Americans to the Pacific; once they realized the presence of many non-Christians there, men and women of different Protestant denominations embarked on foreign travel in order to spread Christianity. The American Board of Commissioners for Foreign Missions sent male and female missionaries to Hawaii for the first time in 1820; Protestant missionaries arrived in Canton, China, in 1829. During the 1890s, these religious workers also exhibited the new nationalist spirit, which had been sweeping the United States during the post–Civil War decades and was most vehemently expressed through the acquisition of overseas territories. Missionaries, inspired by the social gospel movement that preached a Christian responsibility to see that all people had education, sound health, jobs, and good living conditions, enthusiastically took up the task of blending religious instruction with lessons in the American way of life.

Female missionaries figured prominently in these endeavors. Church work constituted an acceptable avocation for American women, since dedication to religion was considered part of their nature, so they enthusiastically participated in organizing Sunday schools, raising funds for church buildings, and training as missionaries to go abroad to spread Christianity. By 1890, married and single women represented 60 percent of foreign missionaries, women who dominated not only by their numbers but also by their determination. In 1900, women from the Women's Foreign Missionary Society of the Methodist Church became the first full-time Methodist missionaries to serve in the Philippines, where they controlled their mission, the largest in the region, ultimately refusing to relinquish their power to male missionaries.[4] Women's missionary work accomplished two contradictory purposes: first, it allowed women to challenge male authority, but only for the sake of God and religion, and second, it spread Christianity, itself a patriarchal institution, with the rationalization that it improved the condition of women.

China, with its millions of non-Christian souls, was a popular destination for female missionaries at the beginning of the twentieth century, where their work represented a way of serving God, a means by which to earn a living, and an adventure. For women who remained single, missionary work gave social sanction to their spinsterhood, ensuring that they would not become economic burdens on their families. Although married missionary women enjoyed a special closeness with their husbands brought about by sharing the same calling, the work also helped them to develop an identity beyond that of wife and mother. Christianity provided the converts with the "proper" religion to save their souls, and it helped lay an Americanized foundation for the Chinese home and family. Anna Kaufman, a Congregationalist missionary in China, maintained that the "greatest sphere for any woman is the sphere of the home" and that she was determined to bring her "deepest and best vision of home and womanhood" to Chinese women.[5] Creating an American Christian home became crucial to the female missionaries as well, because it functioned as a symbol of "civilization" and a reminder of home and family in the United States.

Female missionaries targeted the Philippines for many of the same reasons, but here the connection between Protestantism and nationalism was more plainly articulated because of the colonial relationship between the United States and the islands. At the beginning of the twentieth century, President William McKinley stated that the American acculturation of the Philippines depended upon converting the Filipinos from Spanish Catholicism to Protestantism, and missionaries from a variety of denominations eagerly took up his call. Catholicism, unpopular in the United States with turn-of-the-century reformers who considered it backward and antiprogressive, had to be thwarted and Protestantism introduced if the Philippines were to be modernized.[6] Because of the strong Catholicism introduced by the Spanish, Filipinos proved reluctant to switch from one form of Christianity to another, so the arrival of Protestant missionaries occasioned tensions between the Filipinos and the Americans.

The missionaries persevered and brought not only their religion to the islands, but also a variety of institutions designed to improve the lives of Filipinos, whether the Filipinos wanted them or not. Inspired by the social gospel and progressive movements, the missionaries built hospitals, schools, libraries, and settlement houses. Their responsibility was to save the souls of the Filipinos and to improve their lives on earth as well; the success of these endeavors hinged on the participa-

THE SOUTHWEST PACIFIC AREA (1941)

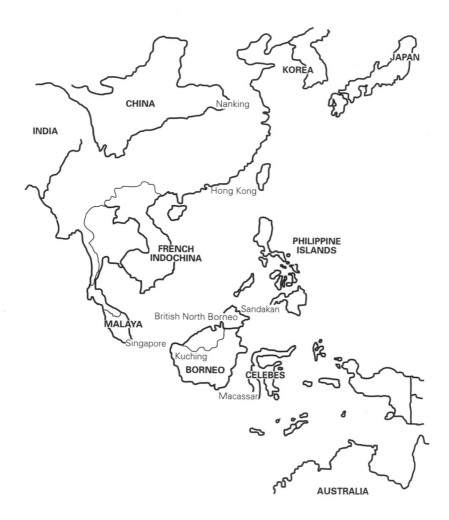

tion of women who had been key players in progressive efforts in the United States. Margaret Payson Waterman, for example, worked at the Rivington Street Settlement in New York City before she headed the Episcopalian settlement house in Tondo in the Philippines.[7]

Since the connection between religion and education was particularly strong, most Protestant denominations established schools in the Philippines, some of which made religious instruction optional rather than mandatory, an indication of the complex and complementary relationship between missionary work and American acculturation. A good example of one of these schools is Silliman University, originally the Silliman Institute. Through a generous gift from a New York business-man, Horace B. Silliman, the Presbyterian Mission in the Philippines established in Dumaguete on the island of Negros in 1901 an industrial school where religion was not among the initial course offerings, but chapel attendance was encouraged.[8]

Although the majority of American missionaries concentrated their efforts in China and the Philippines, a few went to more sparsely popu-lated areas in the Pacific. Darlene Deibler, raised on an Iowa farm, trav-eled with her missionary husband Russell to the Netherlands East Indies (now known as Indonesia) in 1938, settled at mission headquarters in Macassar on the island of Celebes, and carried on their religious work, sometimes together and sometimes separately.[9]

AMERICANIZATION THROUGH EDUCATION

In addition to Christianizing, the U.S. government believed that literacy and education would "civilize" the Filipinos, instruct them in the rights and duties of citizenship, and prepare them for independence. The first appointed American director of education for the Philippines, Fred Atkinson, recruited American teachers to travel to the islands to take part in this progressive endeavor. Thousands applied, and those selected began arriving in Manila in the summer of 1901; the largest single group, about six hundred, arrived in August on board the *Thomas*.[10]

These Thomasites, as the teachers were called, included women in-fused with the progressive spirit, freshly trained at normal schools or more prestigious institutions such as Radcliffe College. Like religious work, teaching acquired a positive reputation as an acceptable type of employment for American women, especially prior to marriage, because the classroom functioned as a kind of home with the students as surro-gate children. Moreover, through education Thomasites not only taught the Filipinos reading, writing, and arithmetic but also the "superior-ity" of the American democratic system. The Division of Education of Cebu issued a report about American teachers in 1902, stating that "every interest of the United States which is properly the concern of an American citizen becomes a matter which we must not only attend to punctiliously, but must rouse zeal for in others who are now under the same flag." These lessons had to start with the basics. Alice M. Kelly arrived in Baguio in October 1901, on an army mule, and began a school for boys, determined to make the Filipinos speak to her "in my own tongue." By 1906 she had set up a school for Igorot girls and succeeded in teaching them not only how to read and write English but also how to weave cloth, thereby making them economically useful in their village. American politicians and educators also believed that teaching the English language to the Filipinos was central to Filipino participation in the expanding Pacific trade, that it would cultivate a "spirit of democracy" in the Filipinos, which would help lead them to self-rule.[11]

Teaching, like missionary work, was not an easy or glamorous job. For the teachers assigned to areas outside of Manila, both housing and schooling facilities appeared crude by American standards, so some women had difficulties turning their new environment into a real "home." Classes often convened in makeshift buildings, teachers usually found themselves without adequate materials, and students frequently skipped classes or showed up late to school. Teachers complained about standards of cleanliness in their houses. Mary Cole, a teacher on Leyte, wrote her parents that pigs ran around her house and that "you never know when the cook is going to wash his feet in the dish pan or wipe them on the tea towel."[12] Mary could not wait for her one-year teaching contract to expire; she had apparently given up on domesticating her students and on turning her house into a home.

However, not all of the American teachers felt this way. Mary Fee, another Thomasite who arrived in 1901, taught in Capiz on the island of Panay, and while her observations about her students characterized the typical paternalistic attitudes of the Americans toward the Filipinos, she possessed a spirit of adventure and an intellectual curiosity about her surroundings. These gave her a different perception of her life and work than Mary Cole had of hers. Mary Fee believed that the Filipinos were a capable people but required firm guidance and much teaching before they could hope to reach their fullest potential. She found that in the presence of firm and fair teachers, Filipino students were "far easier to discipline" than American children, but that at any sign of weakness, the young Filipinos became "infinitely more unruly and arrogant" than their American counterparts. Despite these comments, Mary criticized Americans who had the "habit of uttering generalities about one race on the authority of a single instance." During her six years in the Philippines she also came to regard the islands as very safe and civilized: Mary was impressed by the fact that in all the time she was there, she never locked her house and never heard of any "indignity and disrespect" directed toward American women.[13] When she returned to Chicago, though, she kept her bedroom door locked and for a time feared to walk outside alone, as "civilized" took on a different meaning to her after her years in the Philippines.

FAMILY WOMEN

Other women, in their roles as wives or mothers of government employees, military personnel, and businessmen, also functioned as purveyors of the white, middle-class American way of life. They exhibited an adventurous spirit and adaptability to unusual circumstances, since life and travel in the Pacific region was something novel and daring during the first half of the twentieth century. Caroline Shunk, the wife of a U.S. Army colonel, who arrived in the Philippines in 1909, wrote letters home containing vivid descriptions of Filipino life and culture, much of which was totally alien to her. While writing a letter that spring, she calmly observed that "a band of these wild men [headhunters] is passing the house, walking in single file, led by the chief of the clan, who wears a brilliant scarlet shirt, which comprises his entire costume." Caroline appeared equally intrigued that these men were bona fide headhunters and that they exemplified the Filipinos' general preference for a minimum amount of clothing. Yet she eagerly traveled around the island of Luzon where she was stationed with her husband, routinely discovering beauty in differences from American traditions— with the exception of the headhunters—and wrote affectionately of what she observed. However, when her husband's tour of duty ended at the close of 1909, Caroline wrote, "We could have hugged the khaki-clad men from 'God's country,' for their coming means that we are going home!"[14] For her, both home and civilization meant the United States.

Another military wife, Margaret Tayler Yates, expressed quite opposite sentiments about the opportunity to stay in the Philippines, because she had a different idea about the meaning of home. In the summer of 1924, Margaret accompanied her naval officer husband Bob and their eleven-year-old son Bennie to the Cavite naval base near Manila, a tour of duty the Yates family had anticipated and planned over the preceding two years. Margaret referred to it as the "thrill that comes once in a lifetime." Like Caroline Shunk, she mostly enjoyed her travels throughout the Pacific, wondrously observing all of the new, "exotic" sights, but unlike Caroline, Margaret embraced the Philippines as a real home and was disappointed that her family was posted there for only two years. A poem she wrote in honor of their time at Cavite, titled "At Home Abroad," began with her definition of home: "We're glad to be at home, here, half way 'round the earth."[15]

Clearly, the reactions of American women to their lives in the Pacific area varied, but all of these women, as early colonizers of the islands, felt distanced from their American roots and cut off from other women. However, as Americans gradually settled into the Philippines and other colonial areas of the Pacific, more women willingly called them home.

THE PREWAR YEARS

Agnes Keith found home, civilization, and female companionship outside of the United States in Sandakan, where she was the only American, part of a Caucasian minority of seventy people who controlled politics, economics, and society on North Borneo. Her acquaintances in that capital city were of different nationalities, and they all shared similar but unidentical perspectives of their situation, perspectives based largely on race and class. As members of the small colonial society, they enjoyed a level of economic comfort and social status that eluded many non-Caucasians on the island. While appreciative of Borneo's natural beauty and fascinated by the activities of headhunters, Agnes also enthusiastically participated in British colonial life, which afforded her the amenities of a golf and tennis club, the Sandakan Junior League, and an array of household servants. She treated her servants well and dealt honestly with others in the non-Caucasian community, and her racial attitudes would prove to be an asset during the war years.

Agnes's colonial life in Sandakan in the 1930s mirrored that of American women in the Philippine Islands. As the United States struggled in the depths of a severe economic depression, women there eked out a living by taking any job, often working themselves to exhaustion within the home by patching and repatching clothes, reinforcing shoes and winter coats with newspapers, and stretching increasingly expensive food items. However, middle-class American women in the Philippines experienced a lifestyle virtually unattainable for their counterparts back in the States, and therefore "work" took on a new meaning. For them it was rarely physical or hands-on; it required directing servants and taking on community projects. Social occasions abounded, food and drink were plentiful, and current fashions arrived regularly from Europe and the United States. Elizabeth Head Vaughan, a well-educated woman originally from Georgia, resided in Iloilo on the island of Panay in 1938 after her marriage to Jim Vaughan, a civil engineer working for the Pacific Commercial Company, comfortably settling into colonial life in this business community of some 100,000 inhabitants. Although not rich, the couple easily afforded several servants, an active social life, and a burgeoning bank account, a pleasant lifestyle that continued even after they moved to the smaller city of Bacolod on Negros. But Betsy McCreary, the daughter of an American businessman also living in Iloilo in the years just before the war, crisply observed of this lifestyle that "if we were big frogs, it was only because we lived in a little pond."[16]

Most prewar socializing took place in segregated communities; while racial separation resembled that of Jim Crow segregation in the United States, it did not carry the same rigid legal restrictions. Americans and other Caucasians in the Philippines sometimes socialized with Filipinos or with mestizos (peoples of a mixed racial heritage), and on occasion well-to-do Americans rubbed elbows with the ruling Filipino elite. However, much of the contact between Americans and Filipinos was limited to a master-servant or employer-employee relationship. Florence Horn, a chronicler of American life in the prewar Philippines, described Americans in Manila as "barricaded" because they "insulate[d] themselves as thoroughly as possible against the life of the country they [were] in."[17] Yet she also acknowledged a fact of colonial life that belied absolute racial segregation or insulation: the growing mixed-race population produced by American men who married or lived with Filipinas or mestizas. Often derisively called "squawmen" by the American elite in Manila, these men found themselves shunned from white colonial society. Americans could socialize and work with Filipinos, but they could not have long-term intimate relationships with them; to do so constituted an affront to the accepted beliefs of racial hierarchy and Caucasian superiority.

The children of these interracial unions had some access to American colonial society, depending on the social position of the American parent. Consider Dorothy Dore, a fairly typical mixed-race child of a comfortable but not wealthy class. Her father, Victor Dore, served with the American army in the Philippines during the Spanish-American War, and after the hostilities ended, he decided to stay in the islands, settling on Mindanao to manage a coconut plantation. After a common-law marriage to one Filipina, he legally married another, Dorothy's

mother, Pauline Cueva, in 1918, and the couple had four children including Dorothy, the only daughter, born in 1925 in Davao City. The
siblings played with each other and with the children of the plantation workers; as school-aged children their playmates came from a
variety of backgrounds. Dorothy recalled that they all "simply accepted each other regardless of how rich or poor, whether Catholic or
Protestant, brown or white."[18] The Dore family routinely entertained
visitors from the United States and England, people Dorothy remembered as "dignitaries." As the children got older, Pauline decided that
they should receive an education that would guarantee them entry
anywhere in American-Filipino society, so she sent Dorothy and two
of her brothers off to Silliman University on Negros for the best education available.

Americans found ways to bend racial barriers when they wanted, proof
of the pliancy of racial attitudes. Natalie Crouter, born into an upper-
crust Boston-area family at the turn of the century, cared little about
societal norms. She married Jerry Crouter, an employee of a Hawaiian
sugar planters' association, in Tientsin, China, in the mid-1920s. When
they settled in the Philippine town of Vigan, Natalie's friends included
not only the other Americans and British nationals, but also many Filipinos and Chinese. Her household servants, Ismael and Nida Bacani,
in the Crouter's next home in Baguio were more than paid workers; the
Bacanis constituted an extended family network for Natalie, all taking
care of each other.[19]

The isolation of areas outside of major towns and cities in the Philippines led other American women to close, but not necessarily personal,
involvement with the indigenous population because these women did
not have access to the privileges of the colonial elite. Margaret Coalson
went to the Philippines in 1936 to marry Bob Sherk, a mining engineer
she had known since childhood. The Sherks soon moved to a mining
camp at Nyac, located over two hundred miles north of Manila, where
Bob worked as a supervisor in an ore mine and Margaret found herself
the only Caucasian woman in an area made up of diverse Filipino
tribes.[20] There Margaret had the services of a Filipino "houseboy," the
standard contemporary term for a domestic servant, so she spent much
of her spare time establishing and running a small medical clinic for
the local Igorots. Still, loneliness prevailed, prompting the Sherks to
begin a family sooner than they had planned; their son David arrived in
1938 after a difficult pregnancy for Margaret. The family then moved
south to the gold-mining town of Suyoc, which contained about thirty

Caucasian men, women, and children, so that Margaret and David would be near a doctor.

Alice Franklin Bryant also lived in a relatively isolated area of the Philippines, the coconut-growing Pamplona Plantation on Negros. Alice, her husband, William (whom she called "the Gov'nor" since he had been the provincial governor there), and their young daughter, Imogene, lived more than twenty miles from Dumaguete, the nearest city. The Bryant home was "unpretentious but comfortable," and Alice relished the solitude: "Many women would have found the life lonely and boresome and have longed for telephones, movies, clubs, and luncheons. I longed for none of these. I was never lonely or bored. No doorbell or telephone disturbed us. No noisy traffic raised the dust. I did not miss these evidences of civilization."[21] Yet she *had* other evidences of civilization to keep her entertained, whether or not she longed for them, including a radio, magazines sent from the United States, and numerous party invitations.

Alice exuded a sense of pride about the pleasant race relations in her province. The small village of Pamplona consisted of Filipinos and Chinese, whom she described as her friends, attributing these "especially harmonious" race relations to the existence of nearby Silliman University, which fostered an atmosphere of friendliness between the races. Alice observed that on the social level there was "intermingling and great cordiality between Americans and Filipinos," yet her family's day-to-day experiences with Filipinos were of the master-servant variety. Though Alice proudly recounted how well she got along with her female house servants, how she did not overwork them, she also paternalistically described them as unsophisticated and ignorant. She expressed no wish to make these young women her friends; she simply wanted them to cook and serve the family's meals properly.[22] Alice counseled the village women on maternal and child medical matters, but her overall view of the Filipinos and other non-Caucasians on the island was condescending: while she lived among and appreciated Filipino culture, she retained the belief that American culture was superior.

Whatever the American women's relationship to the indigenous population, these particular racial issues became less important as world events spiraled into a second world war. American women living in the South Pacific in the late 1930s carefully followed the news of worsening conditions in Europe and the latest Japanese advances in their spot of the world. In these matters, little separated the Americans from the native population; both groups worried about how their lives would change as the war expanded. American women identified with the indigenous population but also with the United States' future allies, because, in spirit, most Americans firmly supported the efforts of the English and French to defeat the Axis powers that threatened freedom across the European continent. Frieda Magnuson, the wife of an American exporter in Manila who had been in the Philippines since 1939, recalled that "because of the Europeans we knew in Manila, we felt very close to it all."[23]

Newspapers, magazines, and radio broadcasts also reported on the Japanese as they moved confidently into China in 1937, expanding their living space and seizing needed raw materials. The media widely publicized the rape of Nanking; people around the world saw what Japanese soldiers were capable of. These Americans lived in the midst of a successful advance by the Japanese, yet few seriously believed that the Japanese would do them any harm because the Japanese had no quarrel with the United States. In fact, when the Japanese first moved into China, they did not molest the Americans living there as long as the Americans did not interfere with their takeover. While most Americans sympathized with the plight of the Chinese and even organized relief programs to help them, few foresaw that Japanese actions there would have any impact on the American presence in the Pacific.

Central to this lack of concern was the issue of race, as most Americans simply presumed that the Japanese did not possess the ability to attack and conquer them. Even though the Japanese had attacked China, they had not succeeded in conquering the country, which Americans took as a sign of their ineptness, conveniently ignoring the ruin that the Japanese inflicted on China during their battles. Despite the tenacity of the Japanese, Americans willingly accepted the "fact" that Japanese soldiers, because of certain alleged psychological problems and physical defects, could not shoot, sail, or fly. They overwhelmingly believed that the Japanese simply would not dare attack the United States.[24]

The Americans' disregard of Japanese military successes and tenacity was compounded by the illusion of American military preparedness in the Philippines, a mirage that proved a costly one for Americans and Filipinos alike. Despite the bluster of American officials, defenses in the Philippines were totally inadequate, and the American military knew it. Just after World War I, the Joint Army and Navy Board reasoned that sheer distance from the United States precluded an effective military defense of the Philippines against the Japanese, who could quickly send hundreds of thousands of soldiers there to be met by fewer than twenty thousand U.S. and Filipino troops. Isolationist sentiment in the United States during the interwar period caused many Americans to fear that military preparedness would lead to war, so they worked for demobilization and disarmament, and the military was aware of these sentiments. During the early 1920s, U.S. general Leonard Wood predicted that the 1921–1922 Washington conference on naval disarmament doomed the Philippines in case of a Japanese attack because it prevented the U.S. Navy from building up its defenses. Throughout the 1920s military planners within the War Plans Division of the War Department disagreed about the strategic importance of the Philippines; in 1930 Douglas MacArthur, the chief of staff, threw his weight behind those who viewed the islands as essential to protecting U.S. interests in the Pacific. The debate was not settled until mid-1941, with MacArthur's appointment as commander of U.S. forces in the Far East and Secretary of War Henry L. Stimson's acknowledgment that the Philippines must be safeguarded. Additional troops and weapons were dispatched to the Philippines, but they were too little and too late.[25]

Unable to significantly improve its military strength in the Pacific, American government and military officials took some steps at the end of the 1930s to safeguard its citizens living there. The State Department deemed the very modest actions of requesting evacuations and denying passports sufficient; since it considered the Philippines impenetrable because of American defenses in Manila Bay, it designated the islands a sanctuary for Americans in the Pacific. The lengthy warfare in China prompted the State Department in 1939 to request American civilians there, many of whom were missionaries, to temporarily relocate to the Philippines until the China situation stabilized. Most left willingly, convinced they could carry on their work in the Philippines. Fern Harrington, a twenty-five-year-old Missourian, secured an appointment from the Foreign Mission Board of the Southern Baptist Convention and went to China in August 1940. After working in Beijing for only a few days, the U.S. Embassy there advised all Americans to leave because of worsening hostilities with Japan, so Fern and the other Baptist missionaries went to Baguio to continue their study of Chinese in anticipation of their return.[26]

Fern was among the last American civilians allowed into China; during the last quarter of 1940, the State Department refused to allow

Americans to land there, a decision that affected some missionaries who had already set sail. Judy Skogerboe, who as a young girl growing up in rural Minnesota "dreamed of a life as a missionary in the Orient," began her career in the fall of 1940 when she set sail for China with a handful of other Lutheran missionaries.[27] The State Department refused to allow Judy's ship to dock in China, so the Lutheran Mission Board ordered the missionaries to Manila where they could study Chinese while waiting for conditions to improve.

The State Department routed American civilians to the Philippines even though American military officials knew that the islands could not be defended. The Japanese had to believe that the Philippines were heavily fortified, because American officials did not want them to turn their attention from China and other parts of Southeast Asia to the Philippines. If too many Americans got wind of the actual military preparedness in the islands, they might evacuate, leaving the Filipinos feeling abandoned and betrayed. Economics was also a motivating factor in keeping Americans in the Philippines, as trade between the United States and the Philippines averaged about $30 million per year during the immediate prewar years. This lucrative arrangement, largely in the hands of American businesses, would collapse if Americans were ordered stateside; consequently, American officials in the Philippines misled the American citizens there about the security of the islands. In April 1941, when Manuel Quezon, president of the Philippine Commonwealth, questioned Francis Sayre, the American High Commissioner of the Philippines, about how, exactly, the United States intended to protect the Filipinos, he received a vague answer.[28]

American officials, both civil and military, had an inkling of what was going to happen, and they could not prevent it. By the summer of 1941, the situation in the Pacific reached a critical point: the Japanese had branched out from their invasion of China and moved into southern Indochina in July, positioning themselves to launch attacks against Malaya, the Philippines, and the Netherlands Indies. President Franklin Roosevelt responded to this latest act of aggression by freezing Japanese assets in the United States, refusing to sell gas and oil to the Japanese, and bringing the Army of the Philippine Commonwealth under the jurisdiction of the United States. This new organization, called the United States Armed Forces Far East (USAFFE), a combined American and Filipino military, was headed by General Douglas MacArthur, who had served as a military adviser to the Philippine government.[29] MacArthur then readied the USAFFE to do battle against the Japanese in an attack he predicted could not occur until the early spring of 1942, a miscalculation that caused immeasurable suffering in the Philippines.

By late 1940, Americans in the Pacific regularly involved themselves in debates over whether and where the Japanese would attack; some believed themselves safe, others did not. In October 1940, Francis Sayre told Americans that despite their fellow countrymen's evacuation from China and Japan, there was "no reason for anxiety or excitement. Manila is one of the safest places in the Far East." Despite the official position on the safety of the Philippines, in May 1941, the U.S. Army sent seven hundred of its dependents back to the United States; the navy soon followed this example. Still, no official evacuation order came for every American civilian, and, paradoxically, the government continued to allow civilians to travel to the Philippines. Helen Brush, the wife of a Methodist minister who arrived in Manila with her husband and two young daughters in the spring of 1941, recalled, "Obviously neither we nor the Methodist Board of Missions believed that the Japanese would attack the Philippines."[30]

By 1941, fears of a Japanese attack had become so widespread that proposed evacuations included civilian men as well as women and children, an indication that the Pacific was now regarded as a likely war zone, suitable only for military personnel. About three hundred Americans in Manila met in January 1941 to form the American Coordinating Committee (ACC), which coordinated efforts between the U.S. military, the high commissioner's office, the president of the Philippine Commonwealth, and civilians for defense of the islands.[31] These Americans considered the Philippines their home, so they wanted to protect their families, houses, and livelihoods and did not believe that officials were doing enough to protect them.

One of the issues the ACC and the civilian population in general consistently raised throughout 1941 was the appropriateness of sending American women and children back to the United States. In times of war or other civil disturbances, women and children are routinely removed from dangerous areas; while all men are potential soldiers, women and children, as noncombatants, get in the way and can become unnecessary casualties of war. The ACC tried to convince Francis Sayre to issue a statement instructing all "non-essential" Americans to return to the United States. Sayre initially approved, then changed his mind at the last minute; Americans would not be ordered to leave.[32] Civilians who questioned the high commissioner's office about the advisability of remaining in the islands were counseled to stay put, that Manila was the safest place in the Pacific.

Despite what the officials said publicly, some Americans had real misgivings about their alleged safety. Margaret Sherk made the long trip to the high commissioner's office in November 1941 to ask if it was still safe to stay in the Philippines. Her husband, Bob, wanted to send her and David back to the United States, but before splitting up the family Margaret sought an official opinion on the situation. An official in the office emphatically told Margaret to stay, that "Manila is the safest place in the Orient," advice that prompted Margaret to return to Suyoc instead of taking David back to the United States. She later reflected that Americans had been living in a "fool's paradise" in 1941 but stressed her belief that officials purposely kept American civilians in the Philippines as visible proof that the United States did not intend to permanently give up the islands.[33]

Frieda Magnuson also rationalized that the high commissioner's office "could not tell us to leave as they were equally committed to protecting the Filipinos," and she decided to stay.[34] She had booked passage for herself and her infant daughter on the *President Hoover* in April 1941 but canceled the reservations about a week prior to departure. Since plane and ship reservations were already at a premium, this decision was irreversible. Reassured by the knowledge that Sayre's staff was remaining as well as the wives of executives in other big American companies, Frieda stayed in Manila because it seemed unnecessary to split up her family. She was seven months pregnant with her second child when the Japanese bombed Pearl Harbor on December 7, 1941.

Grace Nash, an American wife, mother, and violinist living with her family in Manila, did not seek out any official pronouncements on the situation. She had lived in the Philippines since 1936 when she went there to marry Ralph Nash, an American engineer. In addition to raising two small boys, Grace gave violin concerts, taught music classes, directed the Junior Orchestra, and wrote a music column for the *Manila Daily Bulletin*, activities that put her in the same social circles with various American government and military officials. In late 1940 Grace observed that a "growing concern over the imminence of war infiltrated cocktail and dinner parties, civic meetings and newspapers," but the talk usually focused on the belief that the Japanese would not dare attack the Philippines because they knew they did not stand a chance. Grace described herself as an "outcast" in these conversations because she had a "gut feeling . . . that war was coming; that the Islands were defenseless." She stayed despite this premonition, a decision based on personal family concerns that fulfilled her perception of what it meant to be a good woman. Ralph was wedded to his job; he would buy tickets for Grace and their boys Stan and Gale to leave, but he would not go. Contending with wounded pride that he loved his job more than his family and feeling guilty at the thought of leaving Ralph "to face destruction and even death without us," Grace decided to stay to keep the family together.[35]

A few American families were willing to separate, and in these cases it appeared that sending children home was an acceptable solution in times of uncertainty. Alice Bryant took her eight-year-old daughter Imogene back to the United States in the summer of 1940, making her one of these few who, mostly for safety reasons, consented to the separation of her family. Yet Imogene's safety was not the sole reason for sending her back to the States; the Bryants believed that an American child who reached a certain age needed to be in America, presumably for educational purposes. Still, Alice admitted that leaving Imogene with relatives in California was "desperately difficult" because the two of them had been so close since Alice had refused to hire an amah for her daughter. Although Alice willingly allowed the separation of her family, she was not inclined to let William return to Negros alone; with her daughter well taken care of, her place was with her husband. Just after their ship left Hawaii, the couple received a message from the government advising American citizens to leave the Pacific area, but they refused to consider turning back. Alice wrote: "I felt as if the foundations of our life were being suddenly removed, that we were suspended over an abyss. I looked at the Gov'nor. He laughed easily."[36] Despite their concern for the safety of their daughter, the Bryants optimistically concluded that the Japanese would not dare attack the United States.

Outside of the Philippines safety was neither assumed nor ensured, yet American women faced the same anxiety over splitting up their families. Agnes Keith recalled that the American naval officers visiting British North Borneo in the last months of 1941 encouraged all the Caucasian women there to leave as soon as possible, but British officials did not order their civilians to leave, something Agnes believed they should have done. She maintained that women and children should have been evacuated by order, that this decision was impossible for individuals to make: "In wartime the individual is not in a position to know military or defense facts. Those who know these facts should take the responsibility of deciding who may stay in a war zone."[37] But those in the know had, in fact, made their decision: no official order would be given, and so the Allied civilians were left to fend for themselves.

Notions of home, family, and national identity typically prevented Americans from pulling up stakes, despite the increasing danger. First, they would be physically abandoning their homes. Many Americans, especially those in the Philippines, had roots going back a generation or more, or as Betty Foley put it, "We are Americans, but our home is in the Philippines." Betty's parents had come to the islands more than thirty years before the war started, expected to stay only three years, but quickly decided to put down permanent roots; her father, E. J. Halsema, an engineer by profession, eventually became mayor of Baguio. Betty was born in Manila in 1914 and always considered the Philippines her home, the main reason she did not leave before the war started. Such a desertion was not simply psychological; economics factored into the decision as well. Homes represented physical proof of a prosperous life, evidence that leaving the United States had really paid off, plus they contained mementos impossible to replace and too costly to send back to the States. For example, Natalie Crouter and her husband collected Chinese jade. It formed an integral part of their home and would have been very difficult to pack up and send to the States. Agnes and Harry Keith took great satisfaction in their well-decorated home on Borneo. Harry possessed an extensive collection of books about the island, the couple collected Chinese pottery, and Agnes prided herself on her extensive wardrobe.[38] Without all of these things, a home would not be a home.

Second, Americans felt uneasy about leaving their servants and other employees to face the Japanese alone. Servants functioned as a kind of extended family for Americans; they interacted with each other, often over a period of several years, and came to genuinely care for each other. Therefore, Americans worried about the safety of their servants in the event of a Japanese attack. Throughout China and portions of Southeast Asia, the Japanese showed how they dealt with a conquered people, and atrocity stories abounded about how the Japanese routinely massacred civilians. In the six weeks following the fall of Nanking in 1937, Japanese soldiers slaughtered Chinese men and raped and murdered Chinese women, leaving an estimated 200,000 Chinese dead. Americans had no reason to believe that the Japanese would not do the same to civilians elsewhere, but they hoped that there might be safety in numbers, meaning they could not let their native friends fend for themselves. In her diary Natalie Crouter repeatedly expressed her strong attachment to the Bacanis, her servants in Baguio, and also chronicled her efforts on behalf of various Chinese relief programs. Margaret Sherk asserted similar sentiments, pointing out that "some of the servants we had had for years and they were almost like members of the family." Her female servants knew what had happened in Nanking and feared that the same thing would happen to them.[39]

Finally, Americans held a strong belief that no matter how successful the Japanese had been in other areas of the Pacific, the American military would be able to rout them out of any of its territories in a matter of weeks. The Japanese might be capable of attack, but they would not be able to secure American territories. Americans reasoned that if they could hold out through the initial assault, mighty American military help would soon arrive, so it was simply presumptive of Americans to flee. According to the racial views of the times, Caucasian Americans considered themselves inherently superior to the Japanese; running away would challenge notions of racial superiority, and it seemed like an un-American thing to do.

Work was one exception to these home and family reasons as priorities for staying in the Pacific. Female teachers and missionaries were there as working professionals, and during the 1930s a few women journalists angled for overseas assignments, especially to China after the Japanese invasion in 1937. Because of their careers these women purposely put themselves in harm's way and refused to evacuate when conditions worsened. Yet they often expressed their motives for doing so in feminized terms; that is, as women they had something unique to offer in their reporting.

In 1941, journalist Gwen Dew decided to make a movie about the importance of U.S. relief aid to the Chinese. After freelance reporting in China in the late 1930s and interviewing Madame Chiang Kai-shek several times, she reluctantly left China in 1939 when the U.S. government began advising American women to leave, a decision she immediately regretted. In 1941 Gwen applied to the State Department for permission to return to continue her work. It took several months and many applications before she secured it, yet she was determined to go because of a lack of what she considered a necessary perspective about the war in China. She firmly believed that a qualified female journalist should be in China, "someone who was interested in the human details of international affairs and who was not so concerned with military strategy and political expediency that he could not see . . . the human war for the military ways of war."[40] Men could deal with the military and political aspects of war, women with the "human details."

Gwen set sail for China in May 1941, well aware of the rumblings about the Japanese extending their grasp to other areas of the Pacific. In late November, American officials in British Hong Kong tried to convince Gwen to leave, but she refused, telling one official in British slang, "There's going to be a war, and I want to see the balloon go up."[41] During the first week of December, as Gwen watched some of her American and British counterparts leave the colony, she finally lost her nerve and gave in, making arrangements to leave Hong Kong on December 8, the day it would be impossible to leave.

Nursing, another acceptable female profession in the twentieth century, also afforded American women the opportunity to travel abroad to practice their skills. Women came to the Philippines as army and navy nurses, but civilian nurses came as well. Tressa Roka first worked as a nurse in Pittsburgh and New York until she saved enough money to travel. Her maiden journey took her to Europe, where she had so much fun that she worked for several more years to earn enough money to go to "the Orient"—Hawaii, Japan, China, and the Philippines. She spent a lot of time in China, sightseeing and shopping, and when she started to run out of money she took on private nursing jobs, which paid enough to keep her in fine style. Tressa described her time in Shanghai with a great deal of enthusiasm: "Dinner parties, tea and garden parties! Sightseeing and night clubbing and eating strange and exotic foods! And always there had been an abundance of escorts."[42] Not surprisingly, she was reluctant to leave the city, doing so only when the Japanese attacked in 1937 and evacuating to Manila, where she took a job as a civilian nurse at Sternberg General Army Hospital. Even though she worked at a military hospital, Tressa never expressed concerns about the possibility of a Japanese attack. She settled into a very comfortable life in Manila and created a family environment with her young, pregnant Filipina maid, Adoracion, and her beloved pet terrier, Rags. She had no intention of leaving; life was good.

PEARL HARBOR

In the closing months of 1941, thousands of American women had made the decision to stay in the Pacific despite increasing speculation of a Japanese attack somewhere in the area. Most of these women decided to stay because of home and family concerns; a few stayed because of their work. Some believed that the Japanese really would attack, and others believed that they would not dare. When the Japanese struck on December 8, 1941 (December 7 for the vast majority of Americans on the other side of the International Dateline), reactions varied, largely based on what the women had originally believed about the possibility of attack. Grace Nash reacted in anger when she heard about Pearl Harbor: "My lips tightened over clenched teeth. I wasn't numb, I was befuddled and angry. . . . I knew war would come . . . and now it has come!" Grace's most immediate concern was a motherly one: purchasing Christmas presents for her sons in order to maintain some sense of normality in their lives. In Bacolod, Elizabeth Vaughan had been well aware of developments in the Pacific but expressed surprise when she heard about the bombing, writing in her diary on December 8, 1941, "My world collapsed." Her husband, Jim, had gone to Manila on business a few days earlier, leaving her alone with their young children, Beth and Clay, and the servants. Separated from her husband, Elizabeth also had to endure a community in turmoil, observing that there "was absolute panic in Bacolod." William Bryant told Alice of the attack on Pearl Harbor, and she recalled that they "looked at each other aghast, stunned by the impact. It was as if our rock-girt island were melting beneath us and we became terribly conscious of the 7,000 miles of ocean that separated us from the security and protection of our homeland."[43] The Bryants immediately realized their precarious predicament: they were Americans, but they were not within the safety of the United States.

Even after the Japanese expanded their attack, some American women believed that it would take the United States only a few weeks to thoroughly vanquish the enemy. Given these women's general racial attitudes about the inferiority of the Japanese and the superiority of the Americans, this reaction is not surprising, since pride in their race and in their country would not allow them to believe otherwise. Helen Brush recalled that even after the Japanese military began its move on the Philippines, "we believed that we would conquer them at Manila Bay and the war would be over. No efforts were made to get the civilians out." She did not know that Philippine officials belatedly and unsuccessfully tried to evacuate civilians, but the Japanese already controlled the ocean and the sky. Although the Sherks evacuated from Suyoc on December 20 because of the advance of the Japanese army on Luzon, Margaret asserted that "the Americans would whip the socks off the presumptuous Japanese within a month at the very most!"[44]

Despite this optimism, women also aired concerns about what would happen in the immediate future: while the battles raged to push the Japanese out, what would happen to their homes and their families? The successful, rapid advance of the Japanese military brought fear into the homes of Americans living in the Pacific. Paving the way for invasion, the Japanese bombed Luzon, Hong Kong, Malaya, Singapore, and Borneo shortly after Pearl Harbor, continuing throughout the first two-thirds of the month with raids that wiped out Allied planes and warships. On Luzon, despite the fact that General MacArthur had already been notified about Pearl Harbor, the Japanese succeeded in taking out about half of MacArthur's "best aircraft" in one day, severely crippling the USAFFE's ability to fight back.[45] The Japanese would not be driven away easily or quickly, and American women now faced the dangerous consequences of their decision to remain in the Pacific.

Americans living in and around Manila experienced the direct effects of war beginning on December 8. The main location of the American and Filipino military, the city became a prime objective for the Japanese, but Manilans were unprepared for what happened that day. Frieda Magnuson, pregnant with her second child, recalled general confusion and fear, that everyone "moved around in a daze making preparations for we weren't sure what." For her, those preparations included purchasing reserve food items and making blackout curtains for the windows. After Grace Nash finished Christmas shopping for her sons she hurried home, realizing that with the close proximity of Japan to the Philippines, "we could expect bombs any time now and any place." That evening, the Japanese bombed Nichols Field, the U.S. Army base located less than five miles from the Nash home in the Pasay district of Manila. Grace woke when she heard the sound of planes: "We had expected it, yet the fright that comes with those first bombs is indescribable."[46]

In Baguio the bombing also began that morning; while the summer capital was not as large or important as Manila, it sat directly in the path of the Japanese invasion of Luzon. Deciding to forgo a direct invasion of Manila because of its heavily fortified bay, the Japanese came around another way, so Baguio fell to the enemy about a week before Manila. As Natalie and Jerry Crouter listened to the morning news on the radio they heard planes outside. Hurrying outside, they saw seventeen bombers in the air, which they assumed were American, and were stunned moments later when they heard a loud noise followed by smoke pouring out of Camp John Hay, a local military establishment. Natalie watched as the "smoke rolled up and the smell of powder reached us. We could hear screaming and men yelling orders. Suddenly we all ran into the house. The planes passed out of sight over the mines and mountain ridge. Our knees were shaky. We kept staring at each other, wondering if we could believe what our eyes had seen."[47] It was not a mirage. The Japanese bombed Baguio. Then just after noon that same day, their bombers attacked Clark Field and wiped out two squadrons of American B-17s and a squadron of P-40s, a brief assault that hindered the Americans' capability for a vigorous military response.

Americans in other areas of the Philippines had some time to adjust to the fact of war before it touched them directly; even though they did not have to deal with bombings, their lives were nevertheless disrupted and fraught with anxiety. Although the Japanese did not bomb or invade Negros until April 1942, rumors of attacks and invasions began right after Pearl Harbor, one of which Elizabeth Vaughan described on December 11: "Servants running wildly, children screaming because of noise and excitement around them, my heart missing every other beat with fear for children—thinking of horror stories of torture administered by Japanese soldiers and my lips repeating, 'Jim, oh Jim, come home.'" During those first few days of the war Elizabeth realized the uncertainty and chaos that would become an integral part of her life, and she had a nagging fear that she would have to handle it alone. Alice Bryant recalled rumors of enemy parachute landings that circulated in the days following the bombings of Pearl Harbor and Manila and worried that the Japanese could "be upon us in five minutes." She was not optimistic about the immediate future, commenting on the irony of the situation that the "physical Eden-like framework [of Negros] remained, but it was paradise no longer."[48]

Elsewhere in the Pacific, the situations of Americans also deteriorated. Gwen Dew, prevented by the December 8 bombings from leaving Hong Kong, felt alone and frightened, knowing that only twenty-six miles separated Hong Kong from Japanese-held territory in China. Still, she refused to remain idle, so she secured press credentials from the British Ministry of Information that allowed her access to authorized military zones for reporting on the war. Gwen reported on the large-scale landings of Japanese troops that began on December 18, work that provided her with a diversion from constant worry over what was going to happen to her when the enemy inevitably took over Hong Kong.

PHILIPPINE ISLANDS

PHILIPPINE SEA

LUZON

Lingayen Gulf

Baguio

Clark Field

Manila

Cavite

SOUTH CHINA SEA

MINDORO

PANAY

Bacolod

CEBU

LEYTE

PALAWAN

NEGROS

Dumaguete

SULU SEA

MINDANAO

Davao City

BRITISH NORTH BORNEO

Agnes Keith remained resolute in her decision to stay in Borneo and keep her family together even after she heard about Pearl Harbor, passing up a couple of last-minute evacuation opportunities during the third week of December 1941. Agnes later wrote: "I was determined to stay. The more I waited, the more I was determined."[49] The Japanese moved into Sarawak on Christmas Day, occupied the Keiths' area of Jesselton in early January 1942, then rounded up all of the enemy nationals.

In early 1942, Darlene Deibler heard news of the steady Japanese advances on Sumatra, Borneo, and then Java, and while she felt grateful for any delay in the arrival of the Japanese, she knew that Celebes would not be spared. The Japanese invaded Macassar on February 8, "killing right and left as they went," but since Darlene and the other missionaries lived near the Dutch resort area of Malino, in Benteng Tinggi, they were spared the horrors of the initial invasion.[50] They had chosen to remain there, dedicated to their religious work, confident that God wanted them to stay, even after the Dutch had offered to evacuate them in January. On March 5, the Japanese moved into their missionary community, took inventory of the Allied nationals, and warned them not to leave the area under penalty of death. Darlene and the others could only wait for and wonder about what the Japanese had in store for them.

Waiting and wondering characterized the uncertain days between Pearl Harbor and invasion. For some Americans this meant enduring days of bombing, for others it meant coping with the stress of knowing that the Japanese would arrive yet not knowing exactly when, but all speculated about how the enemy would behave during the invasions. Women mostly worried about the kind of treatment they could expect from their conquerors. As the Japanese secured their positions, they proceeded to confiscate private property and count and categorize the enemy nationals, actions that provoked distinct unease among the civilians but did not rival their behavior in China. Allied nationals assumed that all draft-age men would be imprisoned to prevent them from participating in sabotage or espionage, leading to the one thing that women tried to prevent: the separation of their families. The Japanese military did not have a set plan for dealing with civilians, however; though they had to deal with the civilian population in their conquered territories, they had not worked out a comprehensive plan prior to invasion. So American women, as well as all other Allied civilians, faced days of uncertainty about what was going to happen to them.

FEARS OF RAPE, VIOLENCE, AND MURDER

Aside from family separation, female civilians worried about the possibility of rape. During World War I, Allied propaganda portrayed German soldiers as rapists of women and indiscriminate murderers of children, something that American women of a certain age would remember hearing about. For women throughout the world, confrontation with the enemy meant the likelihood of rape, as conquering armies of all races and nationalities had long claimed that privilege for themselves. Since the Japanese were not Caucasians, most white Americans in the 1930s and 1940s regarded them as barbarians, as uncivilized and even inhuman; certainly, the Americans reasoned, events in Nanking had borne that out. The phrase "rape of Nanking" sent chills down the spines of most American women who assumed that the Japanese would treat them the same way as the Chinese women. In the hours that followed the Japanese invasion and occupation of the island countries in the Pacific, women anticipated and dreaded the worst possible treatment from their conquerors. Alice Bryant recalled that in the days just after Pearl Harbor, "everyone was thinking of the rape of Nanking."[51]

Just one step ahead of the invading Japanese army, Margaret, Bob, and David Sherk, carrying little money and few personal possessions, made their way to Manila. On New Year's Eve 1941, Bob, now in need of a paying job to support his family and determined to do his patriotic duty, went off with a group of civilian men to Bataan because the USAFFE, desperate to keep the Japanese at bay, needed engineers. Margaret was alone with David when the Japanese moved into the city on January 2, 1942, wondering, "Were we to be treated as Nanking had been not so long before? . . . I had such vivid imaginative pictures of what could be done to us. Waiting for the Japanese to decide what they were going to do with us was one of the hardest waits of my life."[52] Despite her fears about the rape of Nanking, Japanese soldiers did not physically assault Margaret.

Josephine Waldo exhibited similar feelings as she anxiously watched Manila pass into the hands of the Japanese during the last week of December 1941. She and her husband, Bill, a Goodyear employee, stayed together in their flat in the Michel Apartments as the USAFFE withdrew from the city. In her very first war diary entry on January 1, 1942, Josephine expressed her anxieties about the enemy: "The suspense of waiting for them to come in and decide our fate is almost unbearable.

Who knows what treatment they will deal out to us! Stories from occupied China do not make our future seem any to [sic] bright."[53]

Agnes Keith described the time between the Japanese invasion of
Borneo and their subsequent arrival in Sandakan as the "darkest hours
of all my life." One of the few American women caught outside of the
Philippines, her experiences and treatment differed from women like
Margaret Sherk and Josephine Waldo. The small European community
in Sandakan had the foresight to devise a plan in the event of an invasion, which afforded some comfort to the women. Once it began, Harry
went to his office to await the arrival of the Japanese while Agnes and
George went to the British Government House with the European
women and children. British officials had decided that it would be safer
for civilians if the Japanese did not catch them alone in their homes,
assuming safety in numbers for the women and children, and that the
Japanese might feel less challenged if the men were off separately at
their places of business. When the Japanese arrived in Sandakan, they
rounded up all of these men and imprisoned them on January 19, 1942;
Japanese "shock troops" also poured into Government House, threatening and bullying the women and children there, but, as Agnes pointed
out, "they didn't kill us, or rape us."[54]

After two days the Japanese military authorities, still undecided as
to what to do with these civilians, allowed Agnes to return to her house
with George and two of her servants. Since the Japanese released Harry
from prison to oversee essential food production in his capacity of director of agriculture, the Keiths were reunited for a short time. Even
though they were in their own home, all together, life was not the same,
could not be the same, under the Japanese occupation. One afternoon
when Agnes was ill with malaria, three soldiers came into her house to
interrogate her about the neighborhood, and when she did not answer
their questions quickly or accurately enough, they pushed her, knocking her to the floor, and hit her repeatedly. After the soldiers left, Agnes
recalled, "I became very ill. I was pregnant at that time. That afternoon
I had a miscarriage. We lived like this for four months. You do not die
when such things happen. They are not killing matters. In warfare, they
aren't even serious ones."[55] Agnes possessed the ability, at least in hind-
sight, to prioritize mistreatments during wartime; according to her, a
woman's miscarriage did not matter as much as Allied soldiers fighting and dying to prevent the advance of the Japanese.

On May 12, the Keiths' irregular family life ended when Japanese
military officials ordered all Europeans in Sandakan to report for intern-

ment in gender-segregated camps. The one event—family separation—
that Agnes had tried to prevent finally took place, and despite her stub-
bornness and determination, she could not stop it. Agnes and Harry had
one hour in which to pack enough items to last for an unspecified stay,
perhaps the rest of their lives, in a prison camp. George's amah, Ah Yin,
cried and begged to go along with them, but Agnes, fully realizing the
potentially explosive situation they were caught up in, denied her request, explaining to her that "we would all be killed" if they in anyway
disobeyed the Japanese orders.[56] Later that day, Agnes and George were
separated from Harry and sent to a camp with other Allied women and
children on Berhala Island, just off the coast of Borneo.

When the Japanese moved into Hong Kong just before Christmas,
Gwen Dew experienced similar terrors and uncertainties. She and
other Allied civilians holed up in a Hong Kong hotel while the Japanese trounced the British, but even as the enemy conquered more and
more territory, British officials refused to surrender. British soldiers
abandoned the hotel where Gwen was staying when it became appar-
ent that the Japanese would overrun it, reasoning that if the Japanese
found it full of only civilians, they would not feel compelled to kill
everyone. Gwen wondered, "What were the Japs going to do to us when
they arrived?" believing that "one wrong move, one Japanese soldier
over-greedy for blood, one misleading step by any of the 200 guests
would have meant death for all."[57] Though enemy soldiers arrived in
the hotel lobby with fixed bayonets, no wholesale slaughter ensued;
instead, they questioned Allied civilians, relieved them of their valuables, and assured them they now enjoyed the protection of the Japanese army.

"Protection" was, of course, a euphemism, since Allied civilians had
no one to fear but the Japanese. Gwen understood that they "were prisoners, and the Japanese intended us to know that. This was what I would
have dreaded most in the world if I had thought it would happen to me."
In the suite Gwen shared with several other civilians, a soldier ran the
flat of his bayonet blade across her throat several times, but she managed to keep an impassive face, shrugging her shoulders at him, so he
put the bayonet down. Gwen insisted that she and all of the Allied prisoners "were determined never to let them know on what torturous
treadwheels they were forcing our minds, and almost without exception the Japs never saw any weaknesses in their prisoners."[58] On Christmas Eve the Japanese segregated the civilians by nationality, marched
them through war-torn Hong Kong, temporarily imprisoned them in a

paint factory, moved them to Kowloon, and finally took them back to Hong Kong for internment in Fort Stanley.

Fears of rape, violence, and murder prompted some Americans to attempt evasion. Depending on location, motivation, and ingenuity, some Americans, especially those on Negros, opted to use this period between attack and invasion to try to get away from the Japanese, to hide until American forces could rescue them. Elizabeth Vaughan contemplated trying to get to Manila to join up with Jim but could not work out the logistics. Philippine authorities restricted travel, now a dangerous undertaking, and Elizabeth realized the difficulties of packing up and moving all of the things she and the children needed. She also lamented the likely loss of her household and personal items, "silver, hand-embroidered Chinese linens, and other belongings dear to every woman's heart," if she left Negros.[59] As a compromise, on Christmas Day she moved her family to the Hawaiian-Philippine Central, a sugar plantation in Silay just nine miles north of Bacolod, where she managed to move most of the family's belongings while putting the others in storage. Five other American families plus one British family relocated to the Central, providing Elizabeth a certain amount of relief in living near other Americans.

Not only was Elizabeth separated from her home and her husband, but she also had to take on duties that she had never before performed. She wryly noted in her diary that she "studied as many vocational subjects as possible in college—journalism, typing, shorthand, graduate work in English literature (to teach), graduate work and Ph.D. in sociology (to do social work, research, or teach), but never to have to cook." An untraditional southern woman for her times, the war forced Elizabeth to take on traditionally female tasks and even expand her mothering skills. A generally dispassionate observer of the early months of the war, her emotions surfaced only when a problem arose in her immediate family. For instance, in the early spring of 1942, when one-and-a-half-year-old Clay contracted a bad case of diarrhea, Elizabeth admitted that those "times when children are ill I miss my husband most. Need his comfort and moral support. Japanese don't frighten me like illnesses of the children."[60] Her concerns foreshadowed the problems that would plague women during internment: frustration with their inability to effectively deal with routine mothering actions, such as comforting illness, because of the disruptions of war.

After the fall of Bataan in April 1942, the Central population decided that the Japanese would likely invade Negros soon and evacuated to a camp in the hills where life proved even simpler than it had at the Central. Families crowded into one-room houses, ate canned food, and lived without electricity and a radio. On April 16, Elizabeth reported the first Japanese landing on Negros; three days later she opened her diary entry by announcing that she was drunk, "as drunk as one can be and still be aware of the world about me." The Japanese lurked about ten minutes away from their mountain hideout, but the U.S. Army advised the civilians not to turn themselves in. In the event of possible capture, Elizabeth decided that she "would kill Beth and Clay before destroying myself. These tiny bits of blond humanity . . . could not be left to cry to unresponsive ears nor to hold out their tiny arms to a scornful rebuff."[61] But nothing that violent befell the Vaughans. Negros did not surrender to the Japanese until May 12, and Elizabeth and her children safely entered internment in Bacolod on June 7.

Alice and William Bryant also opted for evacuation as a temporary measure until the USAFFE pushed the Japanese out of the Philippines. Alice could not concentrate on any of her usual activities once war had been declared and found that planning and helping to carry out an evacuation "helped to calm and stabilize us."[62] She mostly worried about William's safety, because he was responsible for guarding the Pamplona airstrip from a Japanese takeover, something Alice believed was impossible since neither William nor any of the other locals had enough weapons to challenge the enemy. She soon convinced her husband to move to a secluded area closer to the island's interior, presumably out of the reach of the Japanese. Alice considered this evacuation a group activity; once she and her husband had chosen a site for their refuge, they invited seven other Americans to join them. This extended family at times provoked tensions, but the establishment of such a community was important to Alice, as it symbolized safety and American solidarity. The Bryants stayed in their mountain camp until July 1942, by which time the Japanese had secured their hold on Negros and had enlisted the help of some Filipinos in rooting out Americans, announcing that continued evasion would result in death upon capture. When the couple could no longer hope to hold out until American reinforcements arrived, they surrendered.

The vast majority of American women survived the war without any direct physical assaults from the Japanese, though some experienced psychological and physical terror. The severity of treatment depended on where the Americans were taken prisoner; women rounded up in the Philippines, for instance, rarely reported any kind of physical mistreatment. Josephine Waldo described the Japanese occupation of Manila on January 2, 1942, as "very orderly" but believed this to be unusual, asking herself, "What more experiences will we have before this war is ended?" On January 4, the Waldos and the other residents of the Michel Apartments prepared themselves, as ordered, to be sent to camp. Their internment was delayed a day because of a lack of transportation, then Josephine and Bill were "herded into an open army truck, guarded by soldiers with guns, and taken to Rizal Stadium."[63] Upon arrival, the Japanese registered them by nationality and sex and transferred the couple to Santo Tomas University for internment with other Allied civilians. Josephine did not report any abuse during this entire process.

After the Japanese occupied Manila, Margaret and David Sherk stayed sequestered in their apartment; it was not until January 7 that Margaret found out about the roundup of all Americans. Japanese soldiers came into the apartment that day and ordered her, as they had the Waldos, to pack enough food and clothing for three days. Margaret expressed relief upon receiving these instructions, because she was then sure that "they were not going to kill us, and they were going to take us somewhere."[64] A Japanese interpreter questioned her patiently but carefully about the men's clothing in the apartment, left behind by her husband, but he fortunately accepted her explanation that Bob had abandoned her. By that evening, Margaret and David were interned in Santo Tomas.

The roundup for internment made for a frightening experience, as American women still feared the possibility of rape. Most had stayed out of the streets during the invasion, but during the internment process they could not avoid coming into contact with Japanese soldiers. Grace Nash bravely sneaked out of her house in the Pasay district to watch enemy troops enter Manila, and when it became evident that they would not be routed out, she went home to prepare herself and her family for whatever might come next. She recalled that women "had been advised against wearing nail polish or make-up and to avoid any likeness to the Japanese geisha girls." Grace complied, and the Nash family entered internment on January 6 without suffering any physical assault. Tressa Roka also took care with her appearance during the roundup, but it was not something she had thought of on her own. As she and her fiancé, Lowell "Catesy" Cates, waited for the Japanese to enter the Malate district, Tressa dressed as usual for the day, expressing surprise when Catesy asked if she had something "less becoming" to put on. It took her a few minutes before she realized that he was going through the "same torture that all men were experiencing at this time over their women."[65] Tressa did as Catesy requested; on January 5 the couple entered internment.

Outside of the Philippines, other women were not as lucky; slapping and threats were more commonplace. Japanese soldiers physically abused Agnes Keith to the point where she miscarried, and psychological abuse also occurred. A Japanese soldier terrorized Gwen Dew by pressing a bayonet to her throat, while Darlene Deibler agonized over the swift separation from her husband. Darlene and the other missionaries experienced a brief respite from the Japanese army after its soldiers quit Benteng Tinggi, but just as they had returned to some semblance of a normal life, the soldiers came back to take the missionary men away, including Darlene's husband, Russell. She raged silently that the Japanese had not even given her the opportunity to say goodbye: "'You sadists, you didn't even let me say goodbye!' I swallowed hard and clenched my fists. 'You'll not have the satisfaction of seeing me cry.'"[66] She refused to give in to the Japanese attempts to demoralize their captives by separation, and throughout the war her hard work and belief in God sustained her.

The kinds of abuse that Japanese soldiers directed at American women, whether physical or psychological, were certainly not of the same caliber leveled at Chinese women, Filipinas, mestizas, and even other Caucasian Allied women. Japanese soldiers routinely raped Chinese women during the long years of Japan's war in China and assaulted indigenous women in the other territories that they conquered after the attack on Pearl Harbor. The Japanese army forced close to 200,000 women, about 80 percent of whom were Korean, to be "comfort women" for their soldiers, a brutal form of sexual slavery.[67]

In addition to the routine rape of indigenous women and girls in conquered territories, Japanese soldiers also occasionally raped and murdered Caucasian women from some Allied countries. When Australian army nurses got caught in Rabaul and Singapore during December 1941, evacuation attempts were not always successful, as the Japanese attacked rescue ships, including the *Vyner Brooke*, which carried away sixty-five of the nurses plus other military personnel and Allied civilians from Singapore on February 12, 1942. Two days later the Japanese sank the ship, leaving about one hundred passengers to make their way to nearby Banka Island where, exhausted, injured, and hungry, they surrendered to the Japanese. After shooting and bayoneting the men in the group, the Japanese ordered the twenty-three women into the sea and shot them as well. Only one nurse, Vivian Bullwinkel, who feigned death, survived.[68]

British nurses in Hong Kong endured similar horrors when Japanese troops moved into that city on Christmas Day 1941. Gwen Dew related the experiences of an unnamed British nurse who worked in St. Stephen's, an emergency hospital in Hong Kong, as Japanese invasion forces burst into the building at six o'clock in the morning. Despite the Red Cross banners clearly displayed on the building, the soldiers bayoneted the two doctors in charge, killed fifty-two patients, then lined up the nurses. According to Gwen's informant, "They took away the first three, and they never came back. . . . Then they took the rest of us, one by one, and raped us time and time again. They kept us in a small room, and whenever a Jap wanted us he came and took us away. All Christmas Day. All Christmas night."[69] The bodies of the first three nurses were found later; they had been raped and murdered.

Gwen recounted this atrocity in a book published in 1943, after her repatriation, not for its lurid literary value and not strictly for anti-Japanese propaganda, although both of these elements certainly characterize the book's contents. Her larger purpose was to show what happened to "good" women during war: they endured the most contemptible assaults on their womanhood but bore them stoically, almost philosophically. Blurring the line between the military and the civilian, Gwen described her nurse informant as "a soldier at her post; she had suffered grievous wounds which would leave scars on her soul forever, but she had gone through this in the line of duty, and she had done her part without fear or failure, just as would any brave soldier."[70] Although these atrocities were committed against British women, Gwen intimated that such would be the fate of any Caucasian women in the path of the Japanese, that it would be their duty to meet their fate as heroically as these British nurses did.

One major question that arises in connection with these reports of rape, murder, and forced prostitution is why such things did not happen to Caucasian American women; here the record is virtually silent. Elizabeth Vaughan recounted the story of a Mrs. Christenson, the wife of an American army captain, whom the Japanese tortured so she would reveal the whereabouts of her husband. According to Elizabeth, the Japanese burnt the woman on the arms with lit cigarettes "until pain became so severe she lost her mind and when released committed suicide, leaving two small children." There is no corroboration of this story, and Elizabeth did not specify whether Mrs. Christenson was American by birth or by marriage. Grace Nash remembered only one story of the rape of an American woman, that of "Mrs. L" who was in northern Luzon on business when the Japanese invaded. The Japanese captured and imprisoned her in a guardhouse where soldiers repeatedly raped and mutilated her until she went insane. Alice Bryant recalled that when the Japanese took over Negros they "immediately opened a red light district, and were not—at least at that time—accustomed to molesting respectable women in Dumaguete."[71] Although it is not clear whether "respectable" referred to class or race, it is likely that Alice considered women like herself, a Caucasian American, as respectable, and apparently she had not heard of any sexual assaults on American women.

Both rape and plunder have been considered to be the "right" of conquering armies, and the fact that Japanese soldiers did not rape white American women represents a startling incongruity. There are several possible reasons why for the most part they were left unmolested, the first of which is racial. The Japanese intended to establish a Greater East Asia Co-Prosperity Sphere to unite all Asians, and within this context, the Japanese viewed Caucasians as inferior. Agnes Keith recounted that the Japanese officers in charge of the civilian internment camp on Berhala Island referred to the Allied women and children as members of a "fourth-class nation." Japanese soldiers may have considered Caucasian women so beneath them that they would not soil their bodies by engaging in sexual contact with them.[72] However, this does not explain the treatment of the British and Australian nurses. Other possible reasons that the Japanese did not abuse American women relate to number and location. The majority of American women lived in well-populated areas of the Philippines when the Japanese attacked; their sheer numbers may have assured their safety. Also, when captured or rounded up, many of the American women had children with them, emphasizing their traditional womanhood, while the British and Australian nurses were single women removed from the family environment. Japanese soldiers seemed reluctant to interfere with the mother-child relationship, and by all eyewitness accounts they appeared very fond of children, even Caucasian children.

The final two reasons are related to the military. First, civilians, whether male or female, fared worse when they encountered regular Japanese soldiers, or "shock troops" as Agnes Keith called them, rather than Japanese officers. Although the soldiers indulged in the traditional conqueror's privilege of rape and pillage, the officers restrained themselves and tried to restrain their troops. In most cases where Americans were rounded up for or surrendered to internment, they dealt either with Japanese officers or Japanese soldiers accompanied by civilian interpreters. Finally, Allied opposition that the Japanese encountered influenced treatment of civilians. In Manila, American forces quickly withdrew and declared it an open city; in Hong Kong, however, British troops held out even after it was plain that they would be defeated, provoking Japanese anger when they finally took control. In April 1942, when the Japanese succeeded in taking Bataan, they instituted the infamous death march that resulted in the deaths of thousands of American and Filipino soldiers. The Japanese had assumed they would have a quick victory on Luzon, became irritated by the American holdout on Bataan, and were unprepared for the number of prisoners they took there. The death march served as revenge while whittling down the prisoner population to a more manageable size.

Fortunately, the Japanese demonstrated an unwillingness to treat the Allied civilians in a similar manner. Direct violence, such as shooting or beating, was rare for female captives. The Japanese also intended to remove any sense of superiority the civilians might have felt, turning to more indirect forms of violence to reinforce the captor-captive relationship. The war proved to be a long one for those interned by the Japanese.

2
THE STRUGGLE TO ORGANIZE

*"We are all standing together to prove to our enemy what stuff
the Americans are made of."*

On April 9, 1942, Josephine Waldo felt a severe four-second earthquake
rock Santo Tomas and noted that although there was "some hysteria
among the women," the internees basically remained calm, which she
viewed as a positive sign that the interned Allied nationals would work
together in a spirit of cooperation. For her, cooperation and putting a
good face forward became important coping mechanisms for surviving internment, ways of expressing a strong national identity, because,
as Josephine observed, "We are all standing together to prove to our
enemy what stuff the Americans are made of."[1] Women as well as
men had to prove their mettle in time of war, but for these women,
generally accustomed to a rather leisurely pace of life in the Pacific,
surviving internment markedly challenged their abilities and ingenuity. During internment, their roles as wives, mothers, daughters, and
sweethearts were tested and altered to meet the changing circumstances of war and imprisonment. American women adapted to internment by creating communities based on principles of democracy but
had to change their perceptions and practices of work as they waited
for America to rescue them, adaptations that did not occur without
struggle and controversy.

Although Josephine did not know this, times were even more difficult for Americans in the Pacific theater than the internees imagined.
Determined to seize the Philippines, the Japanese waged a relentless
campaign against the USAFFE, which had retreated to Bataan and
Corregidor where, cut to half rations, they faced failing health, dwindling medical supplies, and the impossibility of relief. On April 9, 1942,
Bataan surrendered, although forces on Corregidor held out about a
month longer. In the face of this onslaught, the commander of the
USAFFE, General Douglas MacArthur, had evacuated to Australia on

March 11, promising with his now famous phrase that he would return. The last hope for a quick Allied victory in the Pacific vanished.

For American civilians, the uncertainty of what would happen once the Japanese invaded was replaced by concern over what would happen to them as the Japanese consolidated their hold on the Pacific region and rounded up the enemy aliens. Americans assumed that as civilians they would be repatriated to the United States, a standard method of dealing with civilians caught in a war zone, especially women and children. In the United States, officials rounded up Japanese diplomats and journalists after the bombing of Pearl Harbor, detaining them until arrangements could be made to send them back to Japan. Germany and Italy interned a few thousand American civilians until repatriation in the spring of 1942, but the Japanese had tens of thousands of Allied civilians to deal with in the Pacific theater, close to fourteen thousand of whom were American.[2] The Japanese refused to repatriate them mostly because they might later prove to be important bargaining chips, so the only thing the Japanese could do for the time being to ensure that these civilians would not work against them was to intern the entire group.

ENTERING INTERNMENT

During the first days of January 1942, just after they marched into Manila, the Japanese rounded up Allied civilians, curtly informing them that this was for purposes of alien registration so they should pack only enough supplies for three days. The commander in chief of the Japanese Imperial Forces issued a statement explaining that "enemy aliens" had been concentrated in order to "protect their lives," ordering those not yet in protective custody to report to Japanese authorities by January 15 or they would be "severely dealt with." The Japanese considered citizens of all Allied powers, including the United States, Great Britain (excluding the Irish Free State), Canada, Australia, New Zealand, the Netherlands, Poland, and the Federation of South Africa, as enemy aliens.[3] This claim of protection was a self-serving one, since Allied civilians, most of whom had lived in the Pacific for years, had no one to fear but the Japanese.

In the first few days of internment, regardless of location, confusion reigned as the Japanese registered the captive civilians by nationality and gender as a basis for categorizing and separating them. Space limitations in the internment camps usually prevented division by nationalities but not by gender, so Japanese authorities typically ordered the separation of adult men and older boys from women and younger children. However, with thousands of people to deal with, the process proved inconsistent, yet both methods of division demoralized the internees by interfering with family and national solidarity or both.

Emily Van Sickle, the thirty-one-year-old wife of an International Harvester employee in Manila, recalled the ensuing commotion when on January 5 the Japanese came into the popular Bay View Hotel, where some Allied civilians had fled for safety. Emily and her husband, Charles, called Van, packed their bags and went along with the other hotel guests for registration. They met up with some British friends from International Harvester, Helen and Edwin Cogan and their daughter, Isabel, and all were deposited at Santo Tomas University. Spanish Dominican priests had founded the university in 1611, and its present site, occupied since 1927, was located in the middle of Manila. Santo Tomas consisted of several large buildings sprawled across sixty acres; walled in on three sides, it was fenced and gated across the main entrance on Espana Boulevard. The university had few overnight accommodations since its approximately six thousand students were mostly commuters, leaving internees scrambling for places to sleep and for easy access to toilet facilities. The Japanese designated the Main Building, situated in the center of the campus, for internee occupation, but within a few days overcrowding pushed others into the Domestic Science Building, dubbed the Annex, and then into the Gymnasium. After ten days of roundups, over three thousand Allied civilians resided in Santo Tomas, a number that swelled to five thousand at points during the war. An early census of the population showed that Americans made up 70 percent of the internees, including more than twelve hundred women and four hundred children under the age of fifteen in the camp.[4]

The Van Sickles and the Cogans made their way to the Main Building, and when Emily could get no "intelligible direction from this bedlam," the two families simply took over the first unoccupied room they came to. Though separate living quarters had been designated for men and women, they were determined to delay the separation because they wanted to hold on to familiar people and things for as long as possible. As they settled in, some Japanese soldiers glanced into their room, looked around, and left, which Emily took as a bad sign. Van, already ill, then headed to the men's quarters, hoping to forestall a subsequent move when he might be even sicker, but Emily elected to stay with the Cogans "as long as possible before seeking refuge among strangers." Just as the small group fell asleep, the Japanese soldiers returned to count the new internees, but with Van gone, their nationality and gender numbers did not match previous tallies, prompting hours of discussions and counts before the Japanese soldiers, aided by interpreters, straightened out the situation. Edwin Cogan had to go to the room for British men, while Helen, Isabel, and Emily relocated to the room for British women; the next morning, Emily transferred to a room of American women. She observed that separating the internees by nationality "appeared to be a whim of third floor sentries, as no attempt was ever made on the first and second floors to unscramble them."[5] But separation by sex remained a constant in the internment camps.

Emily had quietly parted from Van out of concern for his health, while the general chaos of the internment process caused most women enough exhaustion that they simply did not have the energy to react to separation. The Nash family arrived at Santo Tomas at 9:30 in the evening on January 6 and zealously vied for their few allotted feet of living space. Ralph helped Grace and their two young boys get settled in one of the university classrooms, a process complicated by the fact that young Gale had a fever. The accommodations were filthy, and because of the capriciousness of the Japanese soldiers who rounded them up, the Nashes had not been allowed to bring any bedding or mosquito nets. Luckily, Grace found a colleague from the American School where she taught violin who allowed both of the Nash boys, despite Gale's fever, to share a makeshift bed with her daughter. When this arrangement had finally been settled, all that Grace recalled about the first separation from Ralph was that he "hurried on to the men's section which was in the Education Building next to this one, to get at least a foothold, a place to stand or sit for the night."[6] Acting as a good mother, Grace's concern for her son's health took priority over separation from her husband.

Tressa Roka felt exceptionally irritated and unhappy when she entered Santo Tomas on January 5, not only because of fears for her safety and for the success of the U.S. war effort, but also because that was to have been her wedding day. Instead of a wedding celebration she remembered that "the large iron gates of our prison slammed shut on Catesy, my fiancé, and me with a finality that chilled our hearts." The "bedlam" the couple encountered inside the university grounds, combined with her general disappointment at having missed out on her wedding, left her unsurprised to see men and women separated. As she and Catesy approached a dual stairway in the Main Building, Japanese guards told them that men had to go up the right staircase and women the left, to which Tressa responded sharply, "Sheep to the right, and goats to the left!"[7] Denied her wedding, she did not believe that things would improve much; the physical separation from her fiancé simply confirmed that.

In the cool, green, mountain-rimmed summer capital of Baguio, internment occurred about a week earlier than in Manila because the Japanese began their invasion of Luzon from the north. By December 23, 1941, according to Natalie Crouter, Baguio was "ostensibly" an open city, a designation given to a city or town in wartime to let the invading army know that it would not be defended; consequently, it experiences fewer fatalities and less structural damage as the enemy takes over. Within two days the Crouter family joined other Americans at the Brent School, a private religious institution, in a "sort of voluntary concentration so we would be all together" when the Japanese arrived.[8] In the face of invasion, the Americans reacted the same way as the British in Sandakan; they assumed safety in numbers. Since this first concentration was voluntary and the Japanese had not yet arrived, the Crouters moved back and forth from the school to their house, mostly because of the desire to be in their own home at Christmas. Late in the evening of December 26, the Japanese marched into Baguio and took control of the entire city as well as the Brent School, where soldiers kept the civilians awake for hours, even the children, counting them. Before they finally allowed the prisoners to sleep, the Japanese installed a machine gun aimed at their front door. Three days later, the Japanese divided the internees into three groups—men, children and older women, and younger women—and ordered the groups to walk to Camp John Hay, then a deserted American military post, which served as their first internment camp. Ailing from an undiagnosed malady, Natalie did not comment on her separation from Jerry but was very concerned about the whereabouts of Fred and June, and she was grateful that Jerry was around as much as possible to help with the family's move into internment.

Women who entered internment without the support of a man, even one living in a different part of camp, faced great difficulties. In addition to worrying about exactly where their men were and what they were doing—many had joined the USAFFE—those who were mothers had to take on full responsibility for themselves and their children in this new chaotic environment. Elizabeth Vaughan endured the confusion in waves. After the bombing of Manila on December 8, 1941, most of Elizabeth's servants abandoned the household, leaving her to assume control. Then, fearing imminent invasion, Elizabeth moved to an inland sugar plantation in hopes of waiting out the Japanese occupation until Allied forces liberated the island. When she and the children finally entered internment in Bacolod in June 1942, she saw how husbands and wives were separated, how they could only snatch moments together throughout the day, but at least they had some time together and could help each other. The following month Elizabeth admitted to a "permanent fatigue overtaking me. Constant, unending care of Beth and Clay."[9] In a camp of almost one hundred internees, she had to watch out for her children every minute of the day plus handle all of the chores necessary for survival; no one offered her a respite from duties previously carried out by servants.

Similar problems confronted Margaret Sherk when she entered Santo Tomas with David on January 7, moving into a setting she described as "Macy's during a Christmas rush." Since the Sherks had not lived in Manila, they knew few people in the city and did not have any money, two problems that plagued Margaret throughout most of internment. Now basically a single mother, she had no one to rely on and had few means of purchasing either essentials or luxuries for herself and David. Exhausted the first night in camp, she nonetheless stayed awake tending to her inconsolable child. Appalled at the living conditions—mother and son spent the first night sleeping on the floor without so much as a blanket to cushion them—Margaret lamented that she felt "terribly ashamed" that she had done this to David, even though she had done her best to protect him.[10]

Obtaining food was essential for their survival. During the first six weeks of internment, Margaret used her meager cash reserves to purchase fresh produce and canned goods from the Filipinos who were allowed to trade with the internees through the Japanese-controlled package line. The Philippine Red Cross quickly took on the responsibility for feeding the thousands of internees, but the bulk food it provided proved poor in quality and quantity because the Japanese controlled its food warehouses and imposed a rationing system on the supplies. Margaret had to use the camp food line so that she and David had some source of regular nourishment, whatever the quality. Yet the physical process of carrying the food to a table proved difficult without assistance, for as Margaret pointed out, "Four-year-old boys simply cannot carry food on a tin plate across a room without spilling it. . . . It was heartbreaking. Women with husbands had trays, and the husbands very often stood in line for chow for the entire family."[11] Separated from her husband, Margaret had only herself to depend on for survival, a gross expansion of her mothering duties compared with the prewar years.

On Berhala Island, the Japanese not only separated the men from the women and children, they put the men in a separate camp, so the women could not rely on their men for any help during the day. Agnes Keith described the filthy conditions of the women's camp, which had served as the government quarantine station for new Asian arrivals to Borneo: "There was no furniture, and we slept and ate on the floor. . . . Centipedes lived under us, and rats lived over us. The rats were so numerous that the noise of their fighting, playing, eating, and copulating kept us awake at night." She recalled her first week there as "mental and physical torture" because of all of the work she had to do and because of her constant concern about the effect of internment on George. Agnes, worried that he would end up with a mass of neuroses that could never be cured, resolved to be George's main source of strength, forcing herself "to make a tremendous effort to accept difficulties and dangers, if not calmly, at least without hysteria and tears."[12] She believed that George would survive untraumatized only if he thought her all-powerful, quite an illusion for her to create in a prison situation. Agnes altered her motherhood role to meet this new situation, a change that would not have been necessary in peacetime and one that sapped nearly all of her energy at a time when simply staying alive required tremendous effort.

Darlene Deibler faced a similar marital separation on Celebes, but she did not have a child to worry about. Instead, her immediate concern centered on the constructed family of fellow missionaries she stayed with when the Japanese took her husband, Russell, and the other missionary men and interned them in a police barracks in the city of Macassar. Darlene remained in the missionary settlement at Benteng Tinggi along with the other women missionaries, living with the elderly and ailing Dr. Robert Jaffray, the head of the mission, and his family. Although not immediately interned, the missionaries were put under house arrest and could not leave the area under penalty of death. At the end of 1942, the Japanese finally arrived in trucks to take the remaining women and children to a camp in Malino; civilian men had already been moved to Pare Pare. A few months later the Japanese moved the women again, this time to Kampili, formerly a tuberculosis sanitarium, where Darlene spent her remaining years of captivity in Barracks 8, originally reserved for all non-Dutch internees.

Darlene's experiences differed from the American women in the Philippines, most of whom were rounded up from their homes along with the rest of their family members, because her husband had been taken by the Japanese first and she had already endured house arrest. By the time Darlene and the others moved toward the larger town of Malino, the act of internment was merely a formality, but their quality of life deteriorated with that first move to a small house in a valley across from Malino. Eight adults crowded into a two-room house with only a small cubicle for a bathroom and an open-wood fire in a lean-to next to the house for cooking. Darlene's religious faith kept her from losing heart; while she realized the potential for conflict in their situation, she denied that it ever surfaced: "Take seven very individual, independent women and one gentleman, accustomed to being a leader, put them in cramped quarters . . . and what do you have? Put God in the midst, and you have that rare and beautiful thing known as the fellowship of the saints." The missionaries drew on their faith to improve the circumstances of internment. After their final move to Kampili, Darlene recalled that Barracks 8 remained "a calm center in the eye of the military storm that raged around us. There was a sharing, a concern, and a love that was unique."[13] She attributed this harmony to God.

Japanese camp authorities insisted on separating their captives by sex, a division designed to demoralize the internees and cut down on the possibility of a natural increase in the camp population, both of which the Japanese considered crucial to controlling their captives. In Santo Tomas men and older boys occupied the Gymnasium, women and young children were housed in the Annex, and adult men and women lived on separate floors of the Main Building, disrupting the nuclear families the Americans had been accustomed to. Yet men and women took their meals in a common area and performed camp work, including cooking, gardening, and garbage detail, in mixed groups. Men and women could therefore mingle during daytime hours, as long as they did not touch or kiss, before they separated at night. Even in this the Japanese gradually relented: during the last year of internment they lifted the nighttime restriction, and when the Los Banos camp opened in 1943, married couples could live together there. Although women were not totally cut off from their husbands or sweethearts, the reality of camp life meant that they could not rely on consistent help from them.

In Kuching, Borneo, Japanese authorities worried about rebellion from their captives. Agnes Keith observed that there were few armed Japanese soldiers to guard more than three thousand prisoners there, so the

Japanese instituted an elaborate separation by nationality, military status, civilian status, and sex to lessen the possibility of a physical challenge to their authority. Men and women could not eat or work together; if they accidentally met, they were not to speak or even look at each other. But as Agnes Keith pointed out, the temptation proved "too great," and Japanese authorities soon moved the women's camp "a half-mile further down the road, to where we couldn't see our husbands."[14]

CAMP ORGANIZATION AND POLITICS

Japanese civilian authorities ran most of the camps in the Philippines, choosing one or two male internees to act as representatives for the entire camp population, who then established an organizational structure for the camp within the boundaries of the Japanese command. Drawing on the American heritage of establishing communities and a representative government, the internees quickly learned how to survive in their new surroundings, with organization one of the keys to survival. This is not to say that the Japanese were lax in their control but rather that they preferred to have the internees carry the bulk of the responsibility for their well-being, an approach that created more work for the internees and placed the blame on them if something went wrong.

Organization in Santo Tomas occurred swiftly because of the needs of its large population and because of advanced planning. The Central Committee of Santo Tomas was the wartime successor to the American Emergency Committee (AEC), a special unit of the American Red Cross that formed in Manila in early 1941 to protect American lives and property in the event of a Japanese invasion. Toward the end of December, as Japanese troops neared the city, Frederic Stevens, chair of the AEC, worked out an agreement with the officials of Santo Tomas University for its use as an internment site in order to safeguard the lives of Allied civilians. Since the arrangement had already been made, Japanese officials readily accepted it for civilian internment. When the camp opened on January 4, 1942, the Japanese tapped Earl Carroll, district chairman of the South Malate District for the AEC, to head an internee committee, generally known as the Central Committee, which took on the responsibility for day-to-day operations. Men clearly controlled the Central Committee and its subcommittees. Of the sixteen operating committees, only one, the Recreating Committee, was co-chaired by a woman, an American identified as Mrs. Kenneth B. Day, whose husband sat on the first Central Committee. Shortly after Josephine Waldo arrived, she noted this structure: "In 24 hours the camp was organized along the lines of a small town. The Central Committee with Carroll at the head is our governing body and a go-between between the Japs and ourselves. Committees were formed to handle sanitation, food, police, education, religion, labor, etc. . . . Plumbers, electricians, doctors, carpenters, etc. all volunteered their services and much work was done."[15] Successful organization occurred quickly and remained vital to sustaining an acceptable living standard.

The normal rules of American representative politics had to be altered to allow for the reality of internment. The very fact that these people lived in prison precluded the possibility of establishing true representative politics, because Japanese camp authorities could ultimately overturn any decisions made by camp committees, which existed solely at the discretion of the Japanese. Within this established context, the internees proceeded with as much of a representative government as possible; at the heart of representation lay the ability of the internees to choose and vote for the people whom they wanted to run their committees. Since Japanese officials selected a small group of Allied men to act as representatives, the internees rarely had a say in that matter, and while most expressed gratitude that they did not have to deal with the Japanese on a daily basis, they sometimes resented the choices that the Japanese made and criticized those representatives.

For example, Earl Carroll, certainly no puppet of the Japanese, suffered frequent criticism simply because of the position he held, for as Emily Van Sickle pointed out, he "was not an elected official." After the initial organization of the camp, when it became clear that the Japanese intended to let their prisoners run their daily affairs, most expected that all committee members would be affirmed by vote. Even in a wartime concentration camp, Americans counted on carrying on their own political traditions. Members of the Central Committee initially resisted the call for campwide elections, probably because the first months of internment proved very chaotic and required consistent and stable management. Yet one Central Committee member, Alfred "Doug" Duggleby, allegedly defended appointments over voting by asking Emily and her husband: "Why should Earl and the committee stand for election? We're doing a good job. Most internees haven't brains enough to vote for good men." Emily found this "undemocratic defence [sic]" unfathomable.[16]

By June 1942, with the internees more accustomed to their circumstances, members of the Central Committee also grew uneasy with the "undemocratic" nature of the committee structure and persuaded the Japanese to allow an election for a new Central Committee, which took place in July. The new committee, according to camp chronicler A. V. H. Hartendorp, considered itself "justified in asserting authority with a degree of assurance" unmatched by the first Committee.[17] That new feeling of confidence was brought about by faith in the democratic process, leading the new committee members to believe that their actions had the sanction of the majority of the internee population. To allow as many people as possible to serve on the committee, internees planned on scheduling elections every six months, with the first primary on January 15, 1943. Every adult internee could cast a vote for any other internee, and election rules did not specifically list gender as a criterion for either voting or holding office. But the Japanese, preferring stability and consistency over the democratic process, abruptly canceled the final election scheduled for January 22, declaring that the 1942 committee members would continue in their positions, thereby exposing the realistic incompatibility of imprisonment with elected representation.

There are no detailed voting statistics that show how deeply the women of Santo Tomas became involved in these elections. The two most authoritative studies of the camp suggest that only men received nominations for election to the Central Committee, and that in 1942 and 1943 the same group of men always came under consideration, a strong indication that the original committee had worked to the general satisfaction of the internees. The political participation of women likely mirrored their normal stateside participation during peacetime: they voted but rarely sought or held any kind of elected political office. Given the heightened importance of family and attention to daily survival, it is less likely that women would be interested in pursuing political matters beyond voting. Despite what they may have learned from their suffragist foremothers, politics was not a core component of American womanhood for those in Santo Tomas.

Misinformation and misunderstanding of the political process abounded; with the internee population fluctuating between three thousand and five thousand, rumors and innuendoes about anything and everything constantly flew, despite the presence of an internee newsletter. Since daily life in the camp often swung rapidly from hectic to monotonous, the majority of internees did not pay very close attention to politics, and among the women, few devoted much time to it in their diaries or memoirs. Margaret Sherk discussed internee officials only within the context of what she needed to do to survive; for her, their importance lay not in how they came to their position but rather in how they functioned in that position to help others. Emily Van Sickle did not have a clear understanding of camp politics, because she mistakenly blamed the end of representative government on Carroll Grinnell, believing that he pleaded with the Japanese to keep him in power for the sake of consistency. She labeled the camp a dictatorship, "the very monstrosity that our soldiers were battling to free others from." While Emily passionately abhorred dictatorships and the apathy that brought them to power and comprehended the virtual absurdity of establishing real democracy in a concentration camp, she did not fully understand the circumstances that kept Grinnell in power. Tressa Roka also recorded misinformation, stating that by January 9, 1942, "We already had a Central Committee, a self-governing body of Americans and Englishmen elected by us and approved by the Japanese."[18] But that first committee had been appointed by the Japanese, and its members in turn appointed other internees to head additional committees. Both of these misinterpretations may have stemmed from the abundant rumors that flew through Santo Tomas, from women's lesser involvement in camp organization, or from faulty memory on the part of these women.

Autobiographies do show that women pondered the meaning of politics and democracy during wartime. Internment highlighted the importance of American democratic traditions, defining "American" by focusing on a heritage of participatory politics sacred to Americans since the Revolutionary War period. Emily saw that the internees "cherished more than ever the right of free men to choose their leaders" precisely because of their current predicament and expressed concern about the way the committees managed the camp because she viewed that as a reflection of the success of American democracy. Margaret connected democracy more closely with capitalism, maintaining that democracy provided people with the freedom to work and then use the profits of their labor for their own good. She was appalled to realize that to her Japanese captors the "democratic way of life" meant that each person had exactly the same as another.[19] This misreading of democracy ensured continuing misunderstandings between the Japanese and the internees over camp organization, highlighting the national differences between captives and captors.

Organization and politics in Baguio proceeded along similar lines, but with at least one key difference: women became much more involved. Ethel Herold, a former teacher, wife of a well-known businessman, and mother of two, wrote in her diary that when the Japanese moved the internees into Camp John Hay, they were instructed "to organize ourselves and live as a community," a process she described as "similar to setting up a new United States or something—only we have those damned japs over us—but it surely is an experience in government."[20] The small size of the Baguio camp evoked a family-centered atmosphere that mirrored the division of labor in most twentieth-century American families at that time: men and women both contributed to the family with separate but necessary skills.

The Baguio internees organized a Men's Committee (also known as the General Committee) and a Women's Committee, with the women appointed by and reporting to the men; these two umbrella committees then created subcommittees to recruit volunteers for the crucial daily work. By early January 1942, Ethel found herself in charge of the Work Committee, one of the eight committees established under the Women's Committee, of which she was elected chair. These positions meant a lot of work and responsibility, but they made Ethel one of the most powerful women in camp. When she originally resisted the nomination to chair the Women's Committee because she believed she already had enough work to do, one of the ministers persuaded her, saying, "Ethel, if you are a patriotic American and really want to do something for your country, you will do this!"[21] She gave in and took on the responsibility.

Some of the internees expressed gratitude that people like Ethel took charge to begin improving the camp. Fern Harrington recalled that the only "visible leaders" during the first weeks of internment were Ethel and her husband, Elmer, who had been chosen by the Japanese as the camp liaison.[22] But others found Ethel's leadership too dictatorial, and they criticized, sometimes viciously, her actions. Ethel tried to take all of this in stride, with at least a bit of a sense of humor, as shown in a limerick about herself that she anonymously submitted to the camp newsletter in March 1942:

> There once was a woman dictator
> Who tried to be just and not cater;
>   But from morning 'till night
>   She did argue and fight;
> And oh, how some people did hate her.[23]

Animosity toward Ethel and divisiveness among the women increased the following year when a political debate raged through Baguio, a debate important not only to the organizational structure of the camp but also one that illustrated the general political position of women in the camps. The Baguio controversy centered on the following question: Should women be allowed to vote? More than twenty years after the passage of the Nineteenth Amendment that guaranteed American women the right to vote, the issue of women's ability to participate in politics fractured an American community.

In Camp Holmes, the Baguio internees' second internment site, everyone expected women to carry their fair share of work, but their power was generally restricted to "women's issues" and to exercising indirect influence over the male leaders, activities similar to those within the sphere of their presuffrage ancestors. Only a few women wielded authority in camp. Although Ethel Herold chaired the Women's Committee for only the first eight months of its existence, she continued to serve in other capacities on that committee; she also influenced her husband, Elmer, the head of the Men's Committee. As a couple, the Herolds were recognized as camp leaders, and they were formidable. Even though the Japanese did not usually recognize women as leaders, one of the camp liaisons was a woman, Nellie McKim, fluent in both English and Japanese and knowledgeable of both cultures as well. Dr. Beulah Allen Ream, one of the camp physicians, also had much influence with the internees and the Japanese, who respected her medical knowledge. Despite their actual or potential power, women clearly occupied a secondary position in camp politics because of the war, since internees, both male and female, viewed war as men's business; though they were all civilians, in wartime many wanted and expected men to take the lead in organization.

Notwithstanding these generally strong feelings, no absolute consensus on this matter existed. Precisely because of their altered circumstances, because they lived as captives, exercising the right to vote became all the more precious to some of the Baguio women. Natalie Crouter expressed concern about the women's lack of voting rights in August 1942 when she noted camp election day and described her continued amazement that the General Committee did not want women to take any part in camp politics. The women had their own committee and were allowed to submit ideas to the men's suggestion box but could not do anything beyond that. The General Committee argued that allowing women political participation would result in a "mess," that since the Japanese "don't consider women people," there was no sense in trying to push the point with camp officials. With women denied voting rights, Natalie concluded that "perhaps there never will be any official democracy in here except for the men." Sticklers for absolute equality, she and a group of women continued to push the issue, and on March 19, 1943, the following notice from the Women's Committee appeared on the camp bulletin board: "In Memorium. Deceased— The Spirit of Liberty as expressed in Women's Suffrage. If the Women's Committee being duly elected by the women of the camp is only functioning through the forbearance of the General [Men's] Committee, then why not bring us Women's Suffrage that we women may have a voice in choosing our General Committee?" The call for universal women's suffrage continued over the next few weeks; on March 30, 1943, Natalie copied another memo into her diary that stated that women not only wanted the right to vote in elections but also the right to hold office in a committee made up of both men and women.[24] The following day the all-male General Committee unanimously rejected the proposal.

Undaunted, the Women's Committee pressed the issue, successfully petitioning for a campwide plebiscite on universal suffrage; the vote, cast separately by men and women, was close: 181 yes and 168 no. The General Committee unconscionably interpreted this result to mean that camp politics could continue as usual, and it denied women universal suffrage. Natalie, devastated by the outcome of the plebiscite because it confirmed women's "secondary, subsidiary" position in camp, recounted one woman's angry reaction: "It will be fine for some of these fathers to tell their sons later how they refused equal suffrage—in a Concentration Camp of all places!"[25]

The struggle over women's suffrage concerned not only women's political rights but also the unique factionalism in Baguio. Historically, women's suffrage never has been simply a case of men versus women, traditionalists versus modernists, or conservatives versus liberals, and in Baguio it had to do with the ways in which the internees developed group loyalties. According to Fern Harrington, by the time the internees moved into Camp Holmes in April 1942, there was little need for the Women's Committee because the General Committee coordinated the administration of the camp, a realization that likely prompted some women to later raise the question of universal suffrage. Fern also recalled that Beulah Allen "set out to champion the rights of women through the Women's Committee." What might have been a purely political issue became deeply embroiled in camp factionalism because

Beulah, a strong-willed and dedicated doctor who often vigorously disagreed with the other camp physician, Dana Nance, was a controversial figure. Internees took sides in these critical matters, most of which
concerned food and medicine policies for the camp. When the General
Committee disregarded the outcome of the plebiscite, it justified its
actions by claiming, according to Fern, that "the real issue was not
voting rights but Dr. Allen and her faction." Fern and her missionary
friend Cleo Morrison voted against women's suffrage because they were
not among the "Allenites" and because they believed that the men
"usually acted in the best interests of the whole camp," so they "were
afraid to upset the status quo."[26]

Following the defeat of universal suffrage, some of the internees
moved to dissolve the Women's Committee and turn over all camp
organization to the men. Natalie Crouter opposed this move, arguing
that women still needed to manage their own affairs, that despite the
conflicts that sometimes arose within the Women's Committee, it
accomplished invaluable work. By October 1943 the women still retained responsibility for some or all of the aspects of child care, clothing, food preparation and service, medical services, and health and
sanitation. Despite the intense debate sparked by the proposal for universal women's suffrage, the controversy concluded very quietly. Fern
Harrington simply noted that "everything that Dr. Allen championed
was eventually adopted"; in February 1944 Natalie reported, without
comment, that when the Japanese Imperial Army had taken control of
the camp, the Women's Committee merged with the General Committee, and "we all vote for the one." She credited the Japanese with giving the women the right to vote and the right to serve on the General
Committee, implicitly criticizing the men raised in democratic countries where women enjoyed political participation who did not accord
women those very same rights.[27]

Voting was never an option in Kuching, Borneo, where Colonel Suga
ruled over the headquarters for the eight camps that held three thousand Allied military prisoners of war and civilian internees, although
each was allowed its own representative or "camp master." When Agnes
Keith arrived there, exhausted after a long, churning boat trip from
Berhala Island, she found that only two women were allowed contact
with Japanese authorities, a Catholic nun and a doctor. These selections
made sense, since the Japanese generally respected religious figures and
those with medical training, regardless of gender. The arrival of Agnes
and the others necessitated the appointment of another liaison, and the

women elected Dorie Adams, the wife of a British army official, who Agnes observed "was not the leader type [but] no other woman in camp would ever have had the patience to put up with us, and the Japanese, both."[28] Although the Japanese initially resisted dealing with her, the persistent ill health of Mother Bernardine, the Catholic nun, forced them to accept her first as a temporary replacement, then as a permanent one. Agnes maintained that Dorie's unassuming yet persuasive demeanor ultimately compelled even the Japanese to admire her.

Although Dorie carried the official title of liaison, in reality she held the responsibility for the management of the women's camp, which in Kuching meant a lot of work. In addition to her liaison duties, Dorie made sure that enough women volunteered for work details and that the work was acceptable to camp authorities. Camp masters also endeavored to better the circumstances of internment, a usually futile effort, yet they were not totally powerless to effect change in their circumstances. They met weekly with Japanese authorities to receive work orders, hear reprimands on behavior, learn about the progress of the war, and, after lectures about their duties, typically requested additional food and medicine, requests the Japanese generally ignored.

Thwarted but unrelenting in their efforts to obtain these supplies, the male camp masters adamantly refused to back down on treatment they considered egregious and offensive to gender conventions: capricious punishment of the women. In the aftermath of an attempted rape charge lodged by Agnes Keith against one of the guards in the summer of 1943, the Japanese began a campaign of petty harassments aimed at the women that culminated in the severe beating of "Mrs. B." for wearing a head scarf. Though the camps were separated by distance and by fencing, news circulated on a regular basis. The British military prisoners, always as solicitous of the women's needs as possible, became particularly enraged when they heard about the women's mistreatment, warning their captors "that the soldiers could not be restrained further if the guards continued to strike the women." The situation became serious enough that the camp masters secured permission to present their complaints directly to Colonel Suga. While Suga declared that he would forbid his guards to ever hit a woman again, he did remind the representatives that the guards had the right to enforce discipline. According to Agnes, Suga relented only because he genuinely feared a revolt by the malnourished and unarmed Allied male prisoners, a revolt she predicted would be disastrous. She allowed that while the men could have killed some Japanese guards, they then would have been quickly massacred, with the women and children they sought to protect murdered in retaliation. Agnes concluded that "life was not sweet in prison, but it was sweeter than meeting death by mutilation and torture."[29] By the end of the summer the incidents had been largely forgotten, and life in camp, monotonous as ever, went on. But the prisoners had successfully exerted their will, and even in this peculiar wartime situation, men were able to come to the rescue of women, to uphold the chivalry so familiar to them by reasserting their manliness.

The relationship between strong internee representation and decent treatment was also crucial to the women on Celebes, where Darlene Deibler endured internment with a small group of women, most of whom were not American. In Kampili, Darlene and all the non-Dutch lived in Barracks 8, which the women referred to as the "Heinz Barracks" because it contained nearly fifty-seven varieties of nationalities. Each barracks chose a leader who met on a regular basis with Mrs. Joustra, the Dutch head of the camp and liaison with the Japanese camp commander. The women of Barracks 8 chose Darlene as their representative, a choice she believed was due to her fluency in English, Dutch, and Indonesian. Her responsibilities included calling the women to order for roll call, making announcements, and establishing a work schedule. Even roll call was serious business; therefore, Darlene made sure that everyone was present at the specified time, because the camp commander periodically checked every bed for its proper occupant, and if guards found a woman missing, the "punishment always exceeded the crime."[30]

As a missionary, Darlene believed that her responsibility as barracks leader included the spiritual well-being of the women, so she read a portion of the Bible every night and prayed with the women who chose to stay after the reading of the nightly announcements. Soon some women from the other barracks joined in as well. Through these evening prayer sessions, Darlene maintained that "God kept our barracks a calm center in the eye of the military storm that raged around us," and that the sessions provided a "sharing, a concern, and a love that was unique" plus helped the women to cope with and survive internment.[31]

Although young and not part of the dominant nationality group, Darlene assumed Mrs. Joustra's position in the summer of 1945 when Mr. Yamaji, the Japanese head of the camp, ordered the changeover. Although Mrs. Joustra expressed relief to be out of the position, several women resented Darlene's new authority. Mrs. Joustra defended Darlene's appointment, maintaining that Yamaji wanted the change because he had great respect for Darlene, which stemmed from her nobly endured imprisonment and torture by the Kempetai, the Japanese secret police. Although this experience elevated her in the eyes of Yamaji, many of the other camp women did not accord her any special status for her ordeal. Darlene's main detractor, Mrs. Heiden, allegedly told the other women that Kampili was a "Dutch camp and we will not have an American to rule over us!"[32] The issues were not really about age or nationality but the location of control and power, elements crucial to survival in this tough camp. Mrs. Heiden wanted what Darlene had been given, but she did not get it.

SUPPORT FROM THE OUTSIDE

As much as the internees did for themselves, it is unlikely that so many of them would have survived had it not been for the support of sympathetic uninterned peoples. In the Philippines many internees could count on their Filipino friends and former servants and employees to provide them with food, clothing, money, and war news, all very necessary for survival. With the chaos of invasion and roundup, the Americans had little opportunity to sufficiently pack enough supplies for an unanticipated three-year internment, resulting in an appalling combination: the Americans arrived in internment unprepared, while the Japanese resisted providing them with food and other basic supplies necessary for survival. The internees had to figure out how to get these things for themselves, and their friends on the outside proved to be ingenious suppliers.

Those in Santo Tomas, with the approval of Japanese camp authorities, devised the best and most consistent system for securing outside assistance by establishing a package line during the first weeks of internment. Filipinos and other uninterned nationals stood in line in front of the camp to pass goods to friends inside, leading to chaos as internees and outsiders alike swarmed the fence in hopes of seeing people they knew and of receiving food and other goods. Guards initially reacted with violence, knocking the Filipinos down and threatening them with bayonets, but they kept returning. Josephine Waldo reported that although the Japanese had forbidden any more food to be brought in through the fence, "Filipinos threw bread and canned goods over the fence to us. Some will take no money for it." Grace Nash recalled that through the intervention of the General Committee, Japanese authorities decided to allow outside help, but not without rules. Outsiders could send in packages between 9:00 and 11:00 each morning, were forbidden to talk to those in the camp, had to provide their names and addresses along with their packages, and camp guards inspected the packages before passing them on to the internees. Elizabeth Vaughan, arriving in Santo Tomas in the spring of 1943, provided one of the most colorful descriptions of this process: "The daily package line moves like the body of a huge writhing serpent as men, women, and children, who compose the line, shift and fidget from both impatience and the discomfort of the glare of the sun on the driveway from the Main Building to the gate."[33] The Japanese prohibited current non-Japanese periodicals and all sharp instruments; anyone caught trying to pass them into camp was severely punished. After Emily Van Sickle's husband took on the job of camp censor, messages could pass between the internees and their outside friends as long as they adhered to Japanese specifications. Money changed hands as well, complete with handwritten receipts.

Help from the outside, whether in the form of outright gifts or arranged purchases, drastically improved the internees' lifestyle as friends and servants sent in necessities and luxuries. Tressa Roka remarked in early January 1942 that the internees who had "homes, servants, friends, and business associates on the outside were fortunate indeed!" Tressa and Catesy contacted one of their former servants, Catalino, and he brought them not only food but the utensils, stove, and fuel with which to cook it. Emily and Charles Van Sickle benefited from the food sent in by the cook of their British friends the Cogans; the two couples split the expenses for having food brought in three times a week. Just after camp authorities formalized the package line, Grace Nash received several useful items including two mattresses, mosquito nets, and bed sheets, things that she had not had the opportunity to pack as the Japanese rounded up her family for internment. In addition to these individual acts of generosity, there were occasionally larger ones that benefited everyone. Emily recalled that for Thanksgiving 1943, "two loyal and generous friends," Juan Elizalde and Enrico Pirovano, sent in enough turkeys, chickens, and potato salad for everyone to have a real Thanksgiving dinner.[34] The feast not only eased the culinary monotony but also provided a welcome psychological boost by allowing the internees to celebrate a truly American holiday, accompanied by some of the traditional trimmings.

The benefit of the package line went beyond the strictly material to the psychological, assuring the internees that the Filipinos still supported them. According to Emily, the concern that ranked second—just below obtaining food—was maintaining contact with friends on the outside. This connection helped to ease isolation, as the fragmented socializing with people on the other side of the fence provided the internees with some sense of continuity and normality. But when the number of people congregating outside of Santo Tomas continued to increase, the Japanese, angry at this show of assistance, covered the fence with sawali, a large native palm, so that the internees could no longer see outside of their prison. Emily labeled this action "unfortunate" but pointed out that it was not "unnatural that the Japanese should resent manifestations of sympathy from the Filipinos, whose friendship they were avidly courting for themselves." Tressa Roka insisted that the "one bright spot" in their lives was seeing the number of people lined up each day, sometimes for hours on end, to pass along goods and "messages of cheer." The daily presence of these outsiders made the internees feel that they were not "isolated and alone in an enemy world." The package line also represented the Filipinos' firm belief that the Americans would return to the islands and liberate them from the Japanese. Grace Nash observed that despite the risks involved in passing goods along to the internees, "Filipinos continued to come with unselfish and lasting loyalty."[35]

Since the relationship between the United States and the Philippines began with colonial imperialism, the response of its inhabitants to the internment of the Americans was surprising indeed. Yet the situation in the Philippines was different; the United States had taken over the islands with the express idea of granting them independence in the foreseeable future. Enduring, often affectionate personal relationships developed between Filipinos and Americans as did close political and economic ties, so Japanese promises of establishing a Greater East Asia Co-Prosperity Sphere based on Asian racial solidarity failed to completely sever those bonds. The interned women viewed the generosity of the Filipinos as personal and humanitarian, which to a certain extent was true. Some Filipinos took great risks to help the Allied captives even in the face of the wrath of the Japanese, who expected them to unite along racial lines. However, the Filipinos' continued willingness to support the Americans was also prompted by the harsh treatment the Japanese meted out to the local population and by Filipinos' beliefs that the Americans, not the Japanese, could be trusted to give them their independence.[36]

Despite this general American-Filipino alliance, not all of the outsiders who helped the internees turned out to be totally trustworthy or

completely altruistic. Internees entrusted these people with the knowledge of where they had hidden their food and valuables plus gave them
sums of their dwindling cash supply to purchase additional items. As
the war continued and food and medicine became increasingly difficult
to come by, some of the helpers stole from or cheated the internees,
often because they needed these things for survival, but sometimes
because they wanted to profit at the internees' expense. The bonds
forged between the Filipinos and Americans proved strong but not un-
breakable, especially during the chaos and violence of war.

Such betrayals adversely affected the internees, both materially and
psychologically. In November 1942, Tressa Roka became "depressed,
disillusioned, and hurt" because she found out that her trusted former
servants, Catalino and Adoracion, had been selling her personal property from her apartment. Tressa pessimistically concluded that Japanese anti-American propaganda had finally taken hold in Manila and
that the Filipinos believed the Americans would never return; therefore, some Filipinos felt justified in taking advantage of the Americans.
One of Grace Nash's former servants, Santiago, came to the package
line every day for one week, delivering food and clothing the Nashes
had stored in a friend's home, then disappeared on the day he was to
have delivered Grace's sterling silver, items invaluable for trade or sale.
She later found out that her silver turned up in a marketplace in Manila, put up for sale by a man whose description matched Santiago.[37]

If the support of former servants was erratic, internees had more luck
with friends, business associates, and other acquaintances who, because
of the absence of a master-servant relationship, tended to be more consistently helpful. Tressa Roka received outside aide from Mr. Nagy, a
Hungarian she first met in Shanghai in 1937. Tressa had been born in
Hungary and came to the United States as a small child, and Hungarian culture and romantic intentions on Mr. Nagy's part brought the two
of them together. Because Mr. Nagy retained his Hungarian citizenship,
the Japanese did not intern him, so he did what he could to help Tressa,
including giving a home to her beloved dog, Rags, and sending her treats
and other miscellaneous finery to keep her spirits up. Although part of
his helpfulness stemmed from his hopes to eventually marry Tressa,
he understood the deprivations she suffered in Santo Tomas, especially
of feminine regalia, and did what he could to ease her suffering and lift
her spirits.

For the internees who had no helpers of any kind on the outside, the
package line became a symbol of the growing division between the

"haves" and "have-nots." According to Margaret Sherk, the "Manila people," those who had lived in the city for years before the war, benefited most from the package line, while those without connections in Manila "had nothing to fall back on" during internment.[38] Margaret could only use the package line to arrange for the purchase of food from the outside; no one gave anything to her. Yet the line also served as a form of entertainment, even though it could be a rather psychologically painful pastime. She and David went to the fence every day for awhile just to watch, because it gave them something to do and because of the unlikely chance that someone might have word of her husband, Bob. While Margaret envied the people who received food from the line, she was appalled at the amount of food they threw away, which could have been given to the "have-nots" who went hungry until the establishment of a camp kitchen. Such waste was an affront to her perception of American fairness.

The bounty from the package line ended in early 1944 when Santo Tomas reverted to the jurisdiction of the Japanese military, which closed it, lessening the gap between the "haves" and "have-nots" and signaling tougher times ahead for all internees. Tressa Roka noted in her diary on February 21, 1944: "No more food packages! All contact with the outside world has ceased!" Humiliated by a succession of military defeats, the Japanese no longer felt generous toward the internees and began to punish them. The Americans had expected this reaction from the Japanese as they began to lose the war and became heartened by the impending Allied victory, yet they also realized they would suffer even more until liberation. The Japanese discontinued the package line because they wanted to isolate the internees from the Filipinos, to demoralize them by cutting them off from friends and outside news. This action also accelerated malnutrition by cutting off outside food sources and forcing more people to share the camp food.[39] But despite the serious implications of the loss of this food source, internees tried to keep their spirits up with the belief that liberation must be just around the corner.

Many Americans had lived in Baguio for a generation or more and had strong connections with each other and with the Filipinos, which resulted in a tenacious support system. Fern Harrington, an outsider to this group, recalled that when the Americans first settled in Camp John Hay, some Filipinos brought bags of food to the market to be loaded on the camp supply truck, each bag labeled with the name of an internee. Elmer Herold passed out the bags, after the Japanese inspected them, to the "lucky recipients" who usually waited until dark, until the unlucky hungry internees could not see them, before they opened and consumed their treasures.[40]

Not everyone who received food from the outside hoarded it; even Fern shared in some because her friend, Cleo Morrison, befriended Amy Juhan, who received food packages. Amy had married an American and had an American father, but her mother was a Filipina; therefore, she had relatives who regularly sent her food, which she graciously shared. Ethel Herold had a lot of friends on the outside, mostly former students from the Trinidad Agricultural School where the Herolds taught before Elmer went into the lumber business. These people, plus the Herold family chauffeurs, had small farms in the area and regularly sent food to the Herolds, sometimes "four big lots" daily, which they shared with others who were "so appreciative of what we give them." These food gifts helped to keep the family healthy, even though Ethel lost twenty-five pounds during the first six weeks of internment, and they also eased the burden on camp resources. Faithful friends continued to send food in until Japanese military authorities stopped the practice in February 1944. Ethel expressed gratitude in her diary for the Filipino friends who prevented them from starving, pledging that she and Elmer would work in the Philippines after the war "so we can repay all these good souls."[41]

Natalie Crouter's contact with her former servants, Nida and Ismael Bacani, provided her not only with food but also with information and reassurances that her beloved servants remained alive and well. Her diary entries regularly mentioned the Bacanis as she acknowledged food and other items they sent in to the Crouters, and she took comfort in these deliveries as signs that the Bacanis survived. Natalie recorded in her diary on February 9, 1942, that Ismael sent in a loaf of bread and jam, and two days later the Bacanis sent in twelve loaves of *pan de sal* (salt bread) in honor of Fred's eleventh birthday. Even though most of the food and clothing that the Bacanis sent in came from the Crouters' own storage and were therefore not technically gifts, the Bacanis had not deserted their former employers or profited from their internment. But for Natalie, even greater joy came when she received concrete news from the Bacanis: on March 4, 1942, Natalie obtained a "big surprise of a package and letter from Nida!" It was the first time she received any news from home; she expressed delight that the Bacanis had settled in the Crouter home and described it as a "thrill" to get information "tucked in with two cans of Nestle milk and some consomme."[42] Natalie's elation at receiving this letter reflected a mixture of concerns for the Bacanis and for her own family. She liked the idea of the Bacanis living in her home because it provided them with a good place to stay, but their presence also cut down on the likelihood that the Crouter home would be looted. Concerned about her possessions, many of which were Asian antiques or family heirlooms, Natalie trusted that the Bacanis would protect these things.

The strength of the relationship between the two families came under close scrutiny in May 1942, when the Crouters debated the feasibility and practicality of release from Camp Holmes. Nakamura, a former carpenter in one of the local mines and one of the civilian Japanese camp officials, informed Jerry Crouter that Ismael and Nida offered to take care of the family, to act as protective sponsors, should they be released. Natalie observed that Jerry was "sheepish and pleased at once" by the offer and knew that he was "deeply moved" even though he did not say much about it. Natalie was surprised but more loquacious: "It takes courage and faithfulness to come forward in these times to stand back of denuded Americans. Bless them, I knew they would come through, though not quite so staunchly before we even got out. . . . What a homecoming it will be, even if our things are gone." To Natalie, this offer of sponsorship signified shifting dependencies between Filipinos and Americans, a change she viewed as positive. She claimed that the reversed relationship was "like breathing to me, the realization of one's dependence on another," that it did not matter who depended on whom because "all [were] friends in adversity," since "war makes paupers of everyone." Natalie credited the Japanese with inadvertently creating a "new character, new ties, formed in adversity, more lasting that any built during prosperity."[43] But in the end, Japanese officials decided not to release any of the civilian internees, even under Filipino sponsorship, so the Crouters remained in camp.

For Natalie, the link between the Bacanis and "home" was forged even more strongly as the war progressed. As long as the Bacanis stayed healthy and remained safely ensconced in the Crouter home, Natalie maintained a sense of normality plus a positive belief in the future; when that link weakened, she all but collapsed. On June 25, 1943, Natalie declared that "the heavens fell around us and our world, as we have known it, crashed." The news that caused this breakdown was twofold. First, Nida had fallen gravely ill with appendicitis, and Natalie "mentally sank to the floor as the earth rocked and the rest . . . passed over like a tidal wave after earthquake" when she heard. Second, she learned that the Japanese had gone into her home and taken everything except the stove and piano. While she realized she could do nothing about her stolen possessions, she seethed at her inability to do anything for the ailing Nida. Natalie emotionally considered that "Nida is our family, our sister, our mother, her children are ours and we are welded together now for all time. She is the Philippines to which we are bound indissolubly by old and new ties."[44] For Natalie, family ties cut across blood, race, and nationality lines, to intertwine with a sisterhood of mothering love.

On Borneo, where the colonial alliance had not been as friendly as it had been in the Philippines, relations started out friendly enough with some gifts passed along, but soon outside aid relied on commercial transactions and profit margins. On Berhala Island, Agnes Keith and other women engaged in smuggling out of dire necessity. The Japanese did not provide them with an adequate diet, so to procure more nutritious food for themselves and their children, the women decided to violate camp rules and make outside contacts. Agnes first got involved with smuggling when a local fisherman named Saleh passed along a package of eggs to her that had been sent by a former Asian employee of Harry's. With the eggs came a promise of further packages of food and money, which Agnes viewed as a "pledge of confidence" between Asians and Europeans. But others, especially those who did not receive these smuggled packages, believed that Asians would not do anything for any European once they became "helpless." These pessimists were proved wrong as the packages continued to be smuggled in throughout their internment on the island. The smuggling benefited the internees both nutritionally and psychologically, as the women came "to live on the food and excitement of smuggling," but it also enabled them to continue in their role as strong mothers who could provide for their children.[45]

With their transfer to Kuching, the women became isolated from Asian civilians, making it virtually impossible to bring in goods undetected, and as the war dragged on it was unthinkable to expect even the best of friends to provide supplies. During the spring of 1945, the women participated in a black market swap with local Chinese merchants and their own Japanese guards. Agnes knew that the guards forced the Chinese to sell them food for cash, which had little real value, and in turn the guards traded that food for any remaining valuables the women had. Inflation was astronomical, but Agnes swapped to secure food for George, helping to fulfill her vow that she would retain the strength and resourcefulness necessary to see him through the war. During one exchange, she traded her sorority pin for forty eggs and one bottle of coconut oil, which meant "safety for three more weeks for George" when she divided up the bounty.[46] Commerce, rather than friendship or charity, characterized these exchanges, which for Agnes also expressed proper mothering.

THE SUSTENANCE OF PATRIOTISM

Food nourished the bodies of the internees, and outside assistance made them feel that they had not been forgotten—even provided them with connections to home—but patriotism nourished their souls, strengthening their will to survive. The interned women who left accounts of the war years never lost pride in their American heritage, never really gave up hope that their countrymen would eventually liberate them. Even though other countries fought against the Japanese in the Pacific theater, many internees firmly believed that the Americans would reach them first. Ethel Herold and her daughter Betsy always ended their goodnights to each other by saying, "One day the Americans will come," and according to Elizabeth Vaughan, the Bacolod internees whispered "The Yanks are coming" to each other as a kind of "cheery password." This hope evolved into a belief that the Americans would liberate the camp. Elizabeth even speculated that most of the Americans would willingly spend an extra month or two in camp just so they could be "freed by soldiers under the American flag . . . to join the celebrations."[47] A stretch of her imagination, perhaps, but for Elizabeth it was American soldiers who symbolized true freedom.

If those American soldiers were to arrive, the key question was when. The internees' hopes for a quick rescue crumbled with the USAFFE surrender at Corregidor in May 1942, which marked one of the lowest points in their morale. Natalie Crouter recounted a spirited debate she had with Jerry in which they disagreed over the conduct and progress of the war and about how it would all end. After the defeat of the Philippines, Jerry predicted "a long stay" in internment, at least until the end of 1942, with Natalie countering that events would move more quickly, that the United States would "bomb Japan and use the Navy, clearing up here through negotiation." She took pride in holding up her end of the argument, proof that she paid close attention to military and political matters, and in the end, she believed that their "battle at the fence" had been good because it kept them both sharp.[48] But she had been overly optimistic; internment would last even beyond Jerry's long-range prediction about the end of 1942. Though Lieutenant Colonel James Doolittle and his B-25s made a successful bombing raid over Tokyo in April 1942, the Japanese clearly controlled the South Pacific and had no reason to negotiate the Philippines situation with the United States.

National pride and the desire to keep morale high prompted some internees to make optimistic predictions about rescue, but it did not prevent some from criticizing the U.S. government and the military. They understandably felt stung by abandonment and chastised American officials for allowing a situation to develop that led to their internment. After word of the Bataan death march reached the Baguio internees, Natalie Crouter lashed out at both sides, admitting that they all wanted the Japanese officers to suffer for what had been done to the American and Filipino soldiers. She also held culpable members of Congress and others "who cared so little that their neglect made money and comfort from selling scrap iron and other supplies to Japan during five year's of China's war. Finally the iron and neglect came down on our own boys, men we knew well, in Bataan. We dodged our own metal from the skies and were taken by an energetic enemy because we valued money and what it would buy." On New Year's Day 1943 Elizabeth Vaughan admitted that the Bacolod captives had few hopes for an early release. She imagined one of President Roosevelt's fireside chats wherein he counseled Americans to "have patience . . . the democratic way of life will prevail," gently chastising him: "Not words, Mr. Roosevelt. Action, please."[49] Although these Americans truly loved their country, they felt free to criticize it without jeopardizing their relationship to it.

Despite these mixed viewpoints on their position and the reasons for it, the internees still held to their belief that the United States was the mightiest power on earth, a faith that became concrete when forty-seven-pound Red Cross relief packages reached them during Christmas 1943. Rumors of the relief packages circulated in the Philippine camps after the repatriation of about one hundred Allied civilians the previous September. In the most practical sense, these packages ensured the survival of the majority of the internees, containing such delicacies as SPAM, cheese, margarine, and chocolate, supplies that provided vital nutrition throughout the last year or so of internment. Of that Christmas, Natalie Crouter wrote: "Now we know that America is thinking of us, working for us. . . . Pride in America stretched out as we realized it was covering the world. . . . We are not forgotten. We are remembered." In Santo Tomas, the internees almost did not receive one of the most sought-after items in the packages: cigarettes. According to Elizabeth Vaughan, the Japanese found the label on the Old Gold cigarettes offensive: "FREEDOM. Our heritage has always been freedom. We cannot afford to relinquish it. Our armed forces will safeguard that heritage if we, too, do our share to preserve it." The internees strenuously objected when they found out the Japanese intended to confiscate the Old Golds, but in the end the captors relented and distributed the cigarettes without the offending wrapper. News of the wrapper's message had spread like wildfire through the camp, reviving the spirits of the internees; some lucky internees received the cigarettes with the wrapper still intact, and Tressa Roka recalled that this made them "jubilant."[50] Not only did the internees receive precious necessities, but they came from the United States, the very fact of which bolstered the internees' spirits for several crucial months.

American Red Cross packages reached Kuching in March 1944, and despite Japanese looting, enough came through to make an appreciable difference in the internees' lives, both physically and psychologically. Agnes Keith felt particularly pleased to find out that the packages came from the American Red Cross, recalling that prisoners throughout the camp compound proudly whistled "Yankee Doodle" the day the goods were distributed. One of Agnes's friends remarked that it was a good day to be an American, while another countered that any day was a good day to be an American.[51]

Distribution of the relief packages proved to be an isolated occasion, something the internees could not routinely celebrate, but they could and did regularly express their national pride by remembering patriotic holidays, especially the Fourth of July. On July 4, 1942, the first Fourth of internment in Santo Tomas, Josephine Waldo cheered: "Hurrah for the Stars and Stripes! It seems rather strange to be celebrating the 4th in a concentration camp, but it takes more than that to down the good old American spirit." She described a day of celebration during which she and her husband ate ice cream and chocolate cake with friends, listened to firecrackers going off, and admired everyone's red, white, and blue outfits. The day culminated with a lecture on Thomas Jefferson and the singing of "America the Beautiful." Ethel Herold wrote in her diary on July 4, 1944—the last Fourth of her internment, when conditions in Baguio began to deteriorate—that she "hardly noticed" it. Then she went on to describe how some of the internees came to her room to look at and touch an American flag that the women had been secretly working on: "We women have slowly and lovingly button holed every star and sewed and resewed the seams just to be holding the flag. . . . Whatever becomes of this flag, it serves its purpose in here, by just being secretly looked at and dearly cherished." While the Fourth of July was widely celebrated, more minor holidays such as George Washington's birthday did not pass unobserved. Tressa Roka noted on February 22, 1942, that a group of men in Santo Tomas made an American flag and displayed it during roll call.[52] Japanese camp authorities did not approve of these celebrations, but they often did not understand enough about them to shut them down. They could not prevent thousands of people from wearing clothing that happened to be red, white, and blue, and the internees managed to hide the American flags after their brief displays.

These practices helped the internees to mark time, functioned as outlets for demonstrating their national pride, and also served as bittersweet reminders of their current predicament. Natalie Crouter described the school program put on by the children at the end of October 1942 that celebrated both Halloween and Thanksgiving, dwelling on historical comparisons with their own situation. When one of the children, dressed as a Pilgrim, commented that the Indians would probably scalp all the settlers, the audience laughed "because it sounded like our own situation and rumors." But at the end of the program, when young Fred Crouter spoke the final line, "America is waiting for you," summing up the relationship between the settlers and the new land, Natalie recalled, "We almost wept—for we are waiting for America."[53]

Internees also sang patriotic songs to remind themselves of who they were and where they came from. Japanese guards were understandably touchy about such things, and some understood enough English to know when the Americans sang songs about their country. Alice Bryant remembered that when she and her husband moved to the Bacolod internment camp, they sang to keep their spirits up, especially the popular World War I song "Over There," which Alice sang with "great gusto," emphasizing the line "The Yanks are coming." She realized that the Japanese guards heard her and knew that at least one of them knew English, but she remained safe from reprisals because he apparently did not understand the overall meaning of the song. In the spring of 1944,

Ethel Herold rewrote the World War I song "Loyalty" and renamed it "Drudgery"; the song encapsulated both the daily lives of the internees and their anticipation of freedom:

> DRUDGERY is the word today
> Concentration is like that we say
>   Picking rice or swatting flies
>   Chopping wood or censoring lies
> We have hoped for mighty action
> To clean out this Nipponese faction
>   Drudgery is the price we pay
>   Until we are freed by the U.S.A.[54]

Internees could never know when a particular guard might take offense at hearing any kind of American song, even if he did not understand its lyrics, so the thrill of singing or hearing patriotic songs was combined with fear of possible punishment. Emily Van Sickle recalled that during the spring of 1944 in Santo Tomas, a shanty neighbor, Phil Shaouy, began playing several "brand new, patriotic records" on his record player. Emily marveled at his audacity; since the records were new, she guessed that they had been smuggled in from an American submarine via the guerrillas, an extremely dangerous thing to do, since the Kempetai imprisoned and tortured anyone with possible guerrilla connections. Yet Phil played those records loudly, and when Emily cautioned him to lower the volume, to at least stop playing the most "obvious propaganda songs" like "Any Bonds Today?" and "The Man Behind the Man Behind the Gun," he dismissed her concerns, asserting that the Japanese were too dumb to understand what the songs were about. But Emily noticed that he did not play those records whenever Japanese guards came near his shanty.[55]

In September 1944, the U.S. Third Fleet began attacking Japanese positions in the Philippines, word of which soon reached the internees, and they saw American planes for the first time in almost three years. They could hardly restrain themselves from singing. On September 22, Natalie Crouter listened as Fred and one of his friends sang "The Star Spangled Banner" within hearing distance of one of the guards without repercussions. She also noted that Ruth Culpepper taught the song to her young students, "who have never heard it or seen the Stars and Stripes."[56]

Personal anniversaries and celebrations also became occasions to show patriotism. On June 24, 1943, Ethel and Elmer Herold celebrated their twenty-third wedding anniversary, the same day a birthday party was held for Karen Walker. Ethel described the birthday party that took place in the rice-picking room and the entertainment program for which she sang "The Americans Come," a World War I tune she had sung often at that time. According to her, it deeply affected everyone at that party, causing shivers to run up and down their spines, and Ethel, intensely moved by the experience, never sang the song again in camp.[57]

For Agnes Keith, the Fourth of July marked not only a holiday but her birthday as well, so the day was doubly bittersweet for her. During the first of those internment celebrations, Agnes had a party with a group of women, and they violated camp rules by cooking over an open fire; they conveniently misunderstood the guard's command to put out the fire, rewarding his patience with some cigarettes they had smuggled into the camp. The women ended the evening by singing "God Bless America" and drank a toast with coconut milk: "To America and her Day of Independence, celebrated this year [1942] by British and Americans together."[58] Though this episode also illustrates the camaraderie of the women despite their different national origins, such esprit de corps did not always exist.

Sometimes expressions of patriotism took on racial and nationalist overtones as American internees distinguished themselves from their fellow internees, but given the circumstances and the stresses of internment, this reaction is not surprising. In early spring of 1943, Josephine Waldo wrote in her diary with great optimism for the future as she described a lovely birthday celebration for her husband, Bill, recounted discussions of hopes for repatriation, then interjected "a good word for the Americans." Josephine said that she had "never seen people that could take it on the chin like they can and still come up laughing. . . . I don't know any other race that has that happy go lucky spirit and believe me, it's a wonderful thing. The stuff we're made of and character has certainly been brought to light here in this camp and as a whole the Americans have come out with flying colors." But she was not so complimentary about other nationality groups in Santo Tomas, despite the fact that they were all Allies. She found the British conceited, obnoxious, complaining, and lazy; the Poles dumb but happy; and the Spanish, Filipino, and mestizos "lazy so-and-so's." Josephine admitted, though, that everything she wrote sounded "pretty conceited, I guess, but believe me I'm mighty glad to be a foolish American and I'll blow my horn loud and long for the Stars and Stripes."[59]

Agnes Keith understood that such generalities about nationalistic characteristics stemmed from the stress of internment and close quarters. She referred to this sniping as picking "bare the bones of nationalism," reasoning that fatigue and hunger compelled the women to resort to the "comforting generalities about each other and the meanness of each other's races." Agnes found that this meanness practically disappeared when the Japanese moved the women to Kuching, because by that time they realized that "life was hideous if we surrendered to our hatreds; more livable only when we tried to be decent."[60] National pride was fine as long as it did not turn into arrogance or prevent the women from working together for survival, because living through the war was more important than anything else.

Among at least one group of internees, national superiority and patriotism took a decided back seat to faith in God for ultimate deliverance: interned missionaries consistently placed their faith in God, who in turn would lead the Americans to liberate the camps. Fern Harrington recalled that many internees believed that the missionaries did not contribute anything substantial toward the maintenance of the camp, that prayers and Bible study did not constitute real work. Fern periodically wrestled with the connection between spirituality and patriotism, especially after the fall of Bataan and receiving word that a fellow missionary, Rufus Grey, had been tortured by the Japanese and was probably dead, and she underwent a crisis of faith in God and her country. She admitted that she "wallowed in the mire of self-pity" for a time, questioning all that she had given up in exchange for a suspended missionary career. Fern felt as if both God and the United States had deserted her, so she searched desperately for a sign that God even existed. Not until the internees moved to Camp Holmes, where she saw God's majesty in the mountains behind the new camp, did she regain her faith; Fern's spirituality and patriotism were renewed.[61]

Organization, politics, outside assistance, and patriotism helped American women to survive the rigors of internment. Each provided a combination of physical and psychological support, a combination that proved life-sustaining, but in the process women had to alter their traditional definitions of womanhood in order to meet the challenges of internment. They could not afford to remain dependent on men for support, because day-to-day survival required that they take charge, recognize what needed to be done, and get it done. Into these daily tasks women interwove expressions of patriotism that reminded them they were American and that as Americans they had the strength to get through this ordeal. Even though these women had been stranded and then abandoned in the Pacific theater, they retained their faith in their country by celebrating holidays, singing songs, and surreptitiously creating American flags, but their most effusive patriotic sentiments emerged during liberation.

3

WORK AND WOMANHOOD
IN INTERNMENT

*"Work is the great healer, the strong motive power
which keeps us normal."*

During the first spring of internment, Natalie Crouter observed that, for the internees, work constituted "the great healer, the strong motive power which keeps us normal."[1] Organization, camp political systems, and expressions of patriotism provided them with direction and purpose, demonstrating that Americans were flexible enough to effectively function in different situations. Yet the internees needed more to ensure their survival; they needed to work. In early 1942, with food still plentiful and the captives generally healthy, work provided them all, despite location or gender, with a way of organizing their days, keeping up a semblance of a normal life, and enhancing their chances of survival. Regardless of the proximity of their husbands or sweethearts, women fended for themselves, and for women accustomed to having servants for cooking, housekeeping, and child care, taking on daily chores meant major changes in their lives. They had to learn how to accomplish basic tasks, often regarding them as relief from the monotony that plagued the internees throughout most of the war. However, work required energy, which was at a premium as food supplies dwindled near the end of the war; yet completion of such basic tasks as cooking and cleaning meant staying alive, so women had no choice but to continue working. By late 1944, the tedious hardships of internment turned into a life-threatening situation. Through it all, traditional women's roles were stretched and altered yet also reinforced as womanhood became increasingly associated with a willingness to work for the family as well as for the common good.

GENDER AND WORK ASSIGNMENTS

In Santo Tomas, Frederic Stevens, one of the internee leaders, designed the Work Assignment Committee to keep track of available jobs and match them with volunteers, a major job itself given the three thousand to four thousand internees there. He claimed that a "person's position in society or his civil status before the war was not particularly taken into consideration when these jobs were given out." Frieda Magnuson, initially exempted from internment because of pregnancy, picturesquely explained that "business tycoons and society belles were swabbing out toilets." In reality, not quite as much equality existed in camp jobs as Frederic and Frieda suggested. Emily Van Sickle more accurately recalled that people could submit requests for jobs, "but whether or not they would be given assignments of their choice and capabilities was problematical, for inevitably, now as always, 'pull' was often the determining factor."[2] The organizational structure of Santo Tomas was therefore not strictly democratic; connections with members of the Central Committee or any of the operating committees could put internees in more privileged positions than those without connections.

It was not always just "pull" that mattered in work assignments. Some camp jobs required specialized training, such as teaching, nursing, and plumbing, so not just anyone who wanted these jobs got them. In some cases, money ensured that not everyone had to work, especially in the early years of the war when money still circulated and could be spent on things other than extra food, and some of the wealthy internees paid others to do their share of work. For the most part, however, both men and women worked to make their own living areas tolerable, contributing to the overall welfare of the camp as well. Shortly after settling into the nearly bombed out Camp John Hay, Ethel Herold noted succinctly in her diary: "Reorganization. Trying to put everybody to work—plenty to do in this filthy hole." She took her position as head of the women's Work Committee very seriously and handed out work assignments as she saw fit, at times alienating those who did not understand or accept her way of running the committee. Supervising camp work quickly changed Ethel: "I surely do have to boss people around and lay down the law. And I find I can swear like a trooper—using words I did not know were in my vocabulary."[3] Ethel's duties chipped away at her perceptions of her own womanhood, which she seemed to mourn, but only a bit, because working for survival made alterations acceptable.

For Ethel, a woman's worth was not measured by her appearance, her genteel skills of needlework, her impeccable manners, or how she managed her servants, but by how much work she did, willingly and without complaint, for the camp. She quickly formed distinct opinions as to each woman's usefulness. When Edythe Delahunty slipped and broke her leg in March 1942, Ethel extolled the unfortunate woman's virtues; Edythe was "one of the finest women here: a hard worker, not a gossip, and never a word of boast. If some of these lazy-bones could only have broken their necks." Yet Ethel did not lack compassion for other women, because in shunning equality she adhered to the belief that women should only contribute what they could realistically be expected to. For instance, in September 1943, with some internees already showing signs of malnutrition, she defended the right of Mrs. Morris not to work because the woman's husband was a military prisoner in Cabanatuan, her two children had taken ill, and she was "a skeleton herself." Yet "those cats" on the Women's Committee, the ones who disagreed with Ethel, insisted that Mrs. Morris do her camp work. Since the woman possessed skills in "making over" old clothing and things, Ethel arranged for her to consult and aid in these matters, useful work that allowed Mrs. Morris to do her job while she tended to her children.[4]

In general, most internees wanted to do some kind of camp work, because it gave them a sense of control over their lives and provided unique work experience that they otherwise would not have had. In February 1942, Natalie Crouter approvingly noted a father who believed that camp life supplied his daughter with the "equivalent of a college education," because she learned how to do a variety of chores under stressful circumstances. Natalie herself learned new skills. That spring she described her attempts to fry camotes (native sweet potatoes), observing that "one of the minor miracles of this war will occur if I learn to cook," and later complimented herself on "learning to be a good waitress and charwoman after forty."[5] Natalie had not performed these duties in her own home because she had servants, but she willingly took them on in camp, because if she did not cook, her family would have to subsist on camp food, always a last resort for those with discriminating palates and other options. Such rationalizations about usefulness made internment easier to endure.

Work also supplied activity that constructively occupied the internees' time, diverting their thoughts from speculation on the progress of the war and the likelihood of release. On January 6, 1942, Ethel Herold commented that when she worked she did not "have time to think of my happy home." Work also bestowed a sense of normality; Natalie Crouter not only believed that it kept them normal but also observed that the "happiest and best adjusted" people were the ones who always did their share of community work, while the unhappiest only worked for themselves. Natalie concluded that "There must be a balance between personal and community duties. It must increasingly be a community solution because those who are maladjusted become community burdens."[6]

Women were expected to and did participate in jobs in the camp kitchen, library, school, and hospital, activities that reflected a traditional gendered division of labor—less physically taxing and more domestically oriented work than the men's. The type of work that women did and the number of hours they worked also depended on their place of internment. Most adults interned in the Philippines worked two hours per day at camp jobs, with time off only for medical reasons. But as Margaret Sherk observed in Santo Tomas, successfully running such a large camp meant that there "were many people who worked a great many more [than two] hours a day." Getting women to volunteer for camp work became increasingly difficult, because as they succumbed to boredom, apathy, and illnesses, some shirked their duties. For others, family obligations often superseded camp work. In early 1943, Natalie Crouter observed that the public posting of the work detail sheets in Camp Holmes caused a "big stir," because they showed the number of hours that internees promised to work alongside the number of actual hours worked. The problem proved ongoing, so the Women's Committee issued the following request in June: "Do Not Wait for a Public Call for Workers. . . . Endeavor to feel a sense of responsibility for getting the needed work done, not merely for putting in a certain amount of time. More time is required on some days than on others, but if each does her share the burden will not be heavy for anyone." However, Betty Foley recalled no "more than a dozen shirkers" in the camp and that "they gained nothing from not working."[7] The small size of Camp Holmes deprived internees of anonymity, so most of them carried out the work that had to be done.

Kitchen work was extremely important to the camps since it provided extra food for the workers, so men and women divvied up those duties, with the more physically taxing ones going to the men. Elizabeth Vaughan noted that in Bacolod in early June 1942 men and women had separate kitchen duties: four men cleaned the meat or fish for the daily meals, made the fires, and washed the dishes while four women cooked. Later on in the year, Alice Bryant observed, the men in the kitchen cooked rice and boiled water for drinking, jobs that involved lifting large, heavy pots, while the women prepared vegetables, cooked the food, and served it.[8] These task divisions mirrored those of an earlier time in America when men and women living in newly settled areas both carried out domestic chores according to need and ability. In the mid-twentieth century, war and captivity revived these earlier divisions, and under the circumstances no one found them odd.

Food preparation and cooking were huge jobs because of the large number of people that had to be fed and because of their tastes and expectations. During the first months of internment, before high prices and food scarcity became a problem, internees expected palatable, nutritious meals from the camp kitchen. In Santo Tomas, where the camp population ran into the thousands, this was rarely possible, making repetitive, bland, "on the line" food the rule rather than the exception. But in smaller camps, such as the ones in Baguio that billeted about five hundred people, internees had more culinary hopes. In March 1942, Natalie Crouter described a petition presented to the camp kitchen requesting the use of lesser amounts of red pepper and chili in the food. She viewed this request as a democratic way of handling a group problem, expressing annoyance that the women cooks took offense and "resented any criticism or suggestion" from the internees.[9] But this early on, food quality could still be an issue, though soon enough quantity became more important than quality, and people began to crave things like red pepper and chili to spice up their tasteless rice and vegetable diet.

The supervision of food preparation and cooking, usually assigned to a woman, was fraught with difficulties, as supervisors cautiously guarded against appearances of favoritism or waste, which could threaten survival. Some had difficulties adjusting to cooking the available food for large numbers of people. In September 1942, Elizabeth Vaughan noted a "shakeup" in the Bacolod camp kitchen because the supervisor had been "wasting food, serving too many canned goods, and throwing away native fruits and vegetables which she did not know how to use."[10] Management of the kitchen then passed to a committee of both men and women that more prudently made the choices for food usage and preparation, which the internees viewed as fair.

Because these duties were so lucrative, fears of criticism or unappreciation did not prevent women from taking jobs in the camp kitchens. Women working in camp kitchens had easy access to food scraps, a polite term for remnants that were little more than garbage, so major perks of their job included sneaking extra bites of food while working or taking scraps home for private consumption. In early January 1942, Ethel Herold acknowledged that numerous people in Baguio volunteered for food preparation duty because it gave "them a chance to swipe bites." These bonuses often caused dissension in the camps, because those who did not have kitchen jobs did not accept scrap scavenging as a legitimate right of the kitchen workers. Fairness and equality were at stake; kitchen workers who took foodstuffs provoked an unfair and unequal distribution of food. Natalie Crouter helped draft a petition in April 1942 to the General Committee protesting that able-bodied kitchen workers consumed "special foods meant for the children, and other items from the camp stores." The petition proposed that a "detail of three or four persons of integrity . . . be appointed to work with the serving committee" to ensure that leftovers and extra food be distributed equally in the camp. Natalie had difficulty finding enough women to sign the petition, and while she complained that the women in camp "talk, gripe, criticize, but won't do anything about it," she also acknowledged that everyone was "scared of any possible unpleasantness in such close quarters." Betty Foley's summation of the work situation expressed more optimism: "Some jobs had their graft but our socialistic experiment worked quite well."[11] In the long run, at least in retrospect, even though food sharing was not absolutely equal, which would have made it truly socialistic, it was equal enough.

Internee officials took charges of graft and unfairness seriously, endeavoring to eliminate them as much as possible by reassigning the most flagrant violators or sentencing them to time in the camp jail. Alice Bryant, who performed rice cleaning in the Santo Tomas kitchen, found herself dismissed from the vegetable detail for allegedly stealing camotes. She recalled being "amused" by her firing, because she had never served on the vegetable detail and had never stolen any camotes. When she confronted Phil Holdsworth, head of the kitchen guards, he told her that she had been spotted taking some "few tiny pieces" of rotten camotes out of the kitchen. Alice remembered that she had substituted on a vegetable detail one day, and the woman in charge gave her permission to salvage pieces from a pile of rotten camotes that the women did not even attempt to prepare for camp consumption. Satisfied with her explanation, Phil promised he would "expunge the scandal." Alice summed up the incident by insisting on her own innocence, placing herself in a star position, and claiming she bore no grudges, yet she acknowledged the crimes of others: "However, if I did not really steal camotes, others did. Guards had to watch like hawks and prevent women from slipping small camotes into their pockets or bosoms."[12]

Some women found ways of justifying their reasons for taking extra food that went beyond the idea of an individual job perk. In some cases, the food benefited the kitchen worker's sick friend or a family member who needed additional nourishment to recover, a defensible action because it was selfless and motherly, hallmarks of a good woman. Tressa Roka viewed vegetable duty as a way of securing Catesy's health after he was diagnosed with tuberculosis in early 1942. As a nurse, as a woman in love, she well understood the dangers of the disease and desperately wanted her fiancé to receive enough nutritious food so that he did not succumb to his illness. She needed to use the money that they had been spending to purchase their lunches for a food supply for Catesy, so she decided to take on vegetable duty in the Annex, where she could get her lunch from scraps, thereby saving their lunch money for Catesy's benefit. When he initially resisted this idea, telling Tressa that the four-hour kitchen job was "hard work under these conditions," they both looked at her already work-worn hands, and Tressa laughed and joked, "My hands weren't meant for jewelry by Tiffany, anyway!"[13] She got her way: Catesy went off to the camp hospital, and Tressa took a seat in the camp kitchen in the hopes of keeping him alive. By eating scraps instead of purchasing outside food for her lunch, Tressa deprived herself of sustaining nourishment in order to provide a better diet for Catesy.

Kitchen work, while important and often individually rewarding, was nevertheless tedious and exhausting. Most interned women were not accustomed to doing their own food preparation because they had servants to perform such tasks before the war, and getting used to doing it under camp conditions often proved difficult because of the lack of modern appliances, scarcity of food, and volume of consumers. In November 1942, Elizabeth Vaughan described how Bertha Hill spent three days each week roasting native coffee beans for the entire Bacolod camp. Since only a small wood-burning stove was available for this job, the bean roasting was a "hot, slow process"; although almost everyone in the camp enjoyed the coffee, no one ever offered to help Bertha. A few months later, Elizabeth joined a group of volunteers to pick insects out of the camp's daily rice allotment, kiddingly referring to her tedious work as "hunting small game in rice." Emily Van Sickle worked on the vegetable detail in Santo Tomas, gradually categorizing vegetables by how long it took to prepare them. She detested the dried mongo beans, "a four-to-six-hour job, as the beans crawled with tiny brown bugs that closely matched them in color."[14]

Having a tedious job was not the worst kind that a woman could have. Some work, like sanitation and garbage detail, proved unpleasant, but men usually performed these jobs. Yet women had their own disagreeable tasks. For instance, they had to contend with a lack of sanitary napkins, since few women had the foresight or opportunity to pack them, and the available napkins quickly disappeared even though the women experienced periodic menstruation cessation during captivity. They solved the problem by returning to the old-fashioned, nondisposable cloth napkins. Frieda Magnuson recalled that in Santo Tomas when the new ones got soiled, they had to be washed. Surprisingly, a "former society butterfly" volunteered to do this "unpleasant job" on a hand-crank washing machine, with the napkins, carefully embroidered with each woman's initials, then returned for reuse.[15] While men performed other work related to sanitation, the gendered division of labor most certainly did not extend to sanitary napkins, clearly the preserve of women.

Women performed other, less disagreeable duties in the camps as well, jobs that reflected personal or career interests. Besides roasting coffee beans in Bacolod, Bertha Hill also took on the responsibility of working in the camp library, where she established a children's section, taught kindergarten classes two hours each day, and created handmade books for the children. In Santo Tomas, Margaret Sherk worked at bookbinding and mending, skills she had used to finance her way through junior college in the United States. She recalled that she "had always enjoyed working on books, so I did not mind my detail," and felt "fairly contented" while at work.[16] These women did not have to deal with the additional stress of boredom on top of their work assignments; they engaged in enjoyable duties that they had been trained for.

A very few women held professional jobs such as teacher or librarian, and at least one camp doctor was a woman. Dr. Beulah Ream Allen, wife of an American military officer, mother to a toddler son, and carrying another child, used her work to help her adjust to internment and to cope with uncertainties about her husband's whereabouts. Japanese authorities frequently interrogated Beulah, because they suspected her husband of aiding the anti-Japanese guerrillas on Luzon, so she was under considerable strain trying to cope with all of these changes. Baguio internees praised her tireless efforts to persuade the Japanese to stock the camp hospital adequately and for her willingness to treat anyone at any time of the day or night. Beulah represented the epitome of the good woman: as a wife and mother she fiercely protected her own family while working to better the lives of others. In late January 1942, Ethel Herold detected resentment from some internees when they learned that Beulah received a special cake for her birthday, that members of the Women's Committee plus some "extra hard workers" were invited to have a piece of this cake in the back room of the kitchen. Ethel heard "a lot of grumbeling [sic]" about Beulah receiving a cake "made of community stuff," which Ethel strenuously defended on the grounds that the doctor "works harder and [is] more technically useful than anyone in the camp."[17] According to Ethel, those who worked exceptionally well should be rewarded for their talents and efforts, not as favoritism but simply as compensation, since Beulah's profession and her dedication to the internees justified her elevated position.

While no one challenged the usefulness of Dr. Allen's occupation, occasionally a woman's chosen or preferred job raised the question of whether it was really necessary to the camp and counted as camp work. Internees re-created as much as possible the variety of their normal daily routines and regarded leisure activities as essential parts of their lives, but in camp there existed a fine and often disputed line between what qualified as work and as play. In September 1943, Ethel Herold chronicled such a dispute that had taken place in the Women's Committee concerning Joan Turner receiving work credit for teaching dance. Some women objected to it because they did not believe it constituted real work, and others, mostly missionaries, objected to dancing as immoral. Ethel considered Joan a teacher and believed that dance instruction counted as work just like those who taught any other subject to the camp children. Moreover, she thought that Joan warranted special consideration because her husband was in a military prison camp, leaving her with an infant to care for. Ethel temporarily took over Joan's other community job so that Joan could show the camp the value of her work; on September 9, Ethel reported that the camp thoroughly enjoyed a show put on by Joan's students, and the controversy over her work died.[18]

In addition to teaching, women dominated the nursing profession in the camps, which along with food preparation made up one of the most prestigious camp jobs because it helped to ensure survival. Nurses worked hard, often more than the standard two hours per day, work that proved difficult and frustrating because of the lack of medicine and supplies for treating patients. Soon after internment, Tressa Roka volunteered for duty in the Santo Tomas camp hospital on a daily shift that lasted four hours, plus she gave cholera, typhoid, and dysentery injections to the internees. Her duties often required her to exceed her four-hour shift, but nursing had benefits similar to kitchen jobs, so she rarely regretted working extra hours. Tressa recalled that on December 19, 1943, the nurses received thirty extra packages of cigarettes, valuable for smoking or trading, from the Red Cross because the commandant considered them "worthy workers."[19] These kinds of perks put the nurses in a privileged position, as they had access to things that the average internee did not, but the internees undeniably benefited from the nurses' expertise.

MILITARY NURSES IN CAPTIVITY

Tressa Roka was one of several nurses who tirelessly served fellow internees, but nursing in Santo Tomas proved a bit unusual because the civilian nurses worked alongside captured military nurses. Although the U.S. Army and Navy evacuated dependents from the Philippines in 1941, females nurses were allowed to remain; consequently, the Japanese took these military women prisoner when the USAFFE surrendered. The Japanese, unfamiliar with the concept of women in the military, refused to imprison the nurses with captured soldiers. Although the nurses resented this disregard for their military status, preferring to continue to care for their sick and wounded, the decision of the Japanese to intern the nurses with civilians probably saved their lives. As bad as conditions became in the civilian camps, they were much worse in the military prisons, where more than 50 percent of the soldiers died. Since the Japanese viewed surrender as a disgrace, they treated male military prisoners cruelly, compelling them to struggle for food and medicine, forcing them to work long hours under the hot Pacific sun, and meting out horrendous punishments for the smallest rule infraction. In the civilian camps, however, every single military nurse interned by the Japanese survived.[20]

In addition to their willingness to serve in the military, these nurses shared a zest for adventure, an eagerness to change their lives. Dorothy Still, a young, attractive, vivacious native Californian, began her nursing career as a civilian. In the late 1930s, with tensions heightening in Europe, the U.S. military began to recruit nurses, and Dorothy, finding an application for the Navy Nurse Corps in a nursing journal, joined up. After spending her first two years of duty stateside, Dorothy transferred in 1940 to the naval hospital at Canacao, adjacent to the Cavite Naval Yard on Luzon. For several months she led a routine life, working her hospital shifts and spending her leisure time at the popular Jai Alai Club, casually but properly romancing various suitors. When the Japanese bombed the Philippines on December 8, 1941, they targeted the Cavite Naval Yard, putting Dorothy and the other navy personnel under fire. The nurses' workload dramatically increased as the wounded poured into the hospital; the numbers continued to rise over the following two days as the Japanese destroyed Cavite. Eleven of the navy nurses who had been assigned to Canacao made their way to Manila, where they hoped to avoid the worst Japanese attacks while continuing to treat scores of civilians and military personnel. Dorothy was among those who set up a medical facility at the Jai Alai Building before moving the day after Christmas with the other nurses to the Santa Scholastica School, a women's college run by German Catholic nuns, now transformed into a medical facility.

The nurses remained at the school during the next two weeks as the Japanese moved into Manila, their meager facility swelling beyond its capacity, almost beyond the endurance of the nurses. When it became clear that they would have to surrender to the rapidly advancing Japanese, they refused to leave their posts, remaining steadfast as the enemy moved into the city on January 2, 1942, arriving at Santa Scholastica the following day to inspect the personnel and premises. The Japanese ordered the women to continue working, warning that for each patient who escaped, one nurse would be shot. Laura Cobb, with almost twenty years of seniority, undertook leadership of the nurses during this potentially dangerous time, and she endeavored to protect them and their patients from any Japanese cruelties. She had considerable leeway with the Japanese because they viewed her as unassuming and professional, a partial misperception that allowed Laura to thwart the enemy's intention to deprive her patients of necessary care. When the Japanese told the nurses to itemize all of the medical supplies at Santa Scholastica, Laura and the others realized that the Japanese would haul away the most valuable items for their own use. Viewing this as a life-or-death situation for their USAFFE patients, the nurses inventoried all of the antimalaria drug quinine as common soda bicarbonate, thereby saving those supplies. The Japanese did not detect the deception. They kept the doctors and nurses confined to the school, indulged in frequent face slaps for minor offenses, but otherwise left the medical personnel alone.

Clearly they had not figured out what to do with their prisoners, but on March 8, 1942, after over a month of uncertainty, they moved the nurses to Santo Tomas.

Resentful of the transfer to the civilian camp, Dorothy pronounced it "the world's worst" situation for her, a real "letdown" from their former setup at Santa Scholastica. The navy nurses, she claimed, kept their own company because they did not "have enough in common to make close friends with the other internees." Laura decided that inactivity would be the very worst thing for the nurses, so as soon as they were all settled in, she went over to the camp hospital, took on the position of director of nurses, and volunteered the services of the navy nurses. Laura then told the women that she would not force them to work in the hospital, but they had to work at something while in camp, so they might as well work at what they had been trained to do. The navy nurses dominated the civilian and Maryknoll nurses in the camp hospital until sixty-seven combat-weary army nurses arrived that summer.[21]

Caught up in the fierce fighting at Bataan and Corregidor that did not end until the USAFFE surrendered to the Japanese in May 1942, the army nurses served as actual combat nurses, risking their lives to fulfill their duty to take care of the battle casualties. Rose Rieper, who had just begun her army nursing assignment at the end of October, was working in Sternberg Hospital in Manila when the casualties streamed in by the truckloads from the Cavite Naval Yard. The nurses worked for hours on end, ignoring usual shift rotations, treating soldiers who had been "mangled and shot to pieces" during the Japanese attack. Ethel Blaine, assigned to Fort Stotsenberg, which was located about sixty kilometers north of Manila, helped with the frantic evacuation of patients to Sternberg as the Japanese moved south from their landing point at Lingayen Gulf. She stayed in Manila for just a day before removing with the rest of the USAFFE to Bataan, but while in the city she treated common wounds that soldiers sustained from fighting from foxholes: dirt and other debris in the eyes and shrapnel in the buttocks. Within a matter of days, as the Japanese advanced, the hospital ran dangerously low on medical supplies.[22]

When the USAFFE withdrew from Manila on December 24, the army nurses and one navy nurse, Ann Bernatitus, accompanied them to Bataan, where they became the first army nurses to experience field duty in World War II. Civilian nurses also offered their services; at least twenty-five Filipina nurses went to Bataan with the army, and several American civilians volunteered their services, including Mildred

Roth, the pregnant wife of an army officer, who eventually made her way to Corregidor. Another civilian nurse, Maude "Denny" Denson Williams, had joined the U.S. Army Nurse Corps in the 1930s, eventually serving at the army hospital on Corregidor in 1936. The following year, while vacationing in the southern Philippine Islands, she met Bill Williams, who worked for Caltex Oil, a division of Texaco. The two married in March 1939; because of contemporary army rules, Denny had to resign her position upon her marriage. The couple eventually settled in Manila, where Denny took a civilian nursing job at Sternberg Hospital in the summer of 1940, which left her enough leisure time to play badminton and ride horses.

When the Japanese began their attack, Bill, a graduate of the Virginia Military Institute and a reserve army officer, could not contentedly remain in a civilian job, so he joined the 31st Infantry, moving to Bataan on December 26. Now a civilian, Denny could not go there unless she had special permission, but she longed to be with her husband, to nurse the soldiers, and to feel useful again. Abiding by an old saying from her home state of Texas, "Do something: Either lead, follow, or get out of the way," Denny used her military contacts to secure the necessary permission to get her out of Manila, but Bill had anticipated her desires and on December 30 sent two soldiers to bring her to Bataan. On January 10, 1942, Denny received permission from the USAFFE's executive medical officer to work at Hospital #2, located just west of Cabcaben along the Real River, where she worked as an anesthetist and was considered once again part of the Army Nurse Corps.[23]

Denny and the other nurses toiled constantly on Bataan as the Japanese mounted a relentless offensive. By early February 1942, both the Japanese and USAFFE were exhausted, but whereas the Japanese could stop to wait for reinforcements, the longed-for replacements from the United States did not arrive. Crippled by the attack at Pearl Harbor and hampered by Japanese control of the Pacific waters, the American military could do little to relieve the situation in the Philippines. Meanwhile the nurses, clad in size forty-two Army-issue coveralls, sporting large, clumsy oxfords on their feet that they called "Daisy Mays," attended to their duties, dodged air attacks, coped with poor and dangerous sanitation, and endured restricted rations. By the third week of February, Denny lost twenty-five pounds. When Bill visited her at Hospital #2 that month, he was "far too kind" to remark about her appearance. With "my coveralls hanging loose on my scraggy frame, I looked more like Olive Oyl" than the movie star Myrna Loy. In their brief time together, Bill affectionately referred to her as a "battling belle," but the rest of the USAFFE would remember these nurses as the "Angels of Bataan."[24] Although Denny admitted she believed that womanliness depended in part on a glamorous exterior, her assertion was a bit sardonic given the circumstances. The men on Bataan better appreciated the caring and mothering bestowed by these "battling belles" and "Angels of Bataan" than the sight of a well-dressed woman, and Denny truthfully would not have traded any of her medical supplies or knowledge for a pair of Myrna Loy's earrings.

In preparation for surrender, as the USAFFE evacuated the nurses from Bataan on the evening of April 8, 1942, Minnie Breese thought more about her patients than herself, finding it most difficult to leave the sick and wounded to the mercy of the Japanese. She had "always been a bedside nurse and it's hard to leave your patients like that. So we hung on as long as we could until they forced us to go." Besides leaving patients, some of the nurses also left loved ones behind, including Denny, who managed one last time to visit Bill, now hospitalized with malaria. She wanted to stay with him, to nurse him and take her chances with him when the Japanese arrived, but since Bill wanted her to leave she did, arriving on Corregidor the following morning amidst heavy enemy bombardment. By the end of April both sides knew that the "Rock" could not hold out much longer; the Japanese succeeded in wiping out almost all of the defensive guns on Corregidor, while the USAFFE soldiers gradually became weak, hungry, and ill. The officers decided to evacuate the women rather than allow them to become prisoners of the Japanese, and on April 29, ten army and three civilian nurses left Corregidor by airplane, headed for Mindanao and then Australia. According to Denny, the nurses never knew the rationale behind the selection for this evacuation, but she insisted that "there was no feeling of hostility toward any of the chosen few." Ethel Blaine went on that plane because of her repeated bouts with malaria, prompting her to speculate that the nurses were chosen on the basis of their age, health, and marital status (a couple of nurses married soldiers on Bataan). But she conceded that the selected nurses "were not to tell. It was very secretive." On May 3, just three days before surrender, another dozen nurses left the island, but without Denny, who soon realized that the USAFFE had to surrender or perish. She wondered if and how she would die, hoping that she would be "quiet and brave."[25]

The surrender proved orderly; clustered together as the enemy entered Corregidor's Malinta Tunnel, wearing plain uniforms without any military insignia, the women most of all feared that they would be raped. Gladys Ann Mealer, one of the senior nurses, tried to reduce tensions by joking about the situation. She and some of the other nurses decided that they should give the Japanese "one of the ugliest nurses in the whole bunch. Turn her over to old Tojo's soldiers or something. Just fun, you know, and you know we were really scared." Inez McDonald became "scared spit-less" during the surrender because no one briefed her on how to behave as a prisoner, and she had no idea what to expect—she slept with her helmet on. Denny took quick glimpses of the Japanese as they made their way through the tunnel system, expressing relief that "they did not harm me, they didn't speak to me, they didn't even come close to me."[26] The Japanese simply ordered the nurses to continue their duties. However, soon all the soldiers who could be moved were sent off to a prison camp, and the Japanese removed many of the remaining hospital supplies, leaving the nurses little to work with.

The uncertainty of surrender put an additional strain on these women's lives, because no one knew if the Japanese understood that the nurses were part of the American military. Edith Shacklette grasped that the Japanese did not "have nurses like we had" but doubted that they thought the nurses "were really part of the military." Madeline Ullom conjectured that the Japanese were "simply amazed" to find female nurses on Corregidor, leaving them stymied because their "detailed plan of invasion did not include women." The nurses worried that it would not be a positive thing if the Japanese understood this distinction; they already knew how the Japanese treated soldiers who surrendered. Earlyn Black credited General Jonathan Wainwright with protecting the nurses, because she had heard that upon surrender he made it plain to the Japanese that the nurses were part of the medical corps and so could not be considered part of the combat troops. She also commended the Japanese officers who first occupied the Malinta Tunnel, describing their "high intellect" and their stern orders to their troops to leave the women alone. But Helen Nestor, who had joined the Army Nurse Corps through the American Red Cross, believed that this arrangement confused the Japanese about the actual status of the nurses. Once the Japanese found out that some of the nurses had been recruited through the relief organization, they told the women: "Oh, no. You're not military. You are civilians. You are Red Cross."[27] This may be one of the reasons why the Japanese eventually sent the nurses to Santo Tomas.

When Japanese officers moved into the Malinta Tunnel, the nurses took up residence in two of the laterals close to the main hospital, still apprehensive over their safety because the Japanese occupied a nearby lateral. According to Sallie Durrett, a large sign plainly marked the nurses' quarters, and the Japanese soldiers often looked at it and laughed. Sallie assumed that their laughter meant they thought the nurses "were there for other reasons"—"entertainment" for the soldiers—and she worried that the nurses would become part of this amusement. Her fears were not groundless: one night a Japanese officer went into an area where Mary Brown Menzie and Beulah Putnam slept. Mary noticed him immediately, screamed and shouted in panic, and managed to scramble out of the room, leaving the unfortunate Beulah trapped. When the man awkwardly pinned her down and pulled at her pajamas, she quickly guided his hand to the bulky sanitary pad between her legs, causing him to cease his attack. Beulah, bruised and cut, fled to the safety of the other nurses' lateral.[28] As frightening as the attack was, it proved to be an isolated one.

On June 25, 1942, the Japanese finally decided to move the nurses off of Corregidor but refused to tell them where they were headed; however, after a brief boat ride the nurses realized that they were going to Manila. Denny, very ill with the tropical virus dengue fever, hoped that they would be taken to Sternberg Hospital so that they could continue their duties. Instead, they were deposited at Santo Tomas. Bertha Dworsky resented the separation from her military patients but realized she could do nothing about it. However, Hattie Brantley and some of the other nurses did not intend to get out of the truck because Santo Tomas was for civilians, not military personnel. They found it "degrading to be placed with civilians" but quickly realized that "when you have somebody with a bayonet telling you you're getting off, you get off."[29]

Internees anxious for news of loved ones who had been on Bataan and Corregidor quickly surrounded the truck, calling out greetings and questions, pressing fresh fruit into the hands of the tired, bedraggled nurses. Japanese guards, in an attempt to delay the spread of any military news, pushed the internees away and ordered everyone to be quiet. The nurses, with all of the stories they had to tell, could not get a word in edgewise, as Denny observed that they "were beyond speech, our mouths already crammed full of the sweet fruits we hadn't tasted in six months." The nurses were secluded for two months in Santa Catalina, a former convent across the street from Santo Tomas currently occupied by Catholic nuns. Edith Shacklette speculated that their transfer to Manila and segregation in Santa Catalina occurred because the

Japanese simply did not know what else to do with them: "They didn't want us to be part of the military, but we weren't exactly civilians. So they kept us in that school for six weeks until they claimed they got orders from Tokyo about what to do with us." This time to themselves, away from the endless walking and standing in line that characterized Santo Tomas life, provided the nurses with the opportunity to shore themselves up for the years ahead. Although forbidden to talk to the internees, twice a day people sent them "generous amounts" of food, especially fruits and vegetables that the nurses had not eaten since they were sent to Bataan.[30]

In August the Japanese finally brought the nurses into the main part of the camp, housed them in the Engineering Building, and assigned them work in the hospital, recently moved to Santa Catalina. The navy nurses who had dominated the staff since January felt some resentment toward this large group of nurses who seemed determined to take over the running of the hospital; interservice rivalry persisted even during interment. When Laura Cobb relinquished her supervisory position to army nurse Josephine Nesbit, Dorothy Still concluded that this "was as it should be," because the army nurses outnumbered the navy, a change in command she understood but did not like. Dorothy immediately described Josie Nesbit as a "bellowing bosun's mate," then acknowledged that while the two groups of nurses got along well enough "superficially," the navy nurses developed a strong feeling that they were "merely being tolerated." However, like the rest of the internees, the nurses had to learn to live and work together, no matter what their differences.[31]

The number of army nurses increased in mid-September with the arrival of the ten who had been evacuated from Corregidor to Australia via Mindanao the past April. That evacuation had been unsuccessful because the plane had been damaged, enabling the Japanese to capture its passengers when it landed for refueling. Geneva Jenkins, along with the other nine nurses, spent one night in a hospital near Cagyan, confident that the plane would be fixed the next morning and take them on their way. Instead the Japanese rounded up the entire group and kept them in a hospital for almost three months before moving them to Davao, where they stayed for another month before their final transfer to Santo Tomas.[32]

As professional medical workers, both the army and navy nurses found their skills at a premium in Santo Tomas; among the hardest workers, they at times resented the fact that others did not work as hard. Denny

Williams acknowledged "only a few slackers" but vividly recalled that during one of her hospital shifts a woman came in saying that she had a pain in her neck. Denny proclaimed that the "old hag was a faker, and I resented waiting on her, since I didn't get any more calories than she did." Yet Denny held her tongue, hoping that the doctor on duty would realize what the woman was doing and "discharge her so she'd have to work whether she wanted to or not."[33]

Denny's encounter shows that the nurses refused to relinquish their link to the military, that one of the biggest problems the army nurses faced was getting used to dealing with civilians. The nurses, with their military training and discipline, found it difficult to handle people who did not have the same drive and dedication they did. Geneva Jenkins carefully distinguished herself from her patients, labeling them civilian internees while she and the other army nurses were military prisoners of war. She found that the Japanese had a special respect for the nurses because of their medical training and treated them better than the average soldier, even better than the rest of the internees. Helen Nestor kept company with the other army nurses, and her only routine contact with civilians came through nursing. She credited her survival to her ability to work at something she had been trained to do, asserting that it may sound "crazy," but nursing was part of her "salvation." Mildred Dalton connected her survival to her military training, her nursing, and other personal traits, observing that in addition to her "great inner resourcefulness," she "merely tried to do as my Chief Nurse commanded," orders that included four-hour hospital shifts as well as dormitory cleaning duties. Ethel Blaine, who had been brought up on a farm without electricity or running water, was accustomed to hard work and rough living, so camp conditions did not seem very alien to her. She was "certainly not shocked at all of this and I knew how to cook. I knew how to sew." For her, self-sufficiency, rather than military discipline, proved the key to survival.[34]

The rivalry between the army and navy nurses ended in May 1943, when the navy nurses volunteered for transfer to Los Banos. Two of the Santo Tomas doctors planned on going to the new camp, so they approached Laura Cobb about the navy nurses taking charge of the hospital there, which might boost their morale and their prestige. Laura gathered her nurses together to solicit their opinions. After only a few brief minutes of silence, the nurses decided to cast their lot with the transferees, a change that provided the Los Banos internees with necessary medical expertise while lessening the professional tensions within the Santo Tomas hospital. Others in camp clearly appreciated what the nurses had done for them, regardless of their military branch, for as the navy nurses left on May 14, the internees belted out a rousing version of "Anchors Aweigh" in their honor. The Japanese trucked the nurses to a railroad station in the north of Manila, where they piled into metal boxcars along with the rest of those headed for the new camp.

The nurses took up residence in one of the dormitories of the Agricultural College, and although Dorothy Still found the setting serene, she soon realized that much work lay ahead. The campus infirmary, picturesquely located near a large courtyard, was a mess; parts of the building had been damaged, and equipment and furniture had been looted. Dorothy even found an impaired instrument sterilizer, broken because someone had tried to use it to cook rice. Undaunted, the nurses went straight to work; before the end of June they converted the disheveled infirmary into a functioning twenty-five-bed hospital that would immediately service more than eight hundred people and eventually three thousand. According to Mary Rose Harrington, the nurses sewed sheets for the hospital beds and took pods from kapok trees to stuff homemade pillows. She found Los Banos pleasant, providing four- or five-hour day shifts or nightlong shifts in the camp hospital: "Appendectomy, tonsillectomy, whatever came up we did our best to take care of it." Dorothy Still found the place tolerable, got along well with the other nurses, and even managed to enjoy some romance. Since men made up the first group of eight hundred transferees to the camp, the nurses who were interested found it easy to form romantic attachments, which Dorothy found a nice diversion. Even though her workload increased as more internees fell ill, she maintained that she and the other nurses were glad they had "something meaningful to do."[35]

In addition to the possibilities for romance, the Los Banos men venerated the nurses for their medical knowledge and willingness to pitch in and do whatever was needed, so one wrote a song for them:

> Oh, you Navy gals, are regular gals.
> We're glad you're here with us
> To help each day, in your own sweet way
> And listen to us cuss.
> When days seem years, there may be tears
> As you dream of your old home ties.
> So you won't feel blue, we give three cheers for you,
> You're the pals of us eight hundred guys.[36]

Back in Manila, Denny Williams continued to grapple with the harsh realities of internment. Though she and the other nurses had the opportunity to work at something that they had been trained for, Denny complained that the greatest problem she faced was an "increasing and demoralizing boredom." She described the "great mental and emotional fatigue born of idle hours and inane conversations" but also admitted she found her nursing work less than satisfactory because she could not practice her specialty of anesthesia. Feeling stagnant, at the end of 1943 Denny transferred from the hospital to the outpatient clinic in the Main Building, grateful for the move because she had seen enough starvation patients and men who had been severely beaten by the Japanese. Constantly worried about the health and welfare of her husband, Bill, still imprisoned in Cabanatuan, Denny hated to see the battered men who were brought to the hospital for treatment, only to be taken back to jail. Because of her work, she encountered firsthand the worst horrors of internment and feared that the Japanese were similarly abusing Bill.[37]

Despite the nature and caliber of their work, the army and navy nurses experienced internment much the same as civilians. As female military personnel, the nurses were spared the very worst of the treatment that the Japanese meted out to prisoners of war, but in order to maintain their sense of identity the nurses insisted on distinguishing themselves from the civilian internees. Though they had the opportunity to work within their profession, the nurses suffered from boredom just like everyone else. Since most of them were single women, they had no nuclear families to draw sustenance from, and their military status and pride generally prevented them from melding with the larger internee community. Consequently, the nurses expressed their womanhood by forming a family unto themselves, occasionally letting some patients under their nurturing wings but always remembering that they were military, not civilian.

MOTHERHOOD, COMMUNAL WORK, AND PRIVATE ENTERPRISE

The presence of young children in the camps posed a very traditional dilemma for women as they carried out their daily duties, because in addition to the vast amounts of necessary camp work, the children needed looking after. Since internment altered normal family life by depriving children of their homes—and in many cases their fathers—it proved difficult to compel women to leave their children for even a couple of hours each day to perform camp work. Women felt guilty for endangering their children in the first place and tried to make up for it by acting as model mothers, actions made more difficult by the fact that the bulk of child care, even for women with husbands in camp, traditionally fell to the mothers. This was an age of mothering, not parenting. Luckily, in terms of work burdens, most internees recognized the sanctity of the mother-child bond, especially under these conditions, and loathed interfering with it. So two alternatives presented themselves to women with children.

The first was that mothers could decline camp jobs to spend their time taking care of their children and doing their own room work. Making this decision usually left a woman open to reproach from those who believed that every able-bodied person in camp should contribute to the general welfare and that personal child care did not count to this end. In April 1942, Natalie Crouter criticized forty mothers in Baguio who refused to take part in communal camp work, including one woman who became "furious" at the suggestion that she participate in the vegetable detail, saying that she had two children to care for. Natalie dismissed the woman's excuse, claiming that the woman just believed herself "too good to do hard work," especially as the woman's daughter was old enough to help with family chores.[38] Since both of Natalie's children were old enough to help with family chores and also volunteered for camp duties, she routinely participated in camp work and had little sympathy for those who did not share her communal vision. For her, a good woman took care of both her family and community.

The second alternative involved mothers volunteering for camp duty after finding somebody to take care of their children while they did so. For women like Natalie with older children, this was not a big problem, since most camps established elementary and high school classes to keep school-aged children occupied and prepared for their reentry into schools once the war ended. The classes in turn provided women with teaching jobs, recognized by the internees as work. While school afforded some mothers a convenient, worthwhile place for their children, women with young children, such as Margaret Sherk, had to make other arrangements. When she took on the task of binding and repairing books for the Santo Tomas camp library, she wanted to place David in a kindergarten class, but the camp school did not offer it, so Margaret found a woman who taught kindergarten. The woman charged a fee for her services, compelling Margaret to scrape together four pesos (two dollars) per month, which she earned by mending books in private collections.[39] This arrangement made Margaret a good woman and mother, because she secured a familiar and enjoyable job that occupied her mind for a couple of hours each day, while David got to practice his social skills with other children his age.

In the smaller camps, with the lines between camp work and personal work less rigid, women with children had the opportunity to perform jobs that allowed them to take care of their children while contributing something to the camp. For example, Betty Foley recalled that in Baguio some mothers took on the job of monitoring the children's playground.[40] The playground provided recreation for the children while their mothers worked, and its supervision provided jobs for the mothers who did not want to be too far away from their children.

In addition to working to contribute to the general welfare of the camps, internees also used their specialized skills to earn money or to trade for necessities. Although some disagreed over the appropriateness of specialists selling their skills rather than donating them to the common good, the practice continued in almost every camp. Emily Van Sickle remembered that much private enterprise developed in Santo Tomas and that the extra income helped internees ease the financial burden on the whole camp, which allotted them a small "allowance" each month. The businesses also proved that American capitalism thrived even under these unnatural circumstances. Here again, women capitalized on skills considered typically female; Emily knew women who made extra money as beauticians and dishwashers. One "remarkable girl," Eleanor Stone, the wife of an American military prisoner, earned money by selling candy plus working as a housekeeper for Edwin Van Voorhees, a shanty neighbor of the Van Sickles. Japanese authorities allowed the internees to build shanties (individual outdoor structures) as a way of relieving some of the overcrowding in camp, and for women without husbands or fathers, paid domestic work proved lucrative. Margaret Sherk, practically penniless, traded her cooking skills for extra food with an unattached, generous male acquaintance who invited her to cook for him and his friends in his shanty; in return she shared the food that she prepared. This arrangement tided Margaret over until she secured a more reliable extra food source and until she located some private book owners who would willingly pay to have their books mended.[41]

Yet private enterprise did not strike everyone as equitable and proper. Tressa Roka critically observed one "spoiled and pampered gal" who still had lovely, soft hands in the spring of 1943 because she hired another woman to do all of her hard work. The hired woman was the destitute wife of an American military prisoner who needed to earn money to buy extra food for her family members in camp, an arrangement Tressa deplored. She believed that the "pampered" woman should do her own work because it would help to keep her healthy and that she should donate the money she was paying as salary to the soldier's wife.[42] According to Tressa, this working relationship did not represent good private enterprise; it was exploitation, even unpatriotic, because a serviceman's wife was being taken advantage of.

Women who had been unaccustomed to working prior to internment sometimes found it difficult to concentrate on one job for very long, especially if it was monotonous or if they had trouble finding a job that they liked, so some changed jobs repeatedly. In Santo Tomas, Alice Bryant worked at the sanitation desk, where she issued the spray guns used for fighting bedbugs, but she did not find this satisfying, so in June 1943 she gave it up to teach in the camp high school, a job that also proved to be short-lived. Although Alice stuck it out until the end of the term, she complained of various difficulties: general discipline problems, a shadowy group of female students who wrote anonymous notes and signed themselves "The Black Spots," and the lack of teaching materials. She then moved on to dishwashing, observing that the "respect and consideration which I was always shown as a scullion was a pleasant contrast to the treatment I had received as a teacher, and I liked my new work."[43] Her final job was rice cleaning, a tedious but necessary chore, which she nevertheless enjoyed because of amiable work companions. A naturally gregarious person, Alice craved friendship and stuck with jobs that provided her with interesting coworkers rather than a certain status in the camp hierarchy.

Acutely aware of the needs of the camp as a whole and their families in particular, women performed their camp duties as long as they were physically able to do so. However, poor nutrition, the lack of medicines, pregnancy, and the uncertainty of sanitary facilities often caused illnesses that prevented them from working. When they halted camp work, women remained responsible for their room unless they were so incapacitated that they were hospitalized. In the spring of 1942, Emily Van Sickle had a lengthy bout with enteritis, a common but debilitating intestinal illness, and had to give up her work on the vegetable detail to ensure a complete recovery. Even with the various cleaning and monitoring duties in her room and coping with the exhaustion that accompanied the illness, Emily attempted to contribute something by typing for the censor's office where her husband worked. She did this until Van, concerned that her health was not improving, "refused to let me carry on with it any longer."[44] He tried to convince her to apply for permission to go outside of camp to a hospital, but she avoided doing this because Van himself had been ill ever since they were first interned.

Emily found herself in a bind that plagued devoted wives during internment. Even when ill, she delayed the best treatment available if it meant separation from her husband, so her own health problems never completely went away. Enteritis plagued her in 1943, at the same time that she again stopped menstruating, producing an almost incapacitating lethargy. Van insisted that she hire someone to take over her vegetable detail, which she had resumed after her enteritis attack abated, but Emily resisted because "it seemed a miserable thing to shirk a job." Van finally convinced her that she owed it to him, that if she became too ill he would have no one to take care of him. Viewing her duty as wife as paramount to her duty to the camp and unwilling to have her husband regard her as a bad wife, Emily hired someone to take her place in the kitchen. Although she admitted relief that she did not have to continue with the unpleasant vegetable duty, she would gladly have given up her "privileged status" as a nonworker in exchange for Van's good health.[45]

The hiring of a replacement did not go unnoticed by the camp's Work Assignment Committee, which realized that by the end of 1943, the internees' health had deteriorated to a point that almost everyone could find a legitimate medical reason not to work. Malnutrition manifested itself in a variety of ways, from exhaustion to beriberi to heart failure, yet it remained more necessary than ever that the camp be maintained, and every relatively healthy person had to work. When the director of the committee suggested that Emily work in the garden rather than in the kitchen, Van responded explosively that his wife would not, but the incident proved uncomfortable enough for Emily that she decided to work again, taking a typist job. Van's negative reaction to the work request stemmed from two factors. First, he simply believed that Emily was too ill to do any kind of work; he did not want her to work herself to death. Second, his refusal intimated that he thought gardening beneath Emily, that they enjoyed a high social status that entitled them to refuse certain manual labor if they could afford to hire a replacement. Although Van felt justified in exerting this claim, Emily clearly did not;

despite her weakened condition she did find some work to do, and she was not the only woman who felt obligated to work notwithstanding illness. By November 1944, Tressa Roka was about as ill as her patients, but she could not afford to take time off because too many sick people needed her. She wrote in her diary on November 25: "Distressingly tired and ill again. . . . If only I could stay in bed and get some strength, but nurses and doctors were needed desperately."[46]

During 1944 the Japanese military experienced severe failures: it did well with its offensive against China but gradually lost ground in Burma, encountered increasing difficulties in holding on to the Philippines, and faced a stiff battle for the Marianas Islands, which left most of its naval fleet either destroyed or incapacitated. In frustration, the Japanese refused to authorize the release of foodstuffs to the captives, insisting that they take total responsibility for feeding themselves. Camp gardens took on grave importance; for the internees they were necessary for survival, since the yields provided them with life-sustaining food, yet working in the gardens under the hot Pacific sun made for strenuous, often debilitating work. In the summer of 1944, those in Baguio received orders that every man, woman, and child had to work in the garden, but most tried to avoid it, reflecting a mixed concern of status and ability: few people wanted to do manual labor, and even fewer had the physical capability. Ethel Herold reported that on August 18 Japanese camp authorities threatened to take away the internees' private cooking privileges if they did not volunteer, so "forty-five women and forty-three men volunteered at the point of the bayonet."[47] The bayonet obviously was a major threat but so was the revocation of private cooking privileges, because the camp kitchen had little to offer—it served only tiny portions of tasteless food. The internees who did their own cooking stood the best chance for survival; losing those cooking privileges could be a death sentence.

Along with work that benefited the camp, women had daily domestic chores to attend to, such as cleaning their living space and doing the family laundry, the former assigned on a rotating basis, the latter a personal (and very time-consuming) task. Alice Bryant recalled that in addition to two hours' worth of camp work each day in Bacolod, the women in her room took turns sweeping the floor daily and washing it weekly. Elizabeth Vaughan noted in 1943 that her chore one week in Santo Tomas was mopping the floor of the room that she shared with seven other mothers and their children; each of the mothers took turns sweeping and mopping the entire floor. Maintaining cleanliness in the bathrooms was a health necessity, especially since all of the camps only had very rudimentary facilities. According to Emily Van Sickle, when it came to bathrooms, the Santo Tomas women became "rule-oblivious": they did not clean up after themselves, and they tossed food, garbage, and hair down the outdated, overworked drains. For women unaccustomed to cleaning up after themselves—because of the prewar prevalence of servants and because of their unfamiliarity with plumbing systems—such actions appear logical rather than selfish. Yet within a few weeks of internment, as they acquired more knowledge about their circumstances, the women organized themselves to handle the situation, and, taking turns by room, each "put in an hour of toilet swabbing, drain clearing and, most difficult by far, trying to prevent rule infractions."[48]

Since space was at a premium, a constant source of dissension, living spaces had to be monitored by someone who could oversee disputes and keep count of the room's inhabitants to satisfy the roll calls. Tressa Roka's first room monitor was a southerner she identified as Rainbow, a woman who possessed "an abundance of tact and an even disposition," necessary attributes for dealing with the more than fifty women and children who shared one room. Tressa recalled that the diversity of these roommates, women of different ages, nationalities, races, and temperaments, "spelled dynamite," yet Rainbow served as an effective mediator. In early 1944, Alice Bryant took on the role in her living space, and she registered a series of complaints about this duty, finding it not as congenial as rice cleaning since "no previous monitor had half the work that devolved upon me!" Because of the increasing food shortages, Alice's job included bringing in the room's daily allotment of bread and eggs that were available for purchase, collecting the money, and making change. As women left to live in outdoor shanties, transferred to Los Banos, or went into the hospital, Alice also tried to locate a "desirable roommate" for fear of having an "undesirable" one forced on the room. When the Japanese military took control of Santo Tomas from civilian authorities in February 1944, room monitors assumed responsibility for a twice-daily count of their room's inhabitants, which was recorded on a form then given to the floor monitor for presentation to camp authorities. Discrepancies resulted in a prolonged roll call, which generally taxed the patience and physical endurance of all the internees.[49]

Despite all of the work the internees did, despite their dwindling energy levels, most of them craved some kind of leisure activity to make life seem somewhat normal. During her second month of internment in Bacolod, Elizabeth Vaughan confessed: "Wish I did not feel a compulsion to read, but cannot 'amah' the children continuously without a book under my arm, in case a free moment should arrive." Elizabeth, well-educated, with limited domestic skills, snatched time for pleasure reading whenever and wherever she could, trying to be a good mother to her children while doing something else she enjoyed. Grace Nash used her musical skills as a way of coping with the rigors of internment in Santo Tomas. Playing the violin gave her much-needed respite from her daily chores, and she also broadcasted violin concerts over the camp loudspeaker, which helped alleviate the boredom of the other internees. When the Nashes transferred to Los Banos in the spring of 1944, Grace teamed up with pianist Rosemary Parquette to provide music for the internees there. Grace's talent attracted the attention of a Japanese guard who had been a cellist before the war; he appreciated her music so much that he surreptitiously passed her fruit, sugar, and coffee, treasured food items that benefited the entire family in the last months of the war. She experienced firsthand the compassion of an individual Japanese guard and expressed gratitude for help from an unexpected source.[50]

Work that women performed to benefit the camps was not particularly onerous, at least not until about mid-1944, when malnourishment set in; it continued regardless of illness, boredom, weekends, or holidays. In January 1943, Natalie Crouter congratulated herself because she had not "laid off work one single time of mopping or serving" despite having endured a year of "defeat and adversity." In Santo Tomas, Elizabeth Vaughan woke up at six o'clock on Christmas morning in 1943, because "this was the time of my kitchen duty—Christmas or not."[51]

By mid-1944, internees became so weak from the lack of proper food and medicine that work and leisure activities virtually ground to a halt. These deprivations were not totally accidental; as early as May 1942, Natalie Crouter observed that the Axis powers "count on and succeed in using malnutrition and fear which weakens the will to resist."[52] As the quality and quantity of the camps' food supplies abated, Japanese authorities refused to acknowledge that a problem existed, which was tantamount to admitting their imminent defeat. Successful Allied attacks and blockades cut off Japanese supply lines, leaving most people in the South Pacific scrabbling for food. When internee representatives complained that people were starving, the camp administrators shrugged, lied, and informed them that they were being provided with rations equal to those of Japanese soldiers, making no concessions to the fact that Americans were not accustomed to a traditional Japanese diet.

Despite this physical deterioration, camp officials continued to push the internees to their limits. Tressa Roka noted on August 14 that they had devised a new form of torture: "enforced labor." The Japanese directed men to make rope and women to make "envelopes" or sandbag casings, accomplishing these tasks on "half rations" of rice and vegetables.[53] This enforced labor served no real purpose except to punish Allied civilians for the increasing Allied victories in the Pacific theater and to hasten the death of an already debilitated group of people. Late in the year, the internees' movements appeared automatic rather than calculated; at the end of November, the Santo Tomas camp school closed because students and teachers were too weak from hunger to continue. Only the most essential camp services carried on.

MANUAL LABOR OUTSIDE OF THE PHILIPPINES

Outside of the Philippines the Japanese required internees to work up to six hours per day on labor details in direct violation of the 1929 Geneva Convention, which forbade the forced labor of internees and stipulated that any work done by them be for their benefit only. Some of the work assigned to women put them in the position of servants to the Japanese, work designed to humble or humiliate them. Agnes Keith recalled that on Berhala Island, the Japanese sometimes ordered the women "to clean the guardhouse, while guards lay asleep or drunk on their beds." She and another woman "were given the task of dusting the entire length of the wharf with our handkerchiefs and hands." Yet Agnes and the others refused to be humbled by these activities; instead, they usually laughed to themselves as they worked, enjoying the extra food that the guards tossed to them as a reward.[54]

However humiliating this treatment was intended to be, it proved to be some of their easiest work, because when the women and children moved to Kuching, their workload expanded to include what Agnes referred to as "organized labor." In 1943, camp officials put out a call for volunteers to clear a patch of jungle growth for planting, then ordered the women to volunteer. When the women protested that they were too weak from lack of adequate food and from too many illnesses to carry out such work, and that there would be no one to take care of the children, the Japanese dismissed their protests. Japanese women worked on an inadequate diet, the commanding lieutenant told them; moreover, mothers could take their children with them to work. So the women set to their assigned labor, and Agnes recalled that after the first hour of work she felt exhausted: "By the end of four hours I could scarcely walk back to my barrack. I would be so filthy that I could not sit down inside, and so tired I could scarcely stand up to bathe."[55]

Colonel Suga exempted Agnes from this work for a time, directing her instead to write an account of her experiences in camp. Suga had been educated in the United States and had read Agnes's book on Borneo, *Land Below the Wind*, which impressed him. Positioning himself as a patron of the arts, he provided Agnes with writing materials and ordered her to compose a story that he would edit, so she stayed out of the fields writing a version for Suga and one for herself, which she kept carefully hidden in her barracks. This writing assignment did not keep Agnes away from physical labor entirely, because she still had cooking and cleaning duties, plus she served as a substitute field laborer when other women became ill. At the beginning of 1945, when camp authorities cut the internees' rice rations while still expecting them to work in the fields for six hours every day, Agnes's conscience would not allow her to stay away. Her writing enabled her to accumulate extra energy, thanks to Suga, so she remained one of the healthiest women in camp. When she told him of her decision to give up writing and take up field-work, he did little to dissuade her, prompting Agnes's speculation that "perhaps as patron of the arts he had been satisfied. I went back on the work list."[56]

Overwork and malnutrition made the final months of internment on Borneo critical. Agnes did not spot an American plane until March 25, 1945, nearly two months after the liberation of Santo Tomas; it would be almost another five months before rescue arrived. In the meantime, the Japanese attempted to kill their captives with long hours of forced labor and insufficient food. The women got up in the morning before the sun came up, did their domestic chores, went out into the fields to work for the Japanese, and as Agnes recalled, by "nine o'clock in the morning we were worn out." The food the Japanese provided consisted of thin rice gruel, a few tablespoons of cooked rice, and occasionally some greens, salt, sugar, and tea. To augment these meager rations the women scavenged for and ate whatever they could, including "snails and worms [and] all of us were eating weeds and grass. . . . I had meals of banana skins stolen from Japanese refuse barrels and boiled into soup." Agnes observed that the Japanese expected that the women could live on this but also chillingly speculated: "Or did they expect us to live on it?"[57]

The Japanese condemned the Borneo internees to a slow death through neglect and overwork, but since they provided the women with rudimentary shelter and food, they could deny responsibility for the overall health and welfare of their captives. In a time of war, they had more important matters to tend to. Any remaining food and medicine had to go to the Japanese soldiers, not to conquered enemies; if these deficiencies resulted in the deaths of some civilians, little matter, for in the eyes of the Japanese, nothing was more glorious than dying for the emperor. Despite this inhumane treatment, most of the women in Kuching survived because of effective organization and strong will, survival that came with a price. Agnes described the appearance of her fellow internees in late August 1945: "Faces were strained, lined, agonizingly controlled. Hands were stained and blunted and calloused; feet were bare, broken-toenailed, grimy with sores and septic toes; clothes were worn, patched, faded, and scanty. There were only a half a dozen out of the whole two hundred and forty-six who looked at all attractive and alive. Of the rest, some might regain attractiveness, but never youth again. Captivity had taken too much."[58]

Concerns about femininity undergirded Agnes's assessment of the women captives. They were alive, but most of them, including Agnes, had lost their looks and their youth, a realization that undoubtedly caused them some anxiety as they prepared to meet their husbands or sweethearts after years of separation. During the war these women altered colonial middle-class notions of their roles in order to survive: they did without servants, new clothing, cosmetics, and leisure time, instead tackling any work assignment and dealing with any new rules handed out by the Japanese. They became self-sufficient and strong-willed, characteristics imperative for surviving in an internment camp but traits not necessarily recognized as desirable in American women during normal times. Agnes's description of the survivors foreshadowed the adjustment problems these women would face when the war was over.

The situation on Celebes resembled that of the women on Borneo, where the number of civilian internees was likewise small and directly guarded by the Japanese military. Darlene Deibler recalled that when the eight missionaries arrived at their first internment location, they established a work roster so that their small house remained clean, fires were ready for cooking meals, and food was prepared on a regular basis.

When they moved to Kampili and joined others, the workload increased; the women had to tend the piggery, a pet project of the Japanese, who were fond of pork. The piggery's inhabitants, Darlene observed, "were given more consideration and had better accommodations" than their tenders—their work was physically demanding, the conditions revolting. When the internees received word of the Japanese surrender in August 1945, Darlene recalled the "tears rolling down gaunt faces burned deeply while laboring in the sun on roads, in rice fields, in pig pens, on coolie lines loading and unloading trucks, [and] emptying septic tanks."[59] The majority of the women had survived but their health, too, was ruined.

Work ultimately proved to be a double-edged sword for the interned women. It gave them something constructive to do as they waited out the war years, as they repeatedly looked to the sky for American rescue planes. Work provided women with a sense that they were contributing something to their own survival and to that of their families and fellow internees, things that concerned all good women. It also helped to beat back boredom, one of the biggest problems in the camps. Finally, work altered their view of womanhood as they transformed themselves from colonial women of leisure who directed servants and engaged in community affairs to physically hard-working women. While some mourned the conversion, others accepted it as a necessary, but hopefully temporary, wartime measure.

Work also advanced the women's physical deterioration, because it used up precious calories when foodstuffs became scarce. Between forcing their captives to labor and depriving them of sufficient food, the Japanese found ways to torture their captives without lifting a whip or a rope; if internees died from the strain of overwork and undernourishment, that only meant there were fewer for the Japanese to provide for. Under these conditions it is hardly surprising that family, in all of its various forms and meanings, was of prime importance to the women. Family, friends, sweethearts, and lovers nourished the hearts and souls of the women, giving them more reasons to want to live.

4

ROMANCE, MARRIAGE, AND FAMILY LIFE DURING THE WAR

"Connubial bliss was denied people."

The earthquake that rocked Santo Tomas in the early morning hours of April 9, 1942, jolted most internees out of their sleep, but at least a couple of them, according to Margaret Sherk, were interrupted while doing something that Japanese camp authorities had forbidden, for as she elegantly pointed out, "Connubial bliss was denied people." Throughout most of the war the Japanese prohibited "commingling": married couples could not live together, and internees could not kiss, hold hands, touch, or speak endearments to each other. Margaret recalled that in the hours preceding the earthquake one particularly diligent couple found a way around this ban, or so they thought. They located an empty room, locked its door, and "were engrossed in each other when the first strong tremor shook the building. They were sure that the building was going to crumble around their ears, and they could not get the door open. All thought of earthly bliss had definitely flown out the window by the time the building stopped rocking."[1] Margaret's restrained description of a husband and wife's perilous search for a secluded place in which they could make love represents one of the disruptions women faced in their private lives during internment. The ban against commingling had an impact on femininity and romance, marriage, pregnancy and family life, and continued fears of rape, which prompted some women to rethink their definitions of womanhood and others to cling more tightly to them.

A FEMININE APPEARANCE

Despite their South Pacific location during the prewar years, American women regularly obtained fashion and beauty accoutrements available to their stateside counterparts: the latest outfits, cosmetics, perfume,

hair color, and permanent waves. Then, fashion and the wealth necessary to purchase it set them apart from most of the indigenous women
and made them American, a distinction they found comforting during
the war. Upon internment, these women usually had one suitcase of
clothes and makeup that would have to last throughout the war, a deprivation they handled in different ways. Some flaunted their femininity
through fashion and appearance, which Margaret Sherk claimed was tied
to national pride, since women, "particularly American women, have
always prided themselves on their appearance." Margaret always tried
to maintain a neat appearance, believing that even worse than the lack
of privacy in Santo Tomas was the inability of women to look "presentable." She knew some women who always had cosmetics, but "the great
majority of us had to content ourselves with looking even worse than
nature intended for us to look," and there was little comfort that almost every other woman was in the same situation.[2]

Given the restrictions within the camps plus the general lack of available goods, attention to appearance required a great deal of ingenuity.
Josephine Waldo celebrated her first birthday in Santo Tomas on April
7, 1942, describing it as a "very happy birthday for me in spite of the
circumstances" in part because her gifts included toilet water, powder,
a turban, and a new lipstick. These items, typical birthday presents in
normal times, represented exemplary thoughtfulness and expense during internment. Josephine noted just a few days later that American
facial soap had already been used up, so the Red Cross handed out laundry soap, causing the women to worry about retaining their "school girl
complexions." She observed that most people still tried to look nice or
"at least clean and neat" even though it took a lot of time and effort.
Josephine acknowledged that the internees thought they still looked
good but guessed that "if we were set down in the States somewhere
we'd look like a pretty seedy crowd."[3]

Like women in the United States who had to make do with what was
available because of wartime rations, interned women did the same
because of the scarcity of goods and because of the limited amount of
personal items the Japanese allowed them to take into camp. Repeated
wear of a limited amount of clothing plus rudimentary facilities for
doing laundry guaranteed that apparel quickly wore out. By September 1942, Elizabeth Vaughan observed that the Bacolod women looked
"faded," that each had only three or four dresses "which are worn in
rotation."[4] Because of heat and perspiration a dress needed washing after
every wearing, and cheap soap and repeated rubbing of the garment faded

its color and thinned the fabric. Women applied patches to deteriorated clothing in an attempt to forestall obtaining new ones, because replacing them required strategy and skill if one did not have money.

Clothing replacement therefore became a marked event in the lives of the women as exemplified by Josephine Waldo's April 1943 diary entry about "an addition to my wardrobe," a substitute for her tattered everyday housecoat. At thirty-five pesos a new one was too expensive to purchase, so Josephine sent word to a friend still living in the Michel Apartments, asking her to send two of her cotton dinner dresses into Santo Tomas. With the help of Marge Davis, "an excellent seamstress," Josephine fashioned a new housecoat out of one of those dresses, recalling with pleasure that the first time she wore it to the women's washroom "it caused a sensation because anything new these days stands out like a sore thumb." Her success inspired other women in her dormitory to reevaluate their situation to determine if they could make over some of their husband's unused clothing for themselves. Josephine acknowledged that she was lucky; she had extra garments to send for, so she was almost guaranteed of having something new when she needed it. Admitting that she had always been fond of clothes, she found "this experience had made me even more clothes conscious, because after a couple of years of wearing the same old faded and mended things we all want to go haywire when we get home again." During the last six months of the Japanese occupation of the Philippines, almost all of the internees' clothing had worn out, and spot patching gave way to piecing garments together from several sources. Elizabeth Vaughan described the "Santo Tomas 1944 styles" as clothing with "fronts of one color and backs of another, or yokes of one, sleeves of another, and body of another," yet she found the combinations quite attractive.[5]

For Japanese authorities, clothing symbolized another way in which they could control the internees. The camps had rules regarding what the prisoners could and could not wear, regulations based on the whims of the commandant, who demanded that women be "decently" dressed at all times with discreet necklines and long skirts. Because of the almost unrelenting heat, women tried to get away with as little attire as possible while remaining seemly by their own standards, which were influenced by a combination of prewar fashions and internment realities. In Bacolod, Elizabeth Vaughan described women's "almost universal camp uniform" as a V-neck blouse coupled with shorts, which the commandant found acceptable; however, after her transfer to Santo Tomas, she was dismayed to find that the commandant had different ideas—women could not wear shorts. Emily Van Sickle blamed the ban on Earl Carroll of the Executive Committee, claiming that when "he deemed it necessary to protect women against possible Japanese concupiscence," he issued the ban, contending that it came through the commandant's office. However, by the end of 1943, clothing was in such short supply that the Executive Committee convinced Japanese authorities to allow women to wear shorts. Elizabeth noted that the Japanese seemed "to be in an agreeable mood at the moment" and so gave permission for women to don shorts that were no more than four inches above the knee, an acceptable combination of propriety and practicality.[6]

Cosmetics and new fashions provided women with much-needed psychological boosts during internment, as they looked forward to holidays and other special occasions when they could trot out their finery and feel, at least for a while, that life was normal. The lack of these items clearly caused distress. On their first day of internment, Margaret and David Sherk returned to their room to find some of their possessions stolen, including a bottle of Blue Grass cologne that Bob had given Margaret for Christmas, which she had brought into camp "purely for morale building purposes." Elizabeth Vaughan noticed a lack of spirit and cheerfulness among the Bacolod women by December 1942, which she partially attributed to their shortage of clothing and cosmetics. The rigors of internment produced dry and reddened skin, unkempt and lank hair, broken fingernails, callused feet, and brown teeth, prompting Elizabeth to argue that if a woman "feels herself to be unattractive in the eyes of another woman she cannot help but act unattractively." She longed for the "luxury to wallow in a bath of cold cream, to feel softened and genteel again! And, oh! for a dash of perfume to sweeten the soul as well as the nostrils."[7]

To banish feelings of fashion deprivation, the Baguio women celebrated Easter 1942 by attending a sunrise service with their families, then staging a parade during the Sunday night socializing hour. Almost every adult woman created a new Easter hat, long an American tradition, and joined the parade; Fern Harrington recalled that "shrieks of hilarity punctuated the afternoon as the women fashioned their hats." She covered a strawberry basket with a variety of flowers she had picked the day before but declared the "smartest" hat was the one made from a roll of toilet paper tied to a woman's head with a ribbon. Natalie Crouter, who observed but did not participate, described one woman who wore a branch on her head adorned with a paper bird and another who had "onions hanging from her ears as earrings, the long green sprouts on her head." The parade was a big success. The internees laughed as they thoroughly enjoyed themselves, that is, until the Japanese guards heard the commotion and moved in to break up the event, leading Fern to speculate that "the solemnity of the morning and the frivolity of the evening appeared incongruous" to the guards.[8]

Christmas 1943 also became a joyous occasion in Baguio, with the usual celebration amplified by the distribution of the forty-seven-pound Red Cross comfort kits; the addition of familiar American food such as chocolate bars and canned meat spurred the internees on to an elaborate feast. Fern recalled that everyone showed up for Christmas dinner dressed in the best clothes they could find, including some formal dresses that had been kept in a camp storeroom. She especially marveled over the "stunning hairdos" of the women, which she considered a real testament to the skills of the camp beauty operator, because none of the women had been able to get a permanent wave since internment. Another highlight of the day was a "vivacious redhead" who usually wore a turban: on Christmas Day she discarded her head covering and unveiled her natural mane of silvery white hair.[9]

Those Red Cross packages also contained clothing and other items to enhance women's appearances. Natalie Crouter noted the inclusion of two hundred pairs of women's shoes, plus cleaning tissue, cold cream, dresses, sunsuits, underwear, and nightgowns, but "no lipsticks." By New Year's Day 1944, these items had been swapped among the women according to who needed what the most, and Natalie observed that "the feminine contingent blossomed out in soft pastel shades, trotting about the campus like Girl Scouts all in one style of suits. Some say we look like orphans or prisoners, institutional. But to me they look pretty, gay, new, with fresh color and cut, something to talk about and trade or swap or work on. Each woman wears hers 'with a difference.'"[10]

In paying attention to clothing, hair, and makeup, women tried desperately to avoid what Emily Van Sickle referred to as the "Santo Tomas look," which set in after six months of internment. The image in her mirror confirmed her feeling of being eighty years old: "I stared at the scarecrow apparition with pale brown hair skinned back in two long braids, the top screwed up in a string spiral; eyes that were lusterless and deeply shadowed; face drawn and haggard." Tressa Roka became increasingly depressed every time she looked in her mirror, because she saw that her "light-brown hair was dull, stringy and straight as a ruler, giving me the look of a frustrated Vermont spinster." She decided that no matter what the cost, something had to be done. She cashed in one of her few remaining traveler's checks, gladly paying an outrageously inflated 30 percent fee, for one of the camp beauty operators to give her a permanent wave, which not only made her more attractive but also gave her a "mental lift." Tressa came to understand "why beauty parlors in mental institutions were a part of the mental therapy," and she treated herself to permanent waves as often as she could to keep her psyche in shape.[11]

As women recognized their deteriorating appearances, they often grew jealous of those who retained their looks. Even though Tressa did as much as she could to remain coifed and fashionably attired, she registered envy when another women looked more attractive than she did. One day in March 1943, she went to visit Catesy in the hospital only to find that he already had two visitors, a man she referred to as Don Juan and "his current blonde," who wore "suggestively abbreviated shorts," which caused all of the men in the ward to stare at her "long expanse of beautifully proportioned tan legs." Tressa could not compete—she wore a pair of old, faded slacks that did nothing to enhance her figure—making her feel shabby and diminished in the eyes of her fiancé.[12]

Tressa's hairstylist was one of many internees who established thriving private beauty and fashion enterprises in Santo Tomas, but outside entrepreneurs supplied them as well. During the summer of 1942, Emily Van Sickle watched as women dressed up in the evenings in the "freshest slack suits and dresses," which had been purchased from the in-camp branch of Aguinaldo's, a Manila department store, or via outside contacts from stores in the city that gave internees credit. Tressa noted that on October 15, 1942, vendors came into the women's dormitory hawking an assortment of lingerie and dresses, the cost of which was "exorbitant and usually the material was cheap and sleazy, but if one was down to the last slack or sarong, anything would do—providing, of course, one had the money."[13] Although such economic transactions may appear bizarre within an internment camp setting, they actually reflected the determination of the Japanese to make the internees fend for themselves. Also, by allowing such purchases the Japanese could reinforce their claim that the Allied civilians were detainees rather than prisoners—after all, real prisoners would not have the luxury of buying clothing.

Women did what they could to maintain a neat appearance to cement their relationships with men; without physical attraction romance would die, and early in internment women would not allow that to happen. Even while prisoners, women realized that they could use their physical attraction as a way of keeping men interested and in line. Near the end of February 1942, Tressa Roka's fiancé decided to grow a beard until the war ended. Tressa thought the beard made Catesy "appear more handsome," but its association with internment depressed her; she wanted him to shave it off, but Catesy, proud of the new growth, refused. In retaliation, she donned her most unflattering slacks and arranged her hair in a "homely" style, a "Tobacco Roadish" appearance she continued for three days before he caved in and shaved.[14]

As the years of internment wore on and starvation and illness took their toll, women continued to sustain their morale by dressing up. Tressa noticed that in November 1944 the men looked weaker and thinner than the women did and were also less cheerful, a difference prompted by the men's chivalrous insistence that women receive any available additional calories. The younger women in camp, including herself, "despite their scrawny bodies, kept up appearances" and "still used lipstick and wore hibiscus flowers" in their hair. This required tremendous effort, because during that fall, shortages became so severe that women used the cold cream from the Red Cross comfort kits to fry food rather than cleanse and soften their skin.[15]

Convinced that things such as food and work were much more important than fashion, some women tried to wean themselves from it, to adjust their appearance to the realities of internment. As Natalie Crouter headed into her second month of internment in Baguio, she accepted the fact that she would no longer be able to have her hair washed and set as normal. She found that a single braided pigtail fastened with a red and blue tie knitted by her daughter, June, proved more conducive to her surroundings, since her "state of mind has no time for waves, rouge, or lipstick." The following month when she experimented with rouge and lipstick to see how the cosmetics complemented her pigtail, Jerry "nearly fell off the railing" from surprise. Natalie, who returned to her unadorned state, later criticized women who spent hours a day on their makeup, because to her, this attention to fashion was "out-of-place, poor taste, if not vapid," and she admitted that she could not "keep on looking like the Queen of Sheba while emptying garbage."[16]

Agnes Keith initially agreed with Natalie's view of fashion and, while on Berhala Island, gave up using makeup because she was just too tired: "Why look like a woman, and live like a dog?" However, Agnes soon regretted giving away most of her cosmetics, as she found that it "was more necessary than ever in our circumstances to make an effort to look attractive, for the sake of our own morale." She carefully hoarded her remaining makeup for times when her spirits needed a real boost. During her ordeal of reporting an attempted rape to Kuching camp authorities and being tortured for her "lies," Agnes turned to makeup and nice clothing to keep from falling apart, using them to alleviate her psychological stress and physical pain. After returning to her barracks from her first questioning and beating in Lieutenant Nekata's office, Agnes took a bath, then "put on the remnants" of her cosmetics, which she usually saved for the rare meetings with Harry, despondently referring to this day as a "special occasion." Nekata warned Agnes not to tell anyone what had happened in his office, so she was deprived of the relief of sharing her story with friends who would have comforted her. When Nekata summoned Agnes to his office the following day, she dressed herself carefully in her best outfit, applied lipstick and rouge, and fixed her hair into a neat braid. Convinced she was going to meet her death, she was determined to do so looking as feminine as possible.[17]

Agnes also found that her prewar "weakness for nice clothes" helped to ensure her and George's survival, since there were always women in camp who, because they had no children to care for, willingly traded food and medicine for fancy clothing. Toward the end of the war, when black market gouging dramatically increased, Agnes traded a pink taffeta negligee for soda bicarbonate tablets; a black crepe dinner dress, for which she had paid ninety-eight dollars before the war, for six aspirins for George when he had a toothache; and a black velvet dinner dress for a white cotton sheet that she in turn traded with Chinese merchants for food.[18] Morale never had as high a priority as survival, especially when it came to George, and Agnes maintained her role as the strong mother by trading away these useless items.

Fashion provided some women with optimism for the future by putting aside one nice outfit to be liberated in—they considered greeting American soldiers while looking haggard and beaten un-American and unfeminine. At the end of July 1944, Ethel Herold, in the spirit of Scarlett O'Hara, recounted how she made a new dress for herself out of a striped curtain she had saved since 1942 from the country club. Her other two "best" dresses, a red and white checked sharkskin and a blue and white pique, were "worn and patched beyond repair," so for everyday wear, Ethel donned a hand-me-down kimono. She was not about to waste her new dress to wear in camp, writing emphatically that the "new striped dress is to go HOME in."[19]

Women did not agree on the role of fashion in internment. In the prewar years, fashion, femininity, and appearance made up core components of womanhood, but during the war women disputed these meanings. Natalie Crouter found attention to fashion silly and vain; to some extent Agnes Keith agreed, but she willingly used it to boost her morale and to benefit her son's well-being. Tressa Roka and Josephine Waldo also understood the psychological benefits of fashion and, perhaps because they were younger and more swayed by romance, paid closer attention to it. But whether women chose to disregard fashion issues or not, they justified their decision according to their own interpretation of womanhood as it was altered by internment.

CAMP ROMANCES

Interned women continued to long for and pursue male companionship, but within the bounds of prescribed behavior: unattached women formed attachments with single men, courted within the confines of commingling, and planned weddings. The sexual mores of the times plus the realities of internment dictated this conduct, deviations from which usually resulted in group censure. In September 1942, Margaret Sherk challenged the accepted practice of monogamous marriage and notions of proper womanhood when she fell in love with another man. Her infidelity was compounded by the fact of her husband's military prisoner-of-war status; therefore her adultery, under these peculiar wartime circumstances, appeared to others as unpatriotic as well as immoral. On September 13, Margaret chatted briefly with Jerry Sams as she watched a basketball game on the front lawn of Santo Tomas. Jerry, a former marine and a married man with a wife in the United States, had been working as an electronic engineer for the Civil Aeronautics Authority when the war started. Though his civilian work placed him with the U.S. Navy at Cavite, located across the bay from Manila, Jerry did not join the USAFFE, but he aided in the evacuation of Cavite and saved many lives. He then made his way to Manila and was subsequently interned in Santo Tomas.

The relationship between Margaret and Jerry developed very quickly, and Margaret did not delude herself as to its nature. The ban against consorting and the taint of adultery did not constrain her: "I was twenty-six years old and knew exactly how one should go about the business of being a model daughter, wife, and mother."[20] Margaret disregarded those models because Jerry, the most handsome man she had ever met, was resourceful and he also quickly befriended David. Jerry did things for Margaret that in peacetime would have been quite ordinary and even boring but represented excitement and generosity in camp. He made her a washboard, which lessened her laundry chores, and crafted a food bucket for David so that the youngster did not spill any of the precious food he had to carry when they ate on the food line. Jerry invited Margaret to his living quarters to share calamansi (citrus fruit) juice and other food while they sat on chairs, which additionally impressed Margaret, for she had not sat on a real chair since she had been interned.

These activities, minus the adultery, represented a common form of courtship in the camps, where couples could best show affection for each other by sharing scarce commodities. In the summer of 1942, Natalie Crouter observed that in Camp Holmes "various romances are flourishing the only way they can in concentration—stilted, public, leading to no actual courtship, but tender devotion in conversation and looks, with food preparation ending in twosome parties under pine trees or iron-roofed runways."[21] Natalie clearly believed that true courtship had to have a physical element to it as well.

By Natalie's standards Margaret Sherk and Jerry Sams progressed to an actual courtship. Although Margaret never apologized for her romance with Jerry, she did provide a rationalization for why she fell in love with him, enumerating reasons practical and unique to the time: "I most likely would have fallen in love with the devil himself if he had offered me help and food. When I had sympathy and understanding as well, it was inevitable. Added to that, the circumstances were right for it. No one knew what the next day held; we might be dead, we might be liberated, anything might happen and probably would. It made one want to drain the last drop from the minute at hand." Margaret certainly was not the only woman who felt this way nor was she the only interned woman who acted on her feelings, but she has been the only woman willing to write about it. Her memoir of internment can be read as a "quintessential apologia," because she used it to defend her belief in "passionate love," which, according to her, overrode the marital and sexual conventions of the times—when two people truly fall in love, they have no control over their actions.[22] While Margaret did not flaunt her affair with Jerry, the Santo Tomas rumor mill quickly picked up on it.

Stories also circulated about other women, both married and unmarried, who flouted both propriety and the Japanese edict banning fraternization and had affairs. In the summer of 1942, Natalie Crouter recalled rumors that "at least four or five individuals here have three or four wives in various sections, not all in one spot of course." Referring to this as "strange information," she was apparently unwilling to believe it as absolute fact because Baguio contained only about five hundred people. Emily Van Sickle knew a sixteen-year-old girl in Santo Tomas, whom she called Georgie, who shared a shanty with a tall, dark man known as Duke, an arrangement Georgie pursued despite the strong objections of her parents. The problem was not just Georgie's age but also the fact that Duke had a Filipina wife and several mestizo children outside of the camp, yet Georgie followed her "heart's desire," continuing her romance with Duke.[23]

In addition to the alleged polygamy in Camp Holmes, Natalie Crouter noted "numerous petting parties" that prompted the camp guards to step up their after-hours surveillance. She could not understand why couples indulged in such behavior, because there was not "much use stirring up emotions beyond a certain point. Of course it is a strain on the sex instinct to be so near [a loved one] and yet so far!"[24] Although Natalie did not strongly condemn the women who chose to act on their sexual urges, other internees fretted about the consequences of violating a Japanese edict, worried that a natural increase in the camp population would increase the burden on already meager resources. And women having extramarital affairs, like Margaret Sherk, were shunned by most of the other internees for their unconventional and immoral behavior, and they often found it difficult to live under the censure of their compatriots.

Yet romance flourished in the camps despite Japanese restrictions. The Baguio men developed a variety of whistle calls, including cricket chirps and mourning dove coos, to signal to their wives or girlfriends to come to the talking fence that separated the barracks and served as the place of information exchange and of courtship. Natalie Crouter admitted that she got a "long chuckle" out of a young girl's comment that she "used to call my horse the way these men call their wives." In November 1942, Elizabeth Vaughan recorded a pragmatic courtship that took place in Bacolod. Just after the war started, Mr. White's wife died while giving birth to their son Douglas, and White took ill during the early months of internment; the strain of taking care of the baby by himself proved almost too much. White began to recover only when "romance came into his life again—not by his own will, neither against his will," as one very determined single woman in camp targeted him as the man for her. Elizabeth noted that their relationship brought "joy to all in camp who are watching the unembarrassed principals, who—of course—will have not one minute of privacy during their entire stay in camp."[25]

Although not the center of attention except in her own diary, Tressa Roka and Catesy continued their courtship within the confines of the much larger Santo Tomas. She claimed internment brought them closer together, as they determined to continue their relationship as normally as possible; nevertheless, they remained conscious of Japanese restrictions. Shortly after internment, when Tressa and Catesy exchanged a kiss in public on their way to breakfast, they heard a "commotion" next to them—two Japanese soldiers "talking rapidly and moving their hands back and forth in a negative gesture." Tressa could not imagine what had upset the guards so much, but Catesy speculated that "the little runts don't approve of kissing." A couple of days later, the camp commandant issued a proclamation forbidding any "display of affection between married or unmarried couples before any of his junior officers," empowering the "morality squad men" to apprehend violators.[26]

Even within the confines of Japanese rules, flirtations and courtships gave women something to look forward to, provided some sense of normality in their lives, and made them feel feminine. Tressa Roka observed the courtship of her friend Zest, who took particular care with her appearance, wearing a complexion-enhancing green scarf and cutting her hair in a short, flattering style, proving to Tressa that there "was nothing like a man to perk up the appearance and interest of a girl." On Christmas Day 1942, Zest and her boyfriend, Henry, announced their engagement.[27] Both the accoutrements of femininity and an attentive beau helped Zest contend with internment.

MARRIAGE AND FAMILY

For Margaret Sherk the ban against commingling could not further adversely affect her marriage, because she was already separated from her husband. To her, patriotism and notions of men's duties outweighed marital togetherness, because she supported Bob's decision to serve as an engineer and then as a soldier with the USAFFE at Bataan, later commenting, "I felt he was doing what a man should do." In letting Bob go without a fuss, Margaret believed that she was being a good, patriotic woman. Despite these ideals, Margaret quickly learned that having a husband in camp eased many burdens, worries that now fell entirely on her own shoulders. She observed that "smart women" without husbands or male friends attached themselves to single men who built them private shanties, which made sense to her because "men needed women to clean the shanty and cook for them, and women needed men to build a shanty to be cleaned, and to cook for men." Margaret admitted that she envied women who managed to do "something constructive" to improve the awful living arrangements, but the men she personally knew in camp had families and therefore lacked extra time or energy to build her one of the very sought-after shanties.[28] Without a husband to help her and without extra cash to purchase both necessities and luxuries, Margaret seemed destined to remain one of the less-privileged internees in Santo Tomas.

Not every American woman believed she had to give up her husband to the USAFFE to fulfill ideals of womanhood and patriotism. Pragmatic, family-centered Charlotte Brussolo argued with her husband, Vito, an engineer working near Baguio, because he wanted to join the army after Pearl Harbor. A naturalized American born in Italy, Vito believed that when an invading enemy threatened his home and family, he was duty-bound to fight, but Charlotte vehemently protested. The couple had two school-aged sons, and she believed she could not keep the family together and alive during a Japanese invasion and occupation without Vito's help. She strenuously contested that his duty to family, especially under these dangerous circumstances, outweighed his duty to country. For Charlotte, being a good wife and mother meant keeping the family together at all costs; loyalty to country could best be expressed through survival. She prevailed, so the Brussolos spent the war years interned together.[29]

In Baguio, families remained largely intact because American men had had little opportunity for a quick getaway to join the USAFFE. Japanese authorities established separate barracks for adult men and women but allowed them to socialize as long as they followed certain rules. Natalie Crouter observed in February 1942 that "men and women can join on the tennis court till 7 but must talk only family affairs, nothing about 'soldiers.'" In December, she listed the new commingling rules in her diary, including specific times during the week when husbands and wives could walk together, prohibitions against meeting in places other than the parade ground or the barracks, and requirements that boys and girls walk to school separately. In early 1943, one woman, baffled by the complexities of the rules, questioned a guard about the propriety of a woman eating a meal with a man she was not married to. Japanese officials decided that it was appropriate, but that dining couples, married or not, "must make a definite business of eating and on no account to look romantic, for the guards (with their binoculars) are watching and they know all the romantic ones, including those married." Natalie found this ludicrous, wondering how a person could "turn on and off that spigot which releases the romantic look."[30]

Japanese authorities in Bacolod claimed a willingness to let the internees live in a fairly normal manner—adult men and women slept in separate barracks, but the commandant told them that otherwise they "may live freely." In June 1942, Elizabeth Vaughan observed that since work kept married couples busy during most of the day and since they stayed in separate sleeping quarters, they only had about two hours together in the evening, from just after roll call until before lights out. She watched as "husbands and wives kiss each other goodnight on the verandah, before eyes of others crowded in this narrow space before bedtime to get what breeze there is." Rather than viewing this as living freely, Elizabeth concluded that the internees led a "strangely isolated family life."[31]

Visiting, no matter what the restrictions, made for an invaluable lifeline between husbands and wives, as Ethel Herold observed in Baguio that "one can understand how precious that hour [of public visitation] is with wives and husbands." On Berhala Island, the Japanese interned men and women separately, so couples rarely had the chance for more than a fleeting glimpse at each other when the men walked past the women's gate each day. This deprivation early in the war prompted Agnes Keith's belief that she could not survive without her husband, so she plotted meetings with Harry regardless of the consequences. Sometimes a sympathetic guard allowed couples to exchange a few words before the men were hurried away from the women's gate; the Keiths took one such opportunity to establish plans to join later, illegally, at a spot between the two camps. Agnes slipped out of her bed, crawled underneath the barracks and a wooden fence, and emerged in the pitch-black jungle, where she waited for Harry in the rain, convinced that every sound she heard was a snake or a guard, either of which meant real trouble. The couple worked out their meeting routine that first night, determined to continue on the nights it did not rain. Agnes treasured these meetings for the comfort and reassurance they provided her, recalling that alone with Harry, "we would promise each other that the war would be over soon . . . that we would love each other forever and ever, and at least for that moment we would be happy." These secret meetings ended when the Japanese moved their prisoners to Kuching. Agnes admitted that the move probably saved their lives, for if she and Harry had been caught, they may have been beaten or killed outright. She did not regret the risks that they took to meet during those first months, because at the time, not seeing Harry was the worst thing that she could imagine, but, as she wryly observed later, they were both "still looking at the war on a short-term basis."[32]

The guards in Kuching usually proved very strict about social mixing: the men and women lived in separate camps, were forbidden to talk, and had few occasions to exchange more than a fleeting glance at each other. Opportunities arose when Japanese officials planned entertainment in order to celebrate a Japanese holiday, then ordered internees to volunteer their talents. Prisoners from all of the camps attended these shows, but husbands and wives remained separated, according to Agnes, by "several fireproof layers of Roman Catholic Sisters and British and Dutch soldiers." Guards with fixed bayonets patrolled the audience not to prevent escapes but to keep husbands and wives apart, yet couples could not resist trying to make some contact. After dark, the most daring husbands dropped to the ground, crawling across the various human barriers just to be able to sit next to their wives. These violations rarely went undetected, and the offending husbands "would be flicked out of the audience at the end of a bayonet and chased to the guardhouse." Harry declined to participate in this public indignity, no matter how much he wanted to see Agnes, and instead showed his love for her by passing her messages and medicine.[33]

The vaguest threat of strict separation of families caused a great deal of consternation among the internees; those in the Philippines not subjected to stricter gender separation dreaded the thought. Their fears seemed to be realized in early May 1943, when Japanese officials informed the Santo Tomas internees of the construction of another camp at Los Banos and that eight hundred men would be sent there to get the place ready for a larger group. According to the Japanese, unmanageable overcrowding in Santo Tomas required the opening of this new camp, especially since they started revoking out-of-camp exemptions and interning all enemy aliens. This news made people frantic, because they did not trust the Japanese's motives, even when the Japanese promised that once women were sent to Los Banos, married couples could live together. On May 10, Josephine Waldo noticed that Santo Tomas came "alive with rumors and interpretations" about what prompted the Japanese to make such a decision. Rumors abounded that Los Banos was to be for men only, that the Japanese had finally figured out a way to completely separate men and women. Separation was not the very worst envisioned by the internees; they feared that once the Japanese sent the men away they would then either be transported to prison camps in Japan or be executed in the new camp. According to Josephine, people believed that the construction of Los Banos was simply a ruse "to get all the able-bodied men of military age out of here and into a prison camp."[34]

Josephine's concern was immediate and personal, because Bill, her husband of four and a half years, was of military age, so she worried that he would be one of the men to be sent. Early in the day on May 10, she plunged deep into sorrow: "The thought of Bill and I [sic] being separated has hit me harder than anything I have ever had happen to me before. So far, I have been entirely incapable of meeting the possibility. In many ways, I am ashamed of myself for being so weak, because I know how hard it is on Bill." Josephine believed that she was failing Bill as a wife, that she was not being strong enough for him in his time of need. Emily Van Sickle found herself in a similar position, since she and Van were also childless, making him eligible for that first transfer list and prompting Emily's despair that "the thing we had feared from the first was about to happen to us: separation." But good luck spared both couples. As Josephine finished her diary entry that evening, one of her shanty neighbors who served on the Executive Committee stopped by to tell the couple of Bill's exemption because his planning and administering of shanties was considered essential by the Japanese. Emily had to wait an agonizing couple of days to learn of Van's reprieve, granted because of his ill health and his vital camp work.[35]

The method the Japanese devised for choosing the Los Banos men resembled a military draft: men between the ages of eighteen and fifty-five who did not have wives and children headed the list, followed by men of the same ages who had wives but no children. The elderly and chronically ill, along with those who performed indispensable camp duties, like Bill Waldo, received exemptions. The Japanese then drew up a list of names and on the morning of May 12 posted it on the bulletin board, around which almost every internee swarmed, jostling and angling to get a look. Josephine observed that there were "many mistakes on the first list due to the inefficient camp statistics," so a board convened to determine if any of the men on the list had legitimate reasons, such as families, illness, or vital camp jobs, for exemption. Relieved that Bill was not going, Josephine felt terrible for her friends who were being separated from their husbands and sweethearts, noting that the night before the transfer "people walked the halls and the spirit of the whole camp is low."[36]

Desperation to avoid separation from loved ones prompted some internees to resort to elaborate plans to get their names removed from the transfer list. According to Emily Van Sickle, nearly every man who had his name drawn objected, "some with reason, some with merely an overpowering desire not to go," leading her to recount the story of the boyfriend (who also had a wife in camp) of one of her roommates, the "Duchess." Shortly after seeing his name on the transfer list, the boyfriend was seized with a "violent attack of vomiting," so the Duchess summoned a doctor, telling him that her sick boyfriend could not be moved. After a thorough examination, the doctor concluded that drinking a glass of warm soapsuds had brought on the illness, and he ordered the charlatan to report for transfer.[37]

On occasion, women separated from their husbands somewhat willingly, separations that tended to be temporary when the Japanese granted them for illness or other special circumstances. During the first year and a half of the war, authorities in Manila allowed mothers with small children to live outside of Santo Tomas if they chose, also issuing limited-term passes to women and children who required medical treatment only obtainable outside of camp. Grace Nash steadfastly refused to leave Manila prior to Pearl Harbor, because she worried that her work-obsessed husband, Ralph, would not be able to get along without her. At that point in her life, with war still uncertain and the unity of the family paramount, Grace adhered to a devoted-wife role. But during war she privileged the role of mother by availing herself of the opportunity to take her sons out of camp, thereby separating the family. Young Gale had been ill ever since the family's first night in camp, and when a doctor diagnosed dengue fever, Grace received permission to take both boys to the Philippine General Hospital, where Gale could be treated.

As Grace hurried to pack their things, she realized she had to notify Ralph of these latest developments and admitted that her "fears over leaving camp without him blinded me."[38] She hoped that Ralph would be allowed to accompany them, a request the Japanese denied, so for several months she had to take care of her sons at the Assumption Convent, in a city under enemy occupation. Grace gave private music lessons, set up a grade school to earn extra money to purchase food and other necessities, and returned monthly to Santo Tomas to renew her pass and visit Ralph for a few minutes. When Gale contracted a severe case of bacillary dysentery in April 1942, Ralph secured permission to join his family, and in May they all moved into the private home of a missionary family, friends of theirs from the prewar days. Throughout the spring and summer, Ralph moved in and out of camp, gaining temporary passes to visit his family when one of the boys took ill. His episodic presence helped Grace to better manage the family and cope with Gale's and Stan's illnesses; she functioned especially well when she could be both wife and mother. In the fall, when the entire family was finally well, Ralph moved them back into camp, but now the family had another complication to deal with—Grace was pregnant.

Given the Japanese determination to separate couples, it is hardly surprising that a constant struggle ensued between camp authorities and the internees as internees attempted to stretch the rules as far as they possibly could. Natalie Crouter viewed their resistance as part of human nature, observing in Baguio "sex cycles, pent up energy released every so often, all the abnormality of war reaching a peak and exploding regularly." But the internees tried to police themselves, to prevent any such explosions from actually happening. In February 1942, the Women's Committee asked that women pay more attention to the camp rules, advising them to "keep away from the men as much as possible," and the Men's Committee issued a similar warning in June that the internees had reached the limit of stretching the rules. That bulletin reminded internees of the edict against commingling and related a visit by some Japanese officers during which "several couples were sitting together in front of the building and made no effort to separate during the visit, which brought forth warning from the guard." Two months later, infractions were still a problem, causing Elmer Herold to reprimand a man after catching him inside the women's barracks. Natalie worried that "so many take advantage of leniency that it is more overdone every day and we may end up with no more commingling again. As it is, couples can play bridge in the evening and there is pleasant mingling in the dining room. Why some men have to be smart and brag about how much they get away with is just another one of the human mysteries."[39] Although Natalie felt comfortable limiting fraternization to card games, she could not empathize with those who needed much more interaction.

Yet romantic urges continued to tempt couples, with even Natalie succumbing to them but in a characteristically restrained manner. In late March 1943, she recounted that the songs a woman sang one night in camp "stirred gray ashes into flame and sentiment"—caught up in that quixotic fire, Jerry pulled her pigtail "romantically" as they sat on a bench with their son, Fred, between them. The next morning, observing the changing seasons, she remarked that they showed "the length of our abnormal life without permissible sign of affection." Natalie acknowledged that "one hesitates to stir desire even by the holding of hands when affection is near the surface after being unleashed," obliquely referring to the likelihood that casual touching would lead to sexual intercourse, which might in turn lead to pregnancy, a difficult condition to endure in camp.[40]

Without violating socializing rules, couples celebrated anniversaries and holidays in order to express their love for each other, celebrations that required a great deal of effort and ingenuity. In October 1942, the Waldos celebrated their fourth wedding anniversary, during which Bill surprised Josephine with a catered lunch for themselves and nine guests. He presented her with gifts of scarce American soap, hand cream, toothpaste, and a bottle of Coca Cola, prompting Josephine to remark that it "was a happy day for us and I thank God we are together." Within a few months romantic celebrations took a more pragmatic turn, as luxury items became scarcer: for Valentine's Day 1943, Bill's gift to Josephine was finishing the doors on some kitchen cabinets in their shanty. Josephine admitted her disappointment, but blamed Bill's practicality not on internment but rather on the fact that they were "old married people now and I shouldn't expect too much romance." This rationalization made their situation seem more normal for her, believing that despite internment Bill would have given her such a practical gift on a romantic holiday. The following October, the couple celebrated what would be their last wedding anniversary together by going to a play, then eating at one of the camp restaurants for dinner. Josephine pronounced Bill "the best husband in all the world and in spite of internment life I'm really happy to be alive and to be with him here," but wished to spend their sixth anniversary elsewhere, since two years of "maiden life" had been too long for an "old married woman" like her. The Waldos never made it to that next anniversary. Shortly after celebrating their fifth, Bill took ill with what was originally diagnosed as dengue fever. When he could no longer move his legs, a doctor belatedly determined he had polio and moved him to an outside hospital, where he died on October 28.[41]

Although the Japanese did not interfere with these private celebrations, they did maintain the ban on public displays of affection and on sex between men and women. Yet punishments for commingling varied depending on who got caught doing what and on who caught them. In early 1942, Santo Tomas internees established their own "morality squad men," who did little more than reiterate the commandant's statement prohibiting public displays of affection. The campus's west patio served as a getaway spot for hundreds of couples, and Tressa Roka and Catesy took a grass mat there after evening roll call; in the course of quiet conversation, kissing and hugging usually followed. Once a member of the morality squad interrupted them, but Tressa noticed that although the man warned them of their violation, "his heart wasn't in it," and the couple received no punishment.[42]

Japanese guards also proved capricious with enforcement. Natalie Crouter recounted that in April 1942, when Baguio guards caught yet another couple consorting, they merely stepped up their "prowl" of the barracks and secluded areas, but when a new group of guards who had fought at Bataan arrived in camp the following month, commingling regulations were tightened. According to Ethel Herold, men and women were not allowed to talk to each other during the day, even though mixed work details made this restriction impossible, and on May 16 the Japanese erected a double fence to separate husbands and wives during their evening visitations. In October, Natalie noted that "drama, scandal, made its entrance" into camp when a young married couple was discovered at the high school "out of bounds and commingling, both major offenses at the moment" because they were "holding hands, maybe more." After Nellie McKim, one of the camp liaisons, intervened with officials in an attempt to mitigate their punishment, they received banishment to a room in the guardhouse, where they remained for twenty-four hours, with a guard between them. Fern Harrington recalled another incident in which a Japanese guard caught Bill and Jessie Junkin sitting together on a bench reading the Bible, provoking the guard to slap Jessie's face so hard that she went to the camp hospital to make sure there were no internal injuries.[43]

In at least one instance, the fickleness of the Japanese in regard to commingling related to expediency of administration. Upon their internment at Camp John Hay, the Herold family was allowed to share living quarters in the room that had been the camp barber shop, a special privilege accorded because the Japanese had chosen Elmer as the camp's main liaison officer. When the men's barracks opened up, Billy moved into it, while Elmer remained with Ethel in a special section of the women's barracks. Later the couple moved into an old guard room that had a window, a necessary item, as the Japanese guards used it to pass information and orders to Elmer throughout the day. Ethel did not like the fact that the room was so exposed to the Japanese, so Betsy remained in the women's barracks, closely watched by old friends. Though the room the Herolds shared was far from elegant, with its bomb holes in the walls and makeshift shutters on the windows, the couple had more privacy than did other married people.

Not surprisingly, this arrangement provoked a great deal of jealousy among the internees, which Ethel acknowledged in her usual no-nonsense manner, writing in her diary in January 1942 that "a lot of these cats are jealous of me—they wouldn't be as sex has gone by the board." In one brief sentence she stated her belief that anguish over separation included sexual relations as well as simple companionship plus admitted that even though they lived together, she and Elmer did not have sexual relations. A few days later Ethel noted complaints that some of the missionaries "make too much love on the tennis court," causing her friend Rae Hix to jokingly suggest that the Herolds rent their room "to married couples by the 20 minutes or by the hour—the longer the time, the higher the price."[44]

The Herolds continued their privileged cohabitation after the move to Camp Holmes. Their room, sectioned off from the women's barracks with an old cupboard and boasting a short narrow bed, doubled as a storage area, and women freely approached Elmer "any time during the night or day to ask help of any kind." Natalie Crouter deplored this arrangement as a violation of equality and fairness, gleefully noting that upon the reinternment of missionaries (who had been granted a brief exemption) in November 1942, the Herolds had to find separate accommodations in the men's and women's barracks. Natalie saw that Ethel finally learned "firsthand at last, to everyone's delight, what it is to be surrounded and shoved, pushed about and squeezed," which she viewed as a triumph for the "lower classes" of the average internees, who forced the "uppers" to experience real everyday internment life. She credited Elmer with being "good-natured" about the change but admitted that she "chuckled as he stood below the window last night calling to his mate like all the rest of us, to stick her head out so he could speak to her." Ethel, always attuned to the moods and reactions of others, briefly noted that her "enemies are so glad Elmer is out of the women's barracks." Natalie could only gloat for a couple of days, however, because the Herolds resumed their original arrangements at the insistence of camp officials, who wanted to be able to locate Elmer quickly, correctly reasoning that he spent most of his time with his wife.[45]

Camp officials clearly established some rules to demonstrate the power they had over their captives, because they occasionally relaxed restrictions to reward the internees for good behavior or as a gift in celebration of a holiday. Natalie Crouter noted on New Year's Day 1943 that they were "permitted to commingle, as if it were Sunday, all day"; on Christmas Day 1943, when the Japanese handed out the invaluable Red Cross relief parcels, she observed how "fathers joined families and all commingling rules were off." Such special occasions could also be bittersweet, as Agnes Keith observed of Christmas Day 1944, when the guards in Kuching allowed families to mingle for a half an hour in a field outside of the women's camp. The children, thrilled to be outside of the camp, ran wild for those thirty minutes, hardly sitting still for hugs or kisses from the fathers who rarely saw them; in contrast, couples sat together quietly talking, and Agnes later worried that she had misused that half hour, that chitchat was not as important as simply saying "I love you" to Harry. When the men were marched back to their camp, Agnes "looked after them as far as I could see. Was it better, or was it worse, to meet like this, I wondered."[46]

The forced separation of families sometimes brought marital problems to the surface, and while some of these problems may have been present before the war, the stress of internment undoubtedly exacerbated them. The marital troubles of Cecelia and Sanford Ladic provoked tension between the couple, disrupted the quiet of the Baguio camp, and complicated Ethel Herold's life for a time. In early June 1942, Ethel noted that Elmer had the responsibility of policing the Ladics' behavior and that the Japanese advised him "to always carry the handcuffs in his pocket to put on her; she throwing knives and bottles at her husband." The following month Sanford gave his wife "a good spanking" because she tried to steal his food but mistakenly stole someone else's; just a week after the thievery Cecelia received another public spanking from Sanford after a fight. Ethel sympathized with the woman's situation, commenting that Cecelia should "be pitied; she just can't take this awful life," while Elmer, constantly frazzled with trying to keep the Ladics in line, tried unsuccessfully to have Cecelia and her three daughters released to a convent. In November, after a period of calm, the Ladics resumed their public marital squabbles, this time over a bridge tournament, leaving Ethel to worry that Elmer "might crack his ribs all over again in having to get the cuffs on" Cecelia.[47] After these incidents, the Ladics disappeared from Ethel's diary, as other internment issues took precedence.

Ironically, Japanese authorities also attempted to promote fraternization, often in ways that seemed strange to the Americans, leading internees to believe they were not serious about commingling. In early 1942, the commandant of Santo Tomas offered to set up a "love tent" for married couples, which, according to Emily Van Sickle, the internees found "all the more confounding," because no matter how desperate women might be for private time with their husbands, they would never use it.[48] As much as women longed for intimacy with their husbands, their sense of propriety would not allow them to take advantage of a situation where everyone would know what they were doing. Earl Carroll found a diplomatic way to decline this odd proposal, leaving couples to find their own way through the commingling ban.

Other inconsistencies cropped up as well. In April 1942, one sympathetic Japanese guard in Baguio asked Robert Brown if he was married. When he replied yes, the guard said he could visit his wife, and even though it was against the rules, he would not report the visit. This marital visit would indeed have been welcome for Robert, as his wife lived in the United States. In the fall of 1942, a camp guard allegedly approached a man and offered to procure a woman for him, prompting Natalie Crouter to wonder, "Why are men so filthy? This one [guard] was trying to pick up some cash but the enemy would like to undermine that way too." She was concerned that the Japanese would use sex as a coercive weapon against the men to win them over to their side by providing them with needed female companionship, but she could not admit that American men would ever have accepted this offer. A similar potential coercive weapon surfaced in Santo Tomas in October 1942, when Tressa Roka recorded the promises of Japanese authorities to allow wives to visit their husbands in the military prison camps. It is unlikely that the visits were intended to be conjugal, but the wives looked forward to them as reassurance of their husbands' welfare and for the opportunity to bring them food and other necessities. However, the following March, Tressa noted that "wives of military prisoners had given up the beautiful dream" of being allowed to visit their husbands, because the Japanese had not delivered on their promises. The previous month the Japanese permitted a small group of military prisoners to send brief postcards to their wives or mothers, but these fourteen women could not send replies; as far as the Japanese were concerned, the matter was closed.[49]

In the spring of 1943, recognizing the Japanese inconsistencies with the policy and their own dedication to circumventing it, the Baguio

Santo Tomas University, Manila, March 1945. Three thousand to five thousand Allied civilians spent the war years on this campus. (U.S. Signal Corps III-SC-374478. Courtesy of the National Archives)

Shanties in Santo Tomas, 1945. Camp authorities allowed construction of these structures to ease overcrowding in the Main Building. (U.S. Signal Corps III-SC-20214. Courtesy of the National Archives)

Women and their young children in Camp Holmes, Baguio, 1943. This proved to be the best year of internment: women had settled in with their families, and the food supply was still adequate. (Courtesy of William G. Gray)

Wilma Park and Carroll Dickey wed in Camp Holmes, Baguio, on March 23, 1944, after Japanese authorities relaxed commingling restrictions. "To God be the glory." (Courtesy of Jessie Junkin McCall)

Back view of the Park-Dickey wedding. Some guests are visible in the upper lefthand corner. (Courtesy of Jessie Junkin McCall)

Ethel Herold with her husband, Elmer, in the ruins of Manila, February 27, 1945. The couple survived internment in Baguio and old Bilibid Prison prior to their liberation by American forces at the beginning of the month. (Courtesy of C. William Herold and Betsy Herold Heimke)

American army nurses after their liberation from Santo Tomas, February 1945. Their happy smiles help disguise their gaunt faces, a result of malnutrition and long hours in the camp hospital. (U.S. Signal Corps III-SC-200726. Courtesy of the National Archives)

Army nurses reclaiming femininity after liberation, February 1945. (Courtesy of the Army Nurse Corps (ANC) Collection, U.S. Army Center of Military History)

internees began to debate the continued enforcement of preventing couples from cohabiting. The captives had reached the end of their tolerance for this unnatural arrangement; at the end of June, Natalie Crouter recounted the efforts of one woman who was "fighting for SEX and is pulling all the stops she can." This unnamed woman embarked on a "snooping trip" to the camp hospital, where she found husbands and wives together in bed, even men who were with women who were not their own wives. She argued that in the enforcement of the separation of men and women the "rules must cover all or none." By early 1944, after the military takeover of camp administration, even Japanese officials gave up on the logistics of keeping families separated. In March, with the approval of camp officials, some of the internees drew up plans to alter the barracks so that families could live together; the resulting Family Unit Plan produced a heated debate. Natalie, who supported the plan, mourned that it was the "first normal thing that has been put to us and we can't take it!" She believed that even worse times lay ahead and reasoned that family togetherness would provide the internees with the additional support they would need. Natalie maintained that the plan was not solely about sex; those who wanted to risk pregnancy could resume sexual relations, and those who did not want to take the risk could continue to abstain. However, in addition to issues of sex and cohabitation, some internees objected to the plan because it would deprive them of precious inches of living space.[50]

The General Committee put the question of the Family Unit Plan to the internees in the form of a survey, giving those who supported the plan the chance to sign up to take part in it. Natalie, shocked at the small number of families who favored it—just thirty missionaries and eight other couples—described the lack of support as a "devastating analysis of marriage" and deplored those who did not want to "legalize sex and married life." She was aghast that one woman actually told her husband that supporting the plan was unpatriotic because American soldiers and sailors who directly risked their lives in the war had been deprived of their normal family lives. Natalie questioned whether "everyone in the U.S. was foregoing matrimony and eating and living together, just because the soldiers and sailors weren't having it," summing up the whole situation with an exasperated: "Patriotism—what sins are committed in thy name!"[51]

Opponents to the plan outlined their objections in an April petition, which they submitted to the General Committee. They raised the issue of pregnancies occurring at a most "inopportune" time, argued that there were more pressing projects to be completed in the camp, and objected to the "regrouping [of] people in a manner inconvenient, ill-adjusted, offensive to standards of propriety, and even of decency." The opponents contended, in essence, that in normal times family life was just fine, but these were not normal times. Ethel Herold's opinion of the matter straddled both sides; she did not care if families lived together, but she did have concerns about the effects that the plan would have on the camp. She sympathized with those who did not want to move and risk losing precious living space, plus she did not want the camp school turned into living cubicles, but mostly she worried about the likelihood of pregnancies, as she and Elmer did not "want another crop of babies in here. That would be death for mothers as well as babies and God help us who would have to do the work." But Natalie insisted that despite these alleged drawbacks, in "time of war and separation, people seek more than ever for ties that bind and what little affection they can grab from the maelstrom." The final decision struck an obvious compromise: those who wanted to live as families could, and those who did not could remain in separate barracks. At the end of September 1944, Natalie crisply noted that two more camp women were pregnant, "one Family Unit and one not Family Unit, so that ought to shut all mouths."[52]

Japanese authorities similarly relaxed these restrictions in Santo Tomas. The first signs of their weakening toward enforced separation of couples came in December 1943, when they sent wives and girl-friends to join their men at Los Banos, where married couples lived together in barracks divided up into eight-by-twelve-foot cubicles. Emily Van Sickle referred to these women as the "Los Banos widows," recalling that they left for the camp to the accompaniment of the "lilting strains" of Wagner's "Wedding March."[53] At the beginning of February 1944, the Japanese gave permission for families in Santo Tomas to live together in their shanties, a decision based on space limitations, not altruism. During the last twelve months of the Japanese occupation of Manila, authorities revoked exemption passes, so all enemy aliens, regardless of their health or other extenuating circumstances, had to surrender to internment. This change put a huge strain on available living quarters, causing the Japanese to allow families to move into their shanties. Even though the Nashes' shanty consisted of just one room, Grace was thrilled that the entire family could be together under one roof, where she and Ralph could have quiet time together after their sons fell asleep at night. But this change in the commingling policy still did not ease enough of the congestion, so in March 1944 Japanese authorities announced that another five hundred internees would be transferred to Los Banos. Grace and Ralph decided to take their chances in that newer camp, where they hoped that living conditions would be healthier for their children, and made the move the following month. The resumption of cohabitation gave interned couples a sense of normality that would shore them up for the most difficult months of the war.

When camp authorities lifted restrictions on families living together, they also allowed marriages. In March 1944, Carroll Dickey and Wilma Park had an early evening wedding ceremony in Camp Holmes complete with a borrowed wedding dress for the bride, piano and violin music, fresh flowers, a four-tiered wedding cake, and a gift of two bottles of champagne from Japanese officials. Fern Harrington, Wilma's roommate, observed that the "loveliness of the occasion cast a magic spell over most of us so that we momentarily forgot where we were." Encouraged by the "spirit of comraderie [*sic*]" between captors and captives during the wedding week, she affirmed that the wedding, "an event important in all cultures, reminded us of our common humanity." The generosity of the Japanese authorities attests to the human desire to celebrate love and marriage, but the continuing war quickly overshadowed the glow of the moment. Ethel Herold, unsympathetic and unenthusiastic about the marriage, was one of the very few people who did not contribute anything to the wedding cake and expressed outrage at the effort and expense that had gone into the wedding, perceiving it as the missionaries' blissful ignorance of the realities of internment. She also grimly commented that if either of her children "would marry under similar circumstances I would ring their necks." In late November 1944, Natalie Crouter mentioned that another couple wed, complete with a traditional ceremony much like the Dickeys', but Natalie, joyful over the first wedding, now predicted an unhappy future because the internees had been "repressed beyond endurance, with all natural inclinations damned up for three years either by the enemy or our own fanatics."[54]

Despite the restrictions placed on the private behavior of men and women, the internees did manage to joke about the situation occasionally, a trait Americans prided themselves on. Referring to this as "rugged camp humor," Natalie repeated a conversation two men had about marriage in which the first man "raved about marriage and his love for his wife which grows with the years like a flower." The second man replied, "Yes, and how are you managing to keep the flower watered in these times?" In Bacolod, one internee remarked to another that their internment would provide them with tales to tell to their grandchildren; the other replied, "If the celibate lives we have had continue, there'll be no grandchildren!" Tressa Roka encountered a man in Santo Tomas she called Don Juan because of his repeated romances; by late January 1945, he had lost his looks and energy because of malnutrition, and his latest girlfriend had left him for another man who still had a supply of canned goods. Yet he still joked about his situation, telling Tressa that "if Lana Turner stood before me in her birthday suit, I wouldn't give a damn! Unless she had a ham sandwich in her hand," prompting Tressa's observation that sex had definitely "taken a back seat" to food.[55]

For numerous internees the deprivations caused by the war, especially the lack of food, killed their sex drives; because of a lack of nutrition and energy, even those who still had amorous feelings could not act on them. Don Juan's imagined response to Lana Turner in the buff would not have been atypical of internees' interest in sexual activity near the end of the war, when romance and courtship devolved into plain male-female companionship. Analyzing her relationship with a group of Catholic nuns in Kuching, Agnes Keith expressed admiration for their focus on spirituality as the secular women, the "fleshly creatures," more keenly felt the deprivations of the world. One of the greatest weaknesses of these women was their inability to get along without men, but Agnes emphasized that they missed male companionship, "because very soon, with poor food, hard work, and nervous strain, that was all we had the sexual strength to long for, or to offer."[56]

Women also recognized that despite all of the Japanese regulations that governed their private lives, their situation was still much better than their stateside counterparts. In July 1942, Ethel Herold admitted to feeling lonely because Elmer spent so much time tending to camp business while she was occupied with the Women's Committee business plus family chores, but she also acknowledged that she was better off than "those poor women whose husbands are God-knows-where."[57]

PREGNANCY AND FAMILY LIFE

Despite the fact that the Japanese tried to prevent men and women from romancing and despite the lack of consistent food and medicine, interned women did get pregnant. Even with the uncertainties of internment camp life, some of these babies were planned, since some married couples continued to believe that children were natural by-products of marriage. According to Emily Van Sickle, one "unauthorized" father-to-be in Santo Tomas defended his actions by explaining, "My wife and I thought this was a good time to have a baby. There's nothing else to do and it won't cost us a cent." On December 1, 1943, Natalie Crouter noted that one of the Baguio women delivered a baby at a hospital outside of camp, but the baby had been "manufactured" within, the proud father coyly asking the other internees, "Wouldn't you like to know how we managed it?" Ethel Herold, unamused with either the baby or the clever comments about its conception, snapped in her diary, "Thank goodness the japs do not let husbands and wives live together or we would have a crop of babies and weak mothers—all facing starvation." Babies continued to arrive; in February 1944, Natalie attended a baby shower for a woman who was due to deliver in May and recorded a brief verse penned by another woman to commemorate the occasion: "Roses are red, violets are blue, It can't happen here, But it happened to you!"[58]

Camp pregnancies did not amuse Japanese officials in Santo Tomas. As scattered incidents occurred during the first year of internment, mostly among women pregnant prior to internment, the prisoners received stern warnings that there should be no additional pregnancies. At the end of December 1942, the commandant issued another strong statement through the Executive Committee that internees could not indulge in sexual relations; if they did, certain of their camp privileges would be revoked. A couple of weeks later, a woman gave birth in the camp hospital, and when simple addition proved hers to be a camp pregnancy, Japanese officials demanded the names of other pregnant women, the number of which ranged, according to rumors, anywhere from ten to eighty. Josephine Waldo reported that eleven women expected babies and that "some of the girls are unmarried so it is quite a scandal." Only six women, two unmarried, admitted to being pregnant, although several more may have been; because women usually considered this a private family matter, they refused to make their conditions known until they had to go to the hospital. If no one turned them in before that, the Japanese could not do anything. The commandant ordered all pregnant women out of camp and into a home for unwed mothers, then sent the fathers to the camp jail to serve thirty to sixty days in solitary confinement. He prohibited any communication between the couples and forced all internees to evacuate their shanties, undoubtedly in an attempt to prevent additional pregnancies. Josephine, appalled by the conduct of all parties in this scandal, commented that the "idea of being punished and made to bring a baby into the world under these conditions is enough to make one want to fight."[59]

This situation affected Grace and Ralph Nash, because in October 1942 Grace knew she was pregnant. The day the commandant sent the pregnant women out of camp and the fathers into jail, Ralph was at the Philippine General Hospital with Stan. The Japanese refused to let Grace take Gale with her to the Spanish convent, sending him instead to the Holy Ghost Convent, where some other children also stayed, which caused a wrenching parting because Gale had not adjusted well to internment, his repeated illnesses only making him more miserable. Fortunately, this separation proved short-lived. Within a month Ralph managed to get Gale released into Grace's care, placed Stan with a missionary family in Manila, and went into the camp jail to serve his paternity sentence. After Ralph's time ended, the boys came back into the camp to live in the family shanty, Grace delivered an eight-pound baby boy on May 24, 1943, and on June 9 she and her new son, Roy, joined the rest of the family in Santo Tomas.

Margaret Sherk, because of her deep love for Jerry Sams and her desire to tie him to her permanently, chose, even planned, to become pregnant and give birth to his child. As daring as having an affair was because of moral censure, getting pregnant further strained the morality issue and presented physical complications. Possible health difficulties from pregnancy, however common in peacetime, became life-threatening for interned women, and Margaret had had a difficult time with David. At the beginning of internment, the food supply was inconsistent and the Japanese had confiscated most medicines for military use, so even if a woman safely delivered a baby, she had no guarantee that the child would survive or thrive. But when Japanese officials planned to open Los Banos in May 1943, Margaret decided to take the risk. Since Jerry was young, healthy, and without a family, the Japanese certainly would choose him for this primary work detail, a likelihood that presented Margaret with two interconnected worries. One was that Jerry would forget about her once they were separated, the second that she would no longer have the male help she deemed so necessary for survival; therefore, to Margaret, pregnancy was both an expression of love and an assurance of staying alive. It also represented her notion of what it meant to be a good mother in these circumstances, for without the continued presence of Jerry, David's well-being would certainly suffer. So the night before Jerry's transfer to Los Banos, Margaret got pregnant.

For the first two months after Margaret realized that she was pregnant, she kept quiet. After Jerry's transfer she and David occupied his old living space on the landing in the Main Building, an out-of-the-way location that prevented other women from scrutinizing her on a daily basis, and Margaret, hiding her expanding waistline under some cast-off shirts Jerry left behind, began to plan. To curb inaccurate rumors, she had to let both Bob Sherk and Jerry know of her condition before they heard it from anyone else. Prisoners smuggled notes between Santo Tomas and Cabanatuan, the military prison camp, on a regular basis, so she passed a note to Bob telling him that she was pregnant with another man's child. She also got a message to Jerry, who essentially told her, "I love you. Keep your chin up."[60] Next Margaret had to make sure that she had a healthy pregnancy, plus she had to acquire all of the goods necessary for a newborn baby, which proved a challenge given the scarcity of available food and medicine. Finally, she needed to arrange a transfer to Los Banos so that she could be with the father of her new baby, the man she loved and wanted to have a life with. Margaret was willing to flout convention only so far—while remaining honest about her baby's paternity, she did not want to be a single mother, so she constructed a new "traditional" family to replace the old.

Margaret, spurred on by her love, managed to accomplish her goals, finding sympathy and help when she least expected it, yet encountering a good deal of condemnation from people appalled by what she had done. She felt as though she were under a microscope, because once her pregnancy showed, everyone could "look at and talk about and discuss the pros and cons of the affair." A woman that the Sherks had known for years in one of the mining camps shunned Margaret, saying that she could "understand having an affair with Jerry, but to have a baby under these circumstances I cannot possibly understand," a reference to continuing deprivations. When Bob's response to Margaret's news finally arrived, it was simply, according to her, "the most beautiful love letter ever written." Although she declined to elaborate on the exact contents of the note, she insisted that he "forgave me and proved it in a way that I never would have thought about," refusing to consent to his wife's assumption that they would divorce after liberation.[61] As unacceptable as adultery was to some people, Bob apparently did not believe that it automatically meant the end of a marriage; he was willing to work things out, unaware that Margaret had already made her choice. Despite emotional hardships and a scarcity of goods, Margaret delivered a healthy baby girl, Gerry Ann Sherk, on January 23, 1944, and three months later Margaret, David, and Gerry Ann transferred to Los Banos, where they set up housekeeping with Jerry, albeit in separate barracks.

Since the Los Banos internees had been transplanted from Santo Tomas, most of them knew of the affair, leading Margaret to believe that she made a "public spectacle" whenever she went outside of her barracks, that everyone gossiped about her, Jerry, and their baby. Disapproval indeed ran high. The Central Committee forced Jerry to give up his privileged job on the "communications detail," which had provided him the opportunity not only to work at his specialty but also to live in semiprivate quarters. According to Margaret, because Jerry had lost respect and trust, he got bumped to woodcutting detail, a much less prestigious job but one that he took on resolutely. Jerry took these changes in stride, also rising to the challenge of caring for the children when necessary. When Margaret went into the camp hospital with bacillary dysentery, he sanitized everything that the family had touched, plus he fed, clothed, and bathed David and Gerry Ann every day, which Margaret noted ironically was a "man-sized order" that Jerry nonetheless handled smoothly.[62]

Surviving internment often required a blurring and crossover of gender roles, with men sometimes taking on domestic tasks they would not have done in ordinary times. Routine chores of cooking and cleaning required so much physical strength that inventiveness in approaching them and the ultimate mastery of these duties added to, rather than detracted from, definitions and perceptions of masculinity. Internees did not look down on men who took on this kind of women's work, because it ensured survival. Still, this was an era of motherhood, not parenting, and Margaret and Jerry, along with other internees, viewed child care as a woman's realm, taken up by men only when absolutely necessary. In November 1944, the Sherk-Sams family faced a serious crisis when Margaret lost the will to live, so Jerry again took over. Margaret contracted tuberculosis of the lower bowel, underwent exploratory surgery with only the aid of a spinal tap, received an infusion of sulfa drugs, then was sent back to her barracks to recover or not. The doctor could do nothing more for her; if Margaret's body did not heal on its own, she would die. Margaret recalled that she was "simply too tired to care about anything, that when they brought poor little starved Gerry Ann to me to be nursed, every four hours, it seemed like the final straw." Jerry would not allow her to give up. He took the only food then available in camp, a thin rice gruel called lugao, and toasted it until it resembled something other than what it was, hoping to tempt

Margaret's appetite and keep her alive. Jerry fed this to Margaret, spoonful by spoonful, then shamed her into recovering by accusing her of willfully abandoning him and the children, something only a bad woman and a bad mother would do. Jerry's approach proved successful, as Margaret quickly decided to "get out of that [hospital] bed and show Jerry Sams a thing or two if I never did another thing in my life." By Christmas time she was well again.[63]

The ban against commingling did not prevent a natural increase in the camp populations; despite the risks involved, pregnancies gave some internees something to look forward to, reminding them of the continuation of the life cycle and promises of the future. Where there were babies, there was hope. For some women, pregnancy reminded them of their traditional roles and proved that they were still attractive and desirable to their husbands. But Margaret rejected the tradition of monogamy, choosing to have a child who she believed would ultimately guarantee her and David's survival and the continuation of Jerry Sams's love. Pregnancy could be risky for interned women, but it was not their deepest worry.

THE SPECTER OF RAPE

One dreaded intrusion into the women's private lives that did not occur was rape. Given the general psychological stress of internment compounded by different kinds of family separation, routine rape by the Japanese guards would have made captivity unendurable. American women fared better than Asian women since racial beliefs prompted Japanese soldiers to target Asian women for rape and forced prostitution. Besides army nurse Beulah Putnam on Corregidor, only Agnes Keith admitted to an attempted rape, an incident that unlike anything else that happened to her in Kuching demonstrated her utter powerlessness and the cruelty of her captors.

In the summer of 1943, just after the women's camp had been moved to a new location to obstruct contact between husbands and wives, a Japanese guard attacked Agnes. She and George had been very ill with malaria, and she had stayed up all night with him, nursing his high fever. When it broke during the early morning darkness, Agnes took a break out on the barracks steps—to breathe the air and think quietly, to try and get over her utter despair about her inability to be a good mother to George. Suddenly a soldier appeared, offered her a package of cigarettes, "then bent quickly over me, ran his two hands roughly down my breasts, over my thighs, and forced them violently up between my legs." Agnes did not have the strength to fight him off, but fortunately they were near enough the barracks that her cries attracted the other women, who began to call out, asking what was wrong. In the ensuing confusion, Agnes got away from her attacker, but in the dark she never saw his face.[64]

Apprehensive that this attempted assault marked the beginning of repeated abuses, Agnes decided to report the assault to Colonel Suga. Suga and Agnes had a special, though strained, relationship forged from their love of literature, so she believed that he would handle the incident in a just manner. The next time Suga came in to inspect the barracks, Agnes told him about the attack, concluding her account with an appeal for his protection: "Although I am a prisoner, I believe I have the right to live decently, even in prison. I believe that you intend us to do so. For this reason I report this occurrence to you, and as your prisoner I ask you for protection." Although he apparently believed her claim, Lieutenant Nekata, the head of the women's camp, did not, and he attempted to compel Agnes to sign a statement saying that her charges were false. Making a false accusation against a Japanese soldier was a capital offense, so Agnes had to stick to the truth in order to survive. When she refused to sign, one of Nekata's underlings beat and kicked her, cracking her ribs and almost dislocating her shoulder; Nekata then sent her back to the barracks with a warning not to tell anyone what happened.[65]

Agnes feared for her life because she realized that in making her accusation she had become a "thorn in Nipponese flesh" and that the Japanese would likely just get rid of her. She mainly worried about George, because if she was taken away from the camp, he would be alone and he, too, probably would not survive. She had vowed to get him through captivity; now she had jeopardized this promise by not thinking through the implications of her charge. Without explaining what happened in Nekata's office, Agnes elicited a promise from her closest friend to take care of George if anything happened to her. The morning after her first beating, when Nekata again summoned her to his office, she assumed that it was for more of the same. Despite her injuries, Agnes prepared herself for her last round of questioning: "Dressed for slaughter, hair carefully combed and braided, lipstick on colorless lips, rouge on malaria-yellowed cheeks, in neatest white dress, good sharkskin, once very smart—this is how the Well-Dressed Internee will dress to be beaten up." This time nothing happened. When Agnes adamantly stuck to her story, Nekata dismissed her with a warning that if she had lied about the assault, she could be executed, and as she left his office he gave her a bundle containing six eggs, an astounding gift. Agnes had learned, in the most painful way possible, that as a prisoner she had lost all of her rights not to be assaulted, that the Japanese could do whatever they wished to her.[66]

Other recorded close calls with rape did not involve physical violence. Ethel Herold coped with a frightening attempt by Japanese officials to round up young American women to work as "waitresses" at a hotel in Baguio for Japanese officers. On January 19, 1942, a day which Ethel described as "one of the all-time LOW moments of the Camp," Mukaibo, one of the Japanese officials, approached Ethel with a "damned smirk" on his face, informing her that he needed young women to work as waitresses at the Pines Hotel. When she protested that everyone was already overburdened with work in the camp, Mukaibo tried to make the waitressing jobs sound attractive by telling her that the women would be fed and housed at the hotel. Ethel knew what would happen to those "waitresses," so she was determined to prevent any of the girls from enduring such abuse and humiliation.[67]

Ethel managed to put off Mukaibo by telling him that she would cooperate, but the matter had to go before the Men's Committee because of the impact it would have on camp work. She quickly found Elmer and apprised him of the situation, insisting that "we had to think fast and get our puny forces organized." The only thing the Men's Committee could realistically do was persuade the Japanese to drop the idea, because, as Ethel observed, "after all the japs have the guns." She then assembled all of the single young women in camp, told them to organize themselves, to work with or near children during the day, and to make themselves look as unattractive as possible, a strategy that proved successful. Mukaibo dropped his demand for the waitresses; apparently, young women who looked too motherly and too plain would not be useful to the soldiers. Ethel realized, however, that the Japanese could always change their minds, recalling that for "more than 3 years we expected the japs to come for the waitresses—but they did not come." Her motherly concern extended from her own daughter, Betsy, to the parentless girls from the Brent School; in the event that the Japanese did pursue this request, some of the older married women as well as at least one missionary woman volunteered for the waitressing duty to spare the young women.[68]

Agnes Keith recounted a similar incident when Lieutenant Nekata ordered the "Concert Ladies" to sing, decked out in their nicest clothing and makeup, for a visiting general. The women, distressed by this command because of its "early Roman flavor," decided that only the eight oldest singers would appear to entertain the general; the younger singers stayed out of sight. When Nekata realized the women's plan, he ordered all of the singers to appear, insisting that the youngest ones, the "virgins," take their places at the front of the group. The women could do nothing but hope for the best, and luck was with them. Agnes recalled that the general smiled as the women sang, pleasing Nekata so much that the singers were sent back to their barracks, unmolested, with bananas and biscuits as tributes to their performance.[69]

In Baguio, the women had men to help protect them against possible sexual abuses by Japanese soldiers, and while that certainly provided some psychological comfort, it did not assure that the women would not be attacked. Ethel Herold's very astute observation about the Japanese having the guns summed up the women's vulnerability. The Baguio women and the women on Borneo, deprived of male support, understood that the Japanese had the power to compel them to submit. Only quick thinking on their part could save them from possible rape or sexual servitude. Mostly, incredible luck was on their side that the Japanese did not pursue such abuse.

For the interned American women, keeping up their appearance, indulging in romance, maintaining marriage and family structures, and not facing the constant fear of rape helped them to get through the monotony and uncertainty of their captivity. Women clung to romance, marriage, family, and fashion, all normal parts of their lives, but they refashioned these ideals and practices to fit the reality of internment. Single women used cosmetics and clothing to spark romances, courting was limited to public walks or forbidden, punishable assignations, and the exchange of tokens of affection required ingenuity. Jerry Sams's courtship gift to Margaret Sherk of a washboard was not dull; it showed a tremendous amount of affection, and Margaret was appropriately flattered. Although their conditions were far from exemplary and nothing was really the same, the women learned to adapt and improvise, and they survived.

If women improvised too loosely, like Margaret did with her relationship with Jerry, they risked censure from the other internees who still believed in the inviolability of monogamous marriage. But Margaret's views of womanhood changed because of internment; according to her beliefs in romantic love and being a good mother, having an affair and building a family with Jerry was the absolutely right thing to do. For Agnes Keith, struggling to survive on Borneo, being a good mother meant dealing with the black market and willingly giving up pieces of finery to secure food and medicine to maintain George's health.

For most interned women, though, the alterations were much less dramatic and still closely connected to traditions of womanhood and societal expectations. Although commingling was prohibited during most of the war, wives found ways to be with their husbands, and despite concerns about a natural increase to the camps, some even had babies. Interned women willingly altered these aspects of their private lives without risking too much, but a select group of American women found their lives turned even more upside down because of the war.

5

EVADING INTERNMENT

*"We would run to the hills and wait for our
'proof through the night that our flag was still there.'"*

As the Japanese attacked the Philippines, Abby Jacobs, an American teacher at Silliman University on the island of Negros, asserted that Americans would not sit passively awaiting their fate but "would run to the hills and wait for our 'proof through the night that our flag was still there.'"[1] She and her friends and colleagues believed that the U.S. military would quickly win its battle against the Japanese but concluded that their safety in the meantime required them to go into hiding, to evade and resist the Japanese whenever possible. Hiding in remote, sparsely populated areas, keeping at least one step ahead of the Japanese army and Japanese spies and sympathizers required courage, stamina, ingenuity, and faith in an Allied victory. Some American women chose to do so because it seemed the best way to keep themselves and their families safe, healthy, and alive.

THE AMERICANS OF SILLIMAN UNIVERSITY

The professors and employees of Silliman University represent an entire group of Americans who decided to take their chances and elude the Japanese. Even though Silliman was founded by American Presbyterians in 1901, by the start of World War II, the majority of its professors and staff was Filipino, yet Americans still commanded a strong presence. Negros proved to be a good location for Silliman and an enticing one for Americans. One of the main islands of the archipelago, located between Luzon and Mindanao, it was mainly agricultural, with a rural atmosphere and a tropical climate. It was divided into two provinces, Oriental and Occidental; Dumaguete, the provincial capital of Negros Oriental, contained a population of about twenty-two thousand in 1941, including professors, ministers, and missionaries associated with Silliman University. The city boasted a thriving business district, a government trade school, and a provincial high school, and its inhabitants enjoyed most of the consumer conveniences of modern life, regularly shipped in from Manila. During the war, the island provided good cover for hideouts, as Americans continually moved from coastal locations to inland mountainous regions teeming with dense jungle growth. Because of the elevation, malarial mosquitoes were rare, virtually eliminating one of the most common tropical diseases; plenty of raw materials were available for building houses; and enough vegetation grew to supply at least a subsistence diet. Life in hiding was rough and uncertain, but those who chose it believed they would have fared worse in internment.

After Pearl Harbor, few Dumaguete residents expressed concerns for their immediate safety, believing that since Negros held only a small American military presence, it had no strategic value. Given its location about 350 miles south of Manila, they could not imagine why the Japanese would bother to invade this remote location; still, they prepared for emergencies such as bombings or a blockade. Viola Winn, panic-stricken when she heard about Pearl Harbor, hurried into Dumaguete to shop for canned goods, because she worried about providing enough food for her family. The forty-year-old mother of three young children, including four-month-old Elinor, Viola taught Bible classes at Silliman's high school, while her husband, Gardner, taught English and Bible at the university. She relied on two Filipina housemaids to do all of the domestic chores and to handle child care, but she assumed that they would want to return to their own families now that war had come. Viola recalled that she turned to faith in God to give her strength to handle the very basic household chores once the maids left, telling herself that "He will help you do the tasks that are required of you."[2]

Abby Jacobs, living at 10 Langheim Lane in Dumaguete with her sister, Metta, and her brother-in-law, Bob Silliman, a history professor and a distant relative of the university's founder, was putting on makeup in preparation for her seven o'clock English class on Monday morning, December 8. Metta and Bob still lingered in their pajamas, waiting for their cook to serve them breakfast, when the radio broadcast the news of Pearl Harbor. Abby remembered anticipating tough times ahead with bombing and blockading likely, but she was "not then thinking in terms of 'escape' since we honestly did not expect to see a Japanese soldier in Dumaguete."[3] She observed people in the city digging ditches, prepar-

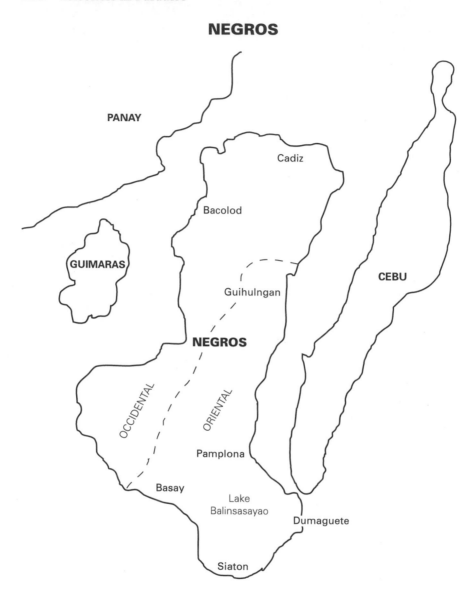

ing sandbags, and hiding valuables just in case of attack, but like others she could not fathom that the Japanese would want anything in that city.

Ethel and Jim Chapman, who since 1916 had been at Silliman, where Jim taught zoology, entomology, and other basic science courses, were likewise getting ready for their day when they heard about Pearl Har-

bor. When they heard the news, Ethel recollected that "we left our breakfast to sit by the radio and gaze blankly into each other's faces as one
awful detail followed another and our peaceful academic world crashed
about us."[4] She could not think of what to do, so she just went off to
her seven o'clock English class at Silliman as usual, leaving Jim glued
to the radio for further news.

Officials of the USAFFE, the provincial government, and Silliman
University quickly established an informational network, which spread
news of the war while attempting to maintain calm among the population. Arthur Carson, Silliman's president, advised the students to head
for home as soon as possible so that the hastily assembled members of
the USAFFE could take over the campus. After Negros Oriental Governor Guillermo Villanueva enacted the National Emergency Act, Roy
Bell, head of the physics department at Silliman, was appointed civil
affairs officer, while other members of the Silliman faculty, encouraged
by Arthur Carson, headed similar emergency committees. Abby Jacobs
observed that Silliman "rose from community influence to virtual community necessity, with almost everyone of its personnel contributing
in one way or another towards the emergency needs of Dumaguete."
The women who remained on campus took part in these preparations
as well; those with home economics training, such as Professor Frances
Rodgers, were in demand to teach classes on camp and emergency cooking. While this type of female knowledge was clearly needed and the
women who possessed these valuable skills did not hesitate to pitch
in, the militarized atmosphere of the university provoked some unease.
Abby described how women "tried to appear as inconspicuous as possible in an atmosphere heavily male-ish," referring to the dominant
presence on the campus of the USAFFE.[5] She gave up dresses in favor
of slacks, a decision based partly on the masculine atmosphere but
strongly influenced by the rigors of evasion.

By mid-December, when it became clear that the USAFFE was having a tough time with the Japanese on Luzon, the Americans realized
that the enemy would reach Negros, so they prepared to go into hiding.
They predicted that despite the USAFFE's difficulties, the American
military would send reinforcements as soon as possible and the islands
would be free of the Japanese within about six months. Thus, they envisioned evasion as a temporary, short-term measure until fresh troops
arrived. The Americans decided to spread out as much as possible, rather
than hide together in one large group, in hopes of discouraging the Japanese from time-consuming hunting expeditions. Some of the Silliman

families lit out as individual units, while others joined forces with one or two other families.

On the advice of Arthur Carson, who as a former missionary in China witnessed firsthand the brutality of the Japanese army toward a civilian population, Silliman families began evacuating Dumaguete in mid-December. Arthur and his wife, Edith, had two children, Robert, age sixteen, and Jean, age ten; the family, initially without Arthur, moved to a small town called Palimpinon, seven miles west of the city, where Edna Bell and her teenage sons, Donald and Kenneth, joined them. Roy Bell had spent his days at Silliman teaching physics and running that department, while Edna served as dean of women and as choir director of Silliman's church. In Palimpinon Edna and Edith not only had their own children to watch over but also a large group of Silliman students, mostly from other islands, who had been unable to get back to their families after the war started. The public school building there temporarily housed these refugees, providing them with quick access to the mountainous interior of Negros should the Japanese pursue territory beyond Dumaguete. Meanwhile, Roy and Arthur remained in the city; secure in the knowledge that their families were safe, they watched over Silliman University, regularly met with USAFFE and provincial officials, and coordinated emergency plans. For the rest of December, Edna and Edith carried on as normally as possible in the school building, taking care of their own children as well as the Silliman students, and occasionally making trips into the city to purchase needed supplies.

Ethel Chapman also took Arthur's advice and headed for the hills, to her and her husband's vacation home at Camp Lookout. Since Jim spent most of his time in the city to carry on his duties as food administrator, the Chapmans spread the word that they wanted guests at Camp Lookout to provide companionship and security for Ethel. During the first few days of the war, Ethel began practicing food and fuel conservation, skills that proved invaluable during the war years. Paul and Clara Lindholm, missionary evacuees from China who served as extension workers for Silliman's theology department, accepted the Chapmans' offer. Clara gave birth to a daughter, Janet, on December 8, giving her four young children to care for; fearing that the Japanese would bomb Dumaguete, the family gratefully moved to Camp Lookout. While Paul worked to enlarge a one-room hut into a livable home, Clara and Janet stayed in the Chapman cottage, where Alvin Scaff and his pregnant wife, Marilee, camped out. A few hundred yards above Camp Lookout sat the cottage of Jim and Virginia McKinley, called Mountain Rest. Jim, who trained ministers at Silliman for the United Church of the Philippines, and Virginia had three daughters; they invited Gardner and Viola Winn and their three small children to join their family. This family cluster worked out particularly well for the Lindholms, because Janet had not been thriving since the family's remove to Camp Lookout, and Viola, who was nursing little Elinor at Mountain Rest, agreed to nurse Janet as well, guaranteeing the good health of the youngest evacuee.

Viola expressed relief not only at having a safe hiding place until the Americans came, but also that her two housemaids, Guillerma and Victoria, decided to join the Winns at Mountain Rest rather than return to their own homes. Viola proved inept at packing even necessary household items for the move; Guillerma provided her with valuable advice on kitchen things, while Victoria knew just what the children needed. During those first days in their mountain hideout, Viola agonized over her relationship with the Filipinos, wondering if the Americans caused them any harm with their attempts to evade the Japanese. In their daily conversations while Viola nursed Clara's daughter, the two women discussed the situation. Clara speculated that the Filipinos had mixed feelings about the situation, that they feared the Japanese and wanted advice and encouragement from the Americans, while Viola admitted that even as she felt guilty for employing maids, she "couldn't get along without them, especially now."[6]

Viola's affection for her maids appeared genuine, but it did not provide her with an instinctive understanding of how they viewed their circumstances. The cultural gap was not automatically bridged by kind feelings, a fact made abundantly clear when the Winns and Lindholms moved to their second hideout further into the interior of Negros. Viola found their living accommodations cramped, as fifteen people, including family members and servants, vied for space in a small frame house. Startled one evening by the sight of Guillerma and Victoria resting together in a small storeroom, she concluded that they would enjoy having a private place to themselves, where they could talk and stretch out to rest, so she had a tent set up next to the house for them. Viola, pleased that she made "better provision for those who were doing so much for us," was crestfallen when Clara revealed that the housemaids intended to leave, because "if they aren't good enough to be in the same house with us, then they aren't good enough to work for us either."[7] Viola assumed that just because she longed for privacy in their close quarters, so did everyone else; she quickly reassured the two young women that no offense had been intended, and they decided to stay. The Winns took down the tent.

At the beginning of January 1942, the Americans felt increasingly vulnerable to Japanese attack, and suddenly Camp Lookout, Mountain Rest, and other locations only a few miles from Dumaguete appeared unsafe. Now uneasily situated in Palimpinon, Edna Bell and Edith Carson, along with their children, scouted out a new location higher in the mountains, ultimately settling in Malabo, a two-hour hike from the road that ended at Palimpinon. Located in the Okoy River valley, this was the site of a small Filipino village whose inhabitants generously allowed the newcomers to build a house near the spring, loaning them an abandoned shed until they completed the new structure. In February, with the new house finished, the Bells and Carsons, along with hired mountain men, carried both families' belongings up a scant mountain trail to their new location, a move that involved a great deal of organization and manpower, as motorized transportation could not be obtained. Alongside the men, women climbed, often barefoot, up steep mountains with meager paths obstructed by overgrowth, mud, and jungle wildlife. Once settled, Edna and Edith kept house under some of the most primitive conditions they had ever encountered: the women washed clothing outside in the spring and, because of a shortage of matches, learned how to preserve embers to keep their cooking fire going day after day. Life was rough but not unpleasant as villagers stopped by daily with food items to trade or sell.

Others moved away from Camp Lookout and spread out because, as Ethel Chapman pointed out, "there was no safety in numbers"; unwilling to concentrate themselves in one area for fear of a roundup after a Japanese invasion, the Silliman families scattered into the hills. [8] The Scaffs moved near a mission hospital at Pamplona, close to Alice and William Bryant's coconut plantation. Bob and Metta Silliman, Abby Jacobs, Charles and Hettie Glunz, and the Chapmans moved to Dalasag, located about eight hundred feet above Camp Lookout in a much more inaccessible area, in hopes that the Japanese would not take the trouble to hunt down each family.

The Lindholms worried more about continuing their religious work and less about when or if the Japanese would ever land on Negros. Paul did not intend for the war to interrupt his job with Silliman, which involved working with local churches, helping them set up Sunday schools, and visiting with Filipino church leaders. In early January, the family approached Gardner and Viola Winn about moving to Guihulngan, about

115 kilometers north of Dumaguete, to work for the Protestant church there, and the Winns, concerned about the safety of Mountain Rest, readily agreed. Ethel Chapman recalled Gardner's uncharacteristically pessimistic parting comment, "See you all in a concentration camp!" which was full of accurate foresight.[9]

In Guihulngan the families found congenial surroundings and active church members; Viola recalled that the group "momentarily [had] forgotten it was wartime in the Philippines, so absorbing did we find the tiny town and its few inhabitants." Luckily the market sold basic household items necessary for setting up new residences, but the ability to forget their circumstances proved fleeting. As Viola helped to settle everyone into their new surroundings, she grasped the realities: "We were at war in a foreign land. The people we knew had all been kind and helpful, but now our two families were to try to live together under circumstances strange to us all. We were taking seven small children into an area where there was no doctor, no medical facility of any kind. . . . And there was no way of knowing how long the war would last or if we would have any way of escaping the country."[10] Viola understood that her roles of wife and mother had to stretch to their limits if she was going to help protect her family.

Abby Jacobs retreated to Camp Lookout along with other Silliman families but spent most of her days, at least during the first months of the war, working at the university. As a single woman, she did not have the family concerns of the others, so she concentrated her efforts on the *Sillimanian*, the university's newspaper, for which her brother-in-law, Bob Silliman, served as general manager. Running the paper became a full-time job for both of them, because as the USAFFE moved onto the campus, it placed huge demands on the press, using it to disseminate information about the war, to run off army forms, and to print emergency money. Newcomers to the press did not understand the workings or limitations of the outdated equipment, which increasingly led to clashes between Bob and Abby, who essentially ran the press, and the USAFFE, which demanded more of its time. One day in February 1942, while Abby worked alone at the press, an American officer, Captain Johnson, ordered five thousand copies of a two-sided information sheet—by early the next morning. Abby found herself "faced with the problem of how to slap down a Captain and still be a lady." The employees had been working ten-hour days, making her reluctant to keep pushing them at such a pace, even for the army; with evening blackouts, the typesetters could not work at night, and there were not enough skilled workers in Dumaguete to spell those already overworked. Her dilemma dissolved with the timely return of Bob who, because of his last name, carried a lot of influence with the USAFFE, so Abby had him deal with the insistent captain, thereby sparing her "facing military combustion."[11] Bob and the captain worked out an acceptable compromise whereby Johnson received his forms, but a bit later the next morning than he had originally wanted. Abby managed to remain a lady and still show the captain who was in charge of the press.

If life in Dumaguete was hectic and tense, life in the mountain hideouts grew increasingly rough. In Dalasag, Ethel Chapman started a vegetable garden of string beans, mongo beans, peanuts, and corn, daily battling the lack of rain and insect infestations. Housekeeping required additional effort as well, as Ethel cooked over an open fire to conserve precious alcohol fuel, building it "on top of the dirt, and pots and pans set over it either on carefully placed stones or on the ring of an iron tripod," a process complicated by a lack of dry wood and matches. Daily chores occupied Edna Bell and Edith Carson in their hideout in Malabo as did thoughts of the war and concern for their husbands' safety. After the Japanese secured their hold over Luzon, they began a steady advance on the other Philippine islands; in April 1942, they targeted Cebu City, the second largest city in the Philippines, located just twelve miles across the water from Negros. When Edna journeyed into Dumaguete for shopping, she and other residents could hear the battle and watch the Japanese warships, which soon turned in their direction. City officials decided to evacuate all civilians, and as civil affairs officer, Roy Bell had the responsibility for coordinating a safe withdrawal. Despite the imminent danger, Edna refused to go back to Malabo or be evacuated with the rest of the Dumaguete residents: "My place is with my husband. When he leaves, I'll leave."[12]

When Edna finally returned to Malabo, Roy accompanied her. Arthur Carson also made the journey, along with an American soldier, who escaped the Japanese in Cebu, and four shipwrecked Norwegian sailors. The American, a radio operator, had valuable communication skills, which made him an especially fortuitous find for the Bell-Carson group, as Roy planned to coordinate guerrilla activities on Negros. Edna, accustomed to dealing with large groups of people, decided to ask the military men "to cast their lot with our already increasing family and, after some conferring among themselves, they decided to accept."[13] With the addition of the sailors, the group numbered fifteen at the end of April.

The Lindholm-Winn assemblage broke up in April, moving to separate locations partially because Viola Winn, unnerved by the fall of Bataan and the Japanese occupation of Cebu, worried that their hiding place was not remote enough to protect them from the Japanese. She received little solace from Gardner, whose devout faith prevented him from doubting that the family would survive. When Paul decided he had accomplished enough religious good around Guihulngan, he moved his family to Pacuan, situated higher and safer in the mountains, to help establish a new church there. Paul invited the Winns to join them, but Gardner determined that his family would be better off living away from other Americans and moved them to Bologo, a mountain town located between Tinnayunan and Pacuan, putting several hours' distance between the two families. Gardner, an uncompromising pacifist, tried to keep his family safe plus keep them away from any situation that might require cooperation with the war effort.

This move proved difficult for Viola, because while it reassured her from a safety standpoint, she missed socializing with Clara, who had quickly become a close friend. The physical distance between the two families and the dangers of travelling prevented them from doing any casual visiting, leaving Viola feeling isolated and edgy. She received a letter from Clara shortly after the Winns arrived in Bologo in which Clara admitted that she had been "too optimistic when I thought we could go back and forth from this distance."[14] So Viola did the only thing she could—she busied herself trying to turn their new house into a home.

In the meantime, Abby Jacobs and Bob and Metta Silliman chose a hiding place in the foothills of Siaton, about fifty kilometers south of Dumaguete, in the opposite direction from most of the other Silliman families. Siaton contained a subsistence level of crops, presumably making its location less attractive to the Japanese than the sugar and coconut plantations in the northern part of Negros. Additionally, the family's two household servants came from the area, where their friends and relatives assured their willingness to help Abby and the Sillimans; support from the local population, the group knew, was essential to successful evasion. In early May 1942, the family made its move to Siaton, to a village called Casala-an, where Joaquin and Nui Funda, former Silliman students with a special attachment to the Americans, soon joined them. According to Abby, this group, including Gliceria, one of their household servants, made up their trinational family: she and the Sillimans were American, Gliceria and Joaquin were Filipino, and Nui was Thai. She pointed out that when a group of people live together in hiding, "when they get scared together and discouraged together—well, the individual components of the groups are no longer 'servants' or 'students' or 'teachers.' They are 'family.'"[15]

The military progress of the war directly affected the choices that this trinational family and other Americans made. When General Wainwright surrendered Corregidor to the Japanese in May 1942, Japanese General Homma Masaharu required him to order the capitulation of the entire USAFFE on all of the Philippine islands. This blanket military surrender affected civilians too, since the Japanese expected Americans and other Allied nationals to turn themselves in for internment. However, even under direct orders from Wainwright, most of the American and Filipino troops on Negros chose to take to the interior and resist the Japanese, actions which, to be successful, required organization and military discipline. American civilians who made the same decision not to give up often found themselves caught up in guerrilla activities: men like Roy Bell organized and aided the guerrillas, while women like Edna Bell supported them by providing food, clothing, and medical attention when necessary. On May 26, 1942, the Japanese landed unopposed in Dumaguete and quickly took over the city, housing their troops on the campus of Silliman University; within a month, two thousand Japanese soldiers occupied Negros Oriental and established headquarters in every large town. They repeatedly called on all Filipino troops to surrender, announced the roundup of Allied nationals, and proclaimed their intention to liberate the Filipinos from the tyranny of Caucasian rule. On the surface, Filipinos cooperated with the Japanese to save their lives, but some also funneled aid to the American and Filipino guerrillas to safeguard their future.

With these new developments, the Bell-Carson group determined that Malabo was no longer safe and moved another two and a half hours inland to Lake Balinsasayao, a location that afforded them better cover and a good freshwater supply. When the Japanese showed no signs of extending their occupation beyond Dumaguete, the Bells, feeling more secure and ambitious, moved back to Malabo, leaving the Carson family at the lake house. Guerrilla activity caused the split. Arthur believed that as a missionary he had no obligation to participate, while Roy believed it was his patriotic duty to help the resistance as much as possible. With the aid of the American radio operator, Edward Chmielewski, Roy established Malabo as a resistance center, organizing guerrillas, creating a hospital for the wounded, and setting up radio contact with other islands, activities that proved crucial to the success of guerrilla warfare on the island.

The surrender of Corregidor also put the Lindholms and the Winns on the move again. Persistent rumors of the Japanese's relentless attempts to root out all Americans plus an actual close call with the Japanese near the end of June convinced the Lindholms to move even further into the interior, to Busilak. Viola Winn, equally frightened about the war developments, had a nerve-racking experience one day in late June 1942, when she looked out of her kitchen window and saw fourteen Japanese soldiers heading for the house. She, the housemaids, and the children had just minutes to flee before the soldiers spotted them, and the group raced to a nearby cornfield. To keep one-year-old Elinor from chattering and attracting the attention of the Japanese, Viola nursed her as they crouched among the stalks. Luckily, this proved to be a false alarm—the soldiers were Filipino, not Japanese. Yet the Winns' troubles were far from over, as the family soon fled again when it received word that the Japanese had moved into Pacuan in an active search for Americans. The Winns took temporary refuge in the tobacco shed of a local family further up in the mountains, huddling together silently while the locals lied to the Japanese soldiers, insisting they had not seen them. Even though the family successfully relocated, they were not safe; the final blow came when a boy named Mateo, whose family had helped the Winns when they lived near Guihulngan, brought them the devastating news that the Japanese would shoot him if he did not turn in Gardner.

Appalled that he should be the cause of anyone's death, Gardner immediately announced that he would go with Mateo to surrender; when Viola realized that he expected her to join him, she resisted. She refused to leave her children in the mountains under the custody of a local family, nor would she subject them to internment. Viola allowed that in their six years of marriage their "physical relationship had been a happy one," but that Gardner would not use "his physical needs as an argument to keep me with him." She believed that their love had reached its "culmination" in the birth of their children and that now her duty as mother took precedence over that of wife, so she told her husband that she would not, could not, go with him. Viola, speculating that the conditions in the internment camps were probably much worse than what they had been experiencing in the mountains, pointedly reminded Gardner that the Japanese had asked for him, not the entire family. Gardner looked at her "with horrible anguish in his brown eyes" as she continued her argument: "We wanted those children so much, each one of them. They didn't ask to be born. They didn't ask to come to the Philippines. How can we let them live in a prison camp until the war ends?"[16] Gardner gave in to Viola's wishes, acceding to her view that the welfare of the children mattered more than having his wife with him, and after blessing the family he went off with Mateo to surrender. Viola remained alone in the mountains with three children and two maids; she now had to call on all of her inner strength to pull her family through the rest of the war.

The surrender of Dumaguete prompted Abby Jacobs and the Sillimans to move from their hideout in Casala-an, which proved not to be as safe as they had hoped. By May 26, several hundred Japanese soldiers were stationed just fifty kilometers away, too close for comfort, according to Abby, especially when a group of them came into Siaton asking about the Sillimans. A severe storm prevented the soldiers from reaching the Silliman sanctuary, providing the fugitives an opportunity to quickly move to Bugual, located deeper in the hills. But Abby disdained her new surroundings: "For companions we had four ignorant hill families, chittering monkeys, wild pigs, iguanas and a slimy assortment of kaingin [patches of burnt jungle] snakes."[17] The house in Bugual was little more than a hovel compared with their accommodations in Casala-an, prompting the group to dub it Hovel Home, but there the family remained until November 1942.

Both women and men in these hidden locations carried on family and community duties, with the bulk of the domestic chores falling to the women. Edna Bell established a Sunday school for the local Filipino children, attracting over thirty of them to her weekly classes, while Clara Lindholm stayed close to her family, filling her days with household tasks made more difficult by the war's deprivations. She made clothing for her family out of old bedsheets, towels, and even a tattered pup tent, items that served not only as cloth but also as thread for sewing, and when Clara ran out of needles, a neighbor made some from the ribs of an old umbrella. The Jacobs-Silliman group established a division of labor based on ability. Metta and Nui ran the kitchen, Joaquin served as interpreter and food provider, Bob executed carpentry and ditch digging, and Abby managed the laundry with Bob's assistance. There were no washing machines and clothes dryers in Bugual, so the two carried laundry baskets a half kilometer to a nearby stream, where they divvied up the washables. Bob made up "near-barroom variety" songs steeped with masculinity, which helped him keep his self-respect while doing woman's work; as Abby observed, he "had never been the type to play in suds or scrub out trousers. Historians seldom are."[18] But this historian did his part, and singing made the work more acceptable to his sense of manhood.

With her husband now interned in Dumaguete, Viola established a home for her family in the forest with the help of some local friends. Although the location was not ideal because of its close proximity to Pacuan, it was the best that the situation afforded at the time, and the family settled into a somewhat uneasy routine. Then Gardner turned up during the third week of July 1942 with the distressing news that the Japanese ordered him to bring in the rest of his family, reassuring him that they could have a house to themselves in town if they cooperated. Viola, still opposed to internment, agreed to go with Gardner to the Lindholms' cave near Busilak to discuss the situation with them. The Lindholms greeted them with surprise—they had heard that the Winns had surrendered and had packed their own suitcases while considering internment. Huddled in the cave, weighing the pros and cons, the Lindholms decided to remain in the mountains, so Viola determined to do the same. Faced with her resolve, Gardner acquiesced again, telling Viola that he would simply inform the Japanese that he did not know where his family had gone; since Paul intended to move Viola and the children to a new hiding place, Gardner would not be compromising his principles by lying. Viola, relieved that her husband did not try to talk her into internment, nevertheless mourned the disruptions the separation would cause the family and lived a lonely but safe existence from August 1942 until May 1943.

From the end of 1942 into early 1943, while the Japanese remained confined to the coast, not making any coordinated efforts to capture the outlaw Americans, the Silliman families' troubles grew. At the end of March 1943, Bob Silliman had been vomiting for three days from an undiagnosed cause and, unable to contact the local doctor, who was working for the guerrillas, asked that midwife Rosa Banogon come to their hideout in Casala-an. He was so ill that he dismissed the ribbing he took for calling a midwife to attend to him, but her presence proved fortuitous for Nui, because she went into labor two weeks early, delivering her daughter on April Fool's Day 1943. Abby expressed relief that they had access to a "town midwife" who had been trained in a hospital in Cebu, which to her was much better than relying on an unsanitary superstitious midwife in Bugual but not quite as good as a hospital birth in Dumaguete. The baby's name represented the outlaw trinational family: Eleanor (American) Sinsook (Thai) Funda (Filipino). Until the end of June the family stayed in Casala-an, where Abby believed that they were "safe enough" but admitted to "occasional flurries, real ones and imaginary ones."[19]

However, the longer the family stayed in Casala-an, the more precarious their situation became, for during the spring of 1943 the Japanese increased their efforts to root out and eliminate the guerrilla forces plus bring in the fugitive Americans. In January of that year, under orders from General MacArthur, Major Jesus Villamor, a Filipino USAFFE officer, made a covert landing on Negros to take command of resistance forces there.[20] The Japanese, who could not occupy every inhabited area on the island with its two thousand troops, became outraged with the continued and increasingly coordinated guerrilla activity. Adding to this affront was the fact that American troops had been making steady advances from island to island in the Pacific, painstakingly forcing the Japanese out of territories they had occupied just a year before. As the Americans approached the Philippines, the Japanese prepared for major battles, but for total victory they had to pacify the civilian population.

These military developments directly threatened the American civilians, putting them on the move. By June 15, 1943, three hundred Japanese soldiers were within two miles of Roy Bell's guerrilla headquarters at Malabo, so along with other Americans in the area, the Bells pulled up stakes and headed for the Carsons' lake home. As the Japanese set fire to Malabo, Ethel Chapman, living in Ta-as Tubig near Dalasag, watched the smoke and was "much disturbed" to hear about the attempted annihilation of the guerrillas. The narrow escape from the Japanese convinced Roy, who recently accepted the rank of major in the American army, that he had to move his family into a more secluded area, that keeping them away from all other Americans was the best way to secure their safety. They moved into the hills above Malabo, into a village called Manalanco, where the men built what Edna referred to as the "Log Cabin Syrup cottage" because of its resemblance to the drawing on the Log Cabin syrup label.[21] However, Roy's involvement with the guerrillas meant that he could not keep his family safe.

Disturbed by frequent Japanese incursions into the interior, Abby Jacobs and the Sillimans decided at the end of June to move from Casala-an back to their Hovel Home in Bugual. Shortly after Metta and Abby made it habitable, the family bolted from Casala-an one step ahead of the Japanese army, but the enemy stayed for only a few days, finally withdrawing to Dumaguete. The family decided to keep both homesteads open and occupied; Bob and a couple of servants stayed in Casalaan so he could carry on his duties as deputy governor of the district while the others stayed in Bugual. Metta and Abby took turns going to Casalaan to oversee the cooking and provide secretarial support to the deputy governor, an arrangement they continued until December 1943.

In July 1943, the Chapmans moved back to Ta-as Tubig from a temporary hiding place, but, Ethel admitted, "life was never normal again for any of us." As the guerrillas became bolder, the Japanese stepped up their patrols, so "alarms were frequent, and rumors kept us always uneasy," an uncertainty they lived with until November. That summer the Lindholms moved to Pacuan in hopes of establishing a school for the local children, but when increased Japanese patrols made this impossible, Clara settled for teaching her two eldest children, Beverly and Dean, with books and other materials that had been donated by the locals. In September they moved again, this time to a location about fifteen minutes away from where the Winns hid, a place where Paul could continue his pastoral work.[22]

Although Viola was overjoyed to be reunited with her friends, a happiness tempered by Gardner's internment, wartime conditions began to wear on her. During one Sunday church service in November when she was supposed to be counting her blessings, she indulged in self-pity, calling to mind all of the bad things in her life. Heading the list was her appearance; Viola lived in three seersucker dresses, which in good times had been stuck in the back of her closet in their Dumaguete home because she did not like them. Now she longed for dainty summer dresses, silk stockings, high-heeled shoes, and the opportunity to have her hair done properly. Viola's attention to fashion also influenced her perceptions of motherhood, because she regretted that her only daughter, Elinor, had to wear pants and shirts instead of dresses. Finally, her concerns revolved around issues that mothers anywhere could relate to—worries that her son Rodger had not learned to read yet and anxiety over the declining health of her other son, Norman. Before the end of the service, Viola chastised herself for dwelling on the negatives: "Who are you, I asked myself, to feel regret for the things you wish you had? Most of the people here haven't even dreamed of the luxuries you once had."[23] While focusing on femininity and motherhood, she also emphasized her national identity; as an American she had had access to items most Filipinos had not, and now she suffered those deprivations.

FAILURES AND SUCCESSES OF EVASION

The Japanese, harassing the area near Manalanco on November 24, 1943, advanced on the Bell home, but the family saw them first and fled through a back window to a hiding place in the woods. With only the clothes on their backs and a tin of milk, they made their way further into the interior—Roy limping and bleeding from a bullet wound in his leg—to seek refuge with the Fleischer family. Although the Bells, Carsons, and Fleischers eluded that Japanese raid, other Silliman families did not. Alvin Scaff, his wife, Marilee, and their two young sons, who lived across the clearing from the Bells, did not have time to escape, but Marilee threw the Japanese off the Bells' tracks by pointing the troops in the opposite direction from where the Bells had run.

A few days later the Japanese finally caught up with Jim and Ethel Chapman. Clearing out of their home after they received word that the Japanese were in Dalasag, the Chapmans headed for their emergency hiding place, carefully concealing their gun and any papers that might give away the locations of other Americans in hiding. When they did not hear anything for several minutes, Jim went back to check out their house and, with the coast apparently clear, called for Ethel to come back. When she arrived at the house, Jim went further down the trail to see if he could get a look at what was going on in Dalasag, a brief separation that put an end to their time in hiding. As Ethel anxiously watched for Jim's return, she saw the Japanese approach. She could have fled from the house, avoiding capture, but she had no way of warning Jim that the Japanese were at the house; by the time he came running up the trail, their opportunity for escape had been cut off. The soldiers and their commanding officer acted polite and reassuring, behavior that surprised Ethel, and while the Japanese did not physically harm the Chapmans, they did loot and then burn their house. Ethel recalled that "with only the clothes we were wearing and a very few things in bags on our backs, we took a last look at the friendly little house and started off once more, prisoners of the Japanese."[24]

The Japanese transported the prisoners to Silliman University for questioning. They separated Jim and Ethel Chapman, interrogated each individually, probing for fresh information about Roy Bell, who still continued his work with the guerrillas. The imprisoned men were kept separated from the women, but occasionally a generous guard allowed the husbands and wives to talk. On December 9, 1943, the Japanese transferred the group to San Carlos, where they were detained for further questioning before being moved to Bacolod. Upon arrival, Ethel and the others struggled to carry their meager belongings down the road to the school that served as their prison, while "Filipinos and Japanese alike stared at the spectacle we presented. Our backs were bowed, but our chins were up. We were still every inch Americans, and proud of it!"[25] Later they were transferred to Santo Tomas to wait out the war.

News of the November raids caused Abby Jacobs and the Sillimans to reevaluate their living situation. In mid-December 1943, the Fundas, now with a baby to worry about and Joaquin's extensive guerrilla activities, decided to leave, breaking up the trinational family to increase their chances of survival. Abby and the Sillimans finally abandoned their home in Casala-an and commenced a rapid series of moves between two different *payags* (hideouts) in Bugual designed to keep them away from the Japanese and informers, but no place seemed safe for very long. On Christmas Day they splurged, opened up the last of their canned food—green beans, tomatoes, and fruit salad—and killed their last two chickens. With their remaining bits of butter, milk, and sugar, they made fudge, creating a Christmas feast that fortified them for their final and most dangerous trip through Negros.

On January 1, 1944, the Japanese landed in Siaton, in the valley just below the family's sanctuary. Abby, Metta, and Bob lived secluded in utter silence for about three weeks, lest anyone passing by the house see or hear them and inadvertently let the information slip to the enemy. On January 23, when their already moldy food supply became barely edible, the trio received word that the Japanese were moving toward the hideout, so they grabbed their prepacked bags and headed across the canyon to yet another location. A day later they bolted again, Abby and Metta crawling on their hands and knees up a muddy bank toward their *payag* across the canyon, which the Japanese found, prompting the women to scramble out of the hut and hide in the bushes until dark, when the enemy left. The next morning the group made its way to the Funda house, where a guerrilla doctor, Jose Garcia, arrived with the astonishing news that an American submarine would land on Negros at the beginning of February to drop off supplies for the guerrillas and evacuate Americans to Australia. Major Villamor had organized a district headquarters on Negros Oriental, establishing a civil government for free portions of the island, and spent much of his time bringing structure and strength to the chaotic resistance movement, which unexpectedly provided most welcome benefits for the American evaders.

Removal to Australia, however, involved a dangerous journey to the coast to meet up with the submarine.

The group made the fifty-kilometer trip around the southern part of the Oriental coast to Basay, mostly traveling at night to avoid detection by the Japanese. Abby brought out her last pair of battered shoes for the trek, recalling, "My mind wasn't working very well, except that part of it which was necessary to keep my feet going. It was just as well not to be thinking too hard. We were going through an area that was a favorite of the Japs for surprise landings."[26] The trio traversed eight rivers, crossed a rickety bamboo bridge, and passed through various small villages in absolute silence before meeting up with the Bells and Carsons to wait for the American submarine.

The terror of the Bells' narrow escape had preyed on the minds of the other evaders, intensifying it when, near the end of December 1943, word circulated that the Japanese captured and executed a group of Baptist missionaries on the nearby island of Panay. Given this serious turn of events, Roy decided the time had finally come to take up the guerrillas' evacuation offer. He had dedicated his time to organizing the Negros guerrillas, fully supporting their efforts, but he knew that Edna, ever conscious of her wifely duties, would not leave the island without him, and he refused to further jeopardize her safety. The Bells and Carsons left on the seven-day trip across the island to Basay on January 22, 1944, a departure made more imperative because the Japanese had decreed that any Americans found in the Philippines outside of internment after January 1 would be executed. The group reached their destination during the first week of February and waited with the others—in separate hiding places—for a week before the submarine arrived.

Reintensified enemy action in the area made their presence especially dangerous, decreasing the likelihood that the submarine would pick them up. However, on February 7, a guerrilla runner delivered the longed-for news that a vessel would surface the next day. On February 8, when they boarded the USS *Narwhal* heading for Australia, Abby gave the guerrilla officers who had delivered the families safely a cheery, "Thanks, fellows—for everything!" but she realized how feebly those words expressed everything that she felt. Safely ensconced in the submarine, Bob jovially put one arm around Metta and the other around Abby and said, "Well, girls, this is the best payag we've ever been in a long time, isn't it?" During their first evening on board, Edna Bell gratefully slept "the sleep of the unafraid" for the first time since Pearl Harbor.[27]

Upon reaching Australia, Abby refused to return to the United States; instead she took a job with the American army, arriving in Manila in April 1945, after the city's liberation. The others also found that they could not stay away from the Philippines: in 1946, the Bells returned to their duties at Silliman, where they stayed until 1959, when their work took them to Thailand, Arthur Carson served as president of Silliman until 1953, and Bob Silliman worked in a variety of administrative positions until he retired in 1962.

In early 1944, despite rumors that the Japanese intended to raid the area where they lived, the Lindholms still debated about leaving. Clara and Paul worried about the trek the family would have to take to get to the submarine, they fretted about the dangers from Japanese ships once they were in the water, and Paul disliked leaving Filipino church members without a pastor. On the other hand, they feared for their continued health and safety. Almost everyone in the family was afflicted with some kind of illness, there was no way to get medical treatment, food was becoming even scarcer, and the children's education suffered.

On April 19, the Lindholms, along with Viola Winn and her children, finally gathered together for the journey to Basay. Viola had not been convinced of the need for such drastic action, but some locals told her that this plan was indeed sensible, pointing out that they would be safer once the Americans left the area. Various Filipinos who had aided the Lindholms and the Winns went into hiding themselves, fearing Japanese retribution; guerrilla leaders in the vicinity urged Viola to leave. She also realized that Gardner would not return to Negros to look for her after the war, that he would assume she and the children had gone back to the United States to wait for him. When she learned that the other Silliman people had arrived safely in Australia, she acquiesced and prepared for evacuation by sewing a pink flowered sundress for her daughter, Elinor, and a new dress for herself, insisting that she and the children look presentable when rescued.

On May 11, after a ten-day trip across Negros and a few days of waiting in Basay, the Lindholms and Winns rendezvoused with the USS *Crevalle.* Waiting for the canoes that would take them to the submarine, Viola feared that the Japanese would come at the last minute to capture them all, but then she looked out and "appreciated the vastness and promise of the ocean, and calm and peace filled my soul." Paul separated from his family as they boarded the submarine, convinced that he had to remain on Negros to continue his work, but the impact of his absence was almost lost to Clara and the children amidst the confusion and joy of being on a rescue vessel. The children excitedly explored their new surroundings, reveling in the abundance of food, something most of them could not remember. When Clara suddenly realized her husband's absence, she asked some crew members to send a loaf of bread to Paul along with the other supplies that the submarine was dropping off, and she encouraged her children to be brave, telling them that their father would write. Clara's own farewell letter to Paul read in part, "God bless you and keep you safely and reunite us all soon. My whole heart is with you and will be always."[28]

The two families found themselves quickly immersed in American culture as they caught up on news from magazines, where they learned about wartime rationing and the American public's reaction to it. The children, raised on chicken, rice, and carabao milk, picked at the ham, potatoes, and peas served for dinner that first night and refused to eat; it took days before they adjusted to their new surroundings. Even more frightening, after five days in the submarine, Clara suddenly collapsed. When the ship's pharmacist examined her, he proclaimed that she suffered from battle fatigue, an emotional ailment not uncommon in soldiers; after he gave her some tranquilizers, Clara bravely boasted that "in a little while I was all right."[29] She would not succumb to weakness just when her family had been rescued.

After eight days at sea, the *Crevalle* docked in Port Darwin, Australia, having successfully evaded Japanese patrols. Viola referred to their arrival as coming out "of the valley of the shadow of death," rejoicing that their "pilgrimage was almost over. No more running. No more hiding. No more crawling on the bottom of the sea. Free." The group remained in Australia for three weeks, after which some members boarded a hospital ship bound for the United States. Although Clara and her children reached San Francisco on June 20, she had no definite word about Paul until she received a telegram on July 9, 1945, stating that he had met up with U.S. forces in Cebu City in mid-April. By the time the telegram arrived, he was already on his way home to Salem, Oregon. Viola heard through the Board of Foreign Missions in New York City that Gardner had been seen alive and well, but thin, in Manila, and in mid-February 1945, he arrived in the United States on the first ship full of those freed from Santo Tomas. When she went to Omaha, Nebraska, to meet him and bring him back to Sioux City, Iowa, where she was staying with relatives, Viola finally found out what happened when he returned to internment without his family. Instead of telling the Japanese that his wife and children had gone into hiding at an unknown location, Gardner told them that Viola had run off with a Filipino, prompting a Japanese officer to respond that "if that was the kind of wife I had, I had done well to be rid of her!"[30] It was the most complete protection Gardner could provide for his family while he was not with them, so even though the story cast Viola in a terribly unflattering light, she registered no objection to this lie.

AMERICAN FILIPINAS: SERVING TWO COUNTRIES

A few Americans in the Pacific theater who evaded capture had limited or no firsthand knowledge of the United States because they were the mixed-race daughters of American-Filipino couples, women who believed themselves doubly duty-bound to resist the Japanese. These women endured changes in their family structures as they struggled to stay alive and contribute to their country's defense in an increasingly hostile environment.

As the Silliman faculty helped prepare Dumaguete for war and made plans for their evacuation into the mountains, students from the other Philippine islands scrambled to get back home. Anxious parents cabled their children, advising them to return; therefore inter-island steamers and private boats quickly filled to capacity. Among this throng of students was fifteen-year-old Dorothy Dore, from the southern Philippine island of Mindanao, who attended the Silliman high school. Dorothy's father, a veteran of the Spanish-American War, settled in the Philippines after the war, eventually marrying a petite, dark-haired mestiza named Pauline Cueva. The couple, who settled on Mindanao near the city of Davao where Victor managed a coconut plantation, had five children, four of whom lived to adulthood. Dorothy was their only daughter. In 1939 Pauline decided that her children needed the best education available, so she chose Silliman, a decision that compelled her to sell some of her own jewelry to pay for the tuition for her three eldest, Samuel, George, and Dorothy.

Dorothy, an enthusiastic high school student who conscientiously studied and eagerly participated in extracurricular activities, lived in Oriental Hall, a women's dormitory for both high school and college students, and belonged to a group of mixed-race young women who socialized almost exclusively with each other. Their fun times ended when the Japanese bombed Pearl Harbor. Even though Roy Bell offered his mountain retreat as an evacuation home for Dorothy and her brother

George, the two—minus Sam, who had already left to take a teaching position—decided to go back to Mindanao, because they knew that their parents were worried about them. Getting home would be quite an ordeal, for it meant traveling a hundred miles by ocean, then another hundred miles across Mindanao to reach their plantation. The wharf in Dumaguete was crowded with evacuees; Dorothy and George doggedly tried for days to find a ship headed for Mindanao that had enough room for them. Finally, on December 14, the captain of one of these ships, who knew Victor Dore, spotted the two at the wharf and offered to take them home, ultimately refusing any payment for his services. After enduring oppressively crowded accommodations for several days on water and then land transportation, Dorothy and George arrived home during the third week of December, just in time for Christmas.

As a family, the Dores had to decide what course of action to take given the worsening war situation. Victor believed that if the family surrendered to or was captured by the Japanese, they would all be tortured and executed because of his nationality and his previous connection with the American military. Yet he insisted that the decision to evade the Japanese be made by the entire family. Victor expected that if they were going to stay out of internment or avoid death, they had to get involved with the USAFFE and actively resist the Japanese invasion of Mindanao. The family unhesitatingly decided to back his plan, so Victor took on a civilian job with the USAFFE, which supported the Dore family in return for his military expertise and knowledge of the island.

Dorothy, an attractive teenager, also cast her lot with the USAFFE, working as a nurse's aide at a military dispensary at Kidapawan. She was issued a khaki uniform and a military cap with a medical insignia on it and, under the direction of American and Filipino military doctors, received on-the-job medical training, helping to treat wounded and sick soldiers and civilians. In March 1942, Dorothy was inducted into the Philippine army as a second lieutenant, a move that ensured that she could ride on army vehicles to requisition medicine and supplies from area pharmacies. The Japanese had the USAFFE on the run in Mindanao in the spring of 1942; amidst their general retreat, Victor and Dorothy were relieved of their duties so they could go back to the family plantation to work out a plan for going into hiding. Dorothy was advised to hide her uniform and her insignia in case she was captured, because the Japanese would likely treat her harshly if they knew she had worked with the USAFFE.[31]

The Dores then headed to the coastal area of Cotabato, where Pauline had family; during the trip they received word that General Wainwright had surrendered at Corregidor and that he had ordered all troops to do the same. Victor, like the majority of the Mindanao soldiers, refused and instead evacuated into the hills, an area unfamiliar to the Dore family. The Japanese detained them in Malaybalay, but since Victor was virtually unknown in that area, he convinced Japanese officials that he was French, an assertion that kept the family out of internment but under the close, watchful eye of the Japanese. During the nine months they remained there, Dorothy made and sold cookies and candies to American military prisoners at a nearby camp, plus she smuggled other goods and information into the camp, even narrowly escaping rape by one of the Japanese officers. In early 1943, during a pitched battle between the guerrillas and the Japanese, the enemy captured the Dores, who in turn were freed in a daring late-night rescue led by local anti-Japanese Moros. Victor and Dorothy then took jobs with the guerrillas, Victor working with the quartermaster and Dorothy taking on medical duties.

The Dores moved to Mailag, where Victor worked in the motor pool under the charge of twenty-four-year-old Captain John "Jack" William Grant, who had made his way to Mindanao after the Japanese bombed Clark Air Force Base in December. Jack and Dorothy fell in love, a quick courtship that resulted in marriage within weeks. Shortly thereafter, the Japanese launched a massive offensive against the guerrillas, and Dorothy's family was forced to flee from the approaching enemy. In the course of this hectic retreat, Dorothy's mother, Pauline, dispirited, exhausted, and plagued with huge blisters on her feet, convinced the rest of her family to leave her under the protection of one of the soldiers and go on without her. Victor remained in a nearby house, awaiting the arrival of his wife before he would go any further. Dorothy, Jack, and Dorothy's cousin, Beth, accompanied by nine Magahat tribesmen whose loyalty caused Dorothy some unease, continued their trek through the jungles of Tigwa. During a rest stop, she was startled to hear Jack's voice sharply calling to her to fire her revolver; by the time she jumped up, gun in hand, to see what was going on, the Magahats had attacked Jack and Beth with bolos and spears. Dorothy watched in horror as one of them thrust his spear through her husband's heart, and when she finally managed to fire the gun, she scared the assailants away. By the time she reached Jack, he was dead. Despite her grief she kept her wits, roused the barely alive Beth, and fled the area before the Magahats could return.

The two young women made their way to a friendly tribe allied with the guerrillas; after Beth recovered a bit, they rejoined Victor, and the news that father and daughter had to exchange was tragic. Although he had already been informed of Jack's death, Dorothy had to fill him in on the details, but Victor possessed information that his daughter had been dreading since the beginning of the war. The Japanese snatched Pauline as she rested in what she thought was a safe place, and they also captured her youngest son, Philip, who had been fighting with the guerrillas. The enemy tortured them both but kept them alive because they wanted to force Victor to give up, leaving him to make the agonizing decision not to surrender because he did not believe that the Japanese would spare the lives of his wife and son. Victor's prediction proved accurate: Japanese soldiers bayoneted Pauline during a mass execution, and Philip was beaten to death while performing forced labor on a Japanese airstrip. Dorothy reasoned that her mother would not have wanted them to surrender, that "she made herself the sacrificial lamb so that we might live to carry on."[32]

Victor's health began an immediate decline, as he not only suffered the loss of his wife and one of his children but also from malnutrition, beriberi, lice infestation, and heart failure. En route to meet up with an evacuation submarine, he died in the mountains of Basak on February 29, 1944, leaving Dorothy an orphan and a widow. But her trials were not over yet; soon after she buried her father, she found out that her swollen stomach was not the result of malaria—she was pregnant. On August 9, with the help of a local midwife, Dorothy delivered a healthy, blonde, blue-eyed baby girl, the image of her American father, and named her Jean Louise Grant. Dorothy stayed close to the American troops for the remainder of the war, eventually bringing herself and Jean Louise to the United States.

Dorothy's experiences on Mindanao are some of the most dramatic of the war. Although her family fell to the enemy and she lost her mother and then became one herself, she not only evaded the Japanese but also actively supported the guerrillas despite any risk to herself. As the daughter of an American father, one who had served with the U.S. military and raised his children with loyalty to that country, and a Filipino mother, Dorothy could make no other choice, but she paid a high price. Most of her family fell victim to the Japanese, yet Dorothy never admitted to losing faith in the United States. During the course of the war she felt increasingly bound to a country she had never seen: in addition to her American father, she had had an American husband, then gave birth to a half-American daughter. Dorothy had risked and lost much, but with Jean Louise, she had every reason to be optimistic about the future.

One of Dorothy's acquaintances from Silliman University, Ida Mason, spent most of the war years outside of internment, helping the anti-Japanese forces in less direct ways than Dorothy had and experiencing fewer losses. When World War II began, Ida's Filipina mother, Aurelia Balandra, lived in Cadiz on the island of Negros with her second husband, while Ida's American father, William Mason, lived with his second wife in Portland, Oregon. William had been a chief sawyer at a lumber mill in Fabrica when he met Aurelia, the principal of the local elementary school; the two married in January 1922, and Ida was born the following November. The Masons lived in the Philippines for a while, then in the United States, where Aurelia and William eventually divorced; Aurelia later took Ida back to the Philippines, believing she could better provide for her daughter there. In the spring of 1941, Ida decided that she wanted to finish college in the United States, so she wrote to her father asking if he would pay her passage to the United States, informing him that, once there, she would find a job and work her way through college. Her father notified her in October that he had booked passage for her on the *President Cleveland*, scheduled to leave Manila on November 27, but Ida's mixed heritage prevented her from leaving that day. Since 1935 when she returned from the United States with her mother, Ida had been a minor on her mother's passport, but now as an adult she needed one of her own. The American embassy in Manila informed her that it required proof of her American citizenship, which meant she needed to provide a copy of her father's birth certificate. It did not arrive in time for the *Cleveland*'s departure, so her ship reservation was transferred to the next one leaving Manila, on December 11, 1941.

When the war started, Ida was staying in the Manila YWCA with a group of university friends. She notified both of her parents by wire that she was safe but was at a loss as to what to do, since no more ships disembarked from the city, either to go to the United States or to other Philippine islands. Ida's one daylong attempt to leave Manila proved unsuccessful—a futile effort to cast her lot with a male protector. Rico, a medical student she had known from Cadiz, invited her to evacuate with him to a small village outside of Manila, where he had friends. They spent the night with the family of one of Rico's classmates, sleeping on the floor of a crowded living room, but when Ida realized that

Rico expected sexual favors in return for his "protection," she went back to Manila to take her chances there. Ida would not trade her chastity, an important component of a young single woman's identity, for any dubious refuge from the Japanese.

After the Japanese took over Manila in early January 1942, they rounded up Ida at the YWCA along with four other American women staying there, and on January 10, she entered Santo Tomas, where she coped with the typical problems of hunger and boredom until September 6. A guard ordered her to report to the commandant's office, where she learned that her mother had secured her release because the Japanese decided to free internees born in the Philippines. Ida's mother found a sponsor for her, a "Mr. Romero," who had known Ida's mother for years, who vouched for Ida, promising she would not leave Manila. Ida and her mother stayed with the Romero family for three days before they decided that it would be prudent to return to Cadiz, for they worried that with hundreds of Japanese around, the city was not a safe place for a young woman. Mr. Romero assured them that if the authorities came looking for Ida, he would report that she had gone out shopping one day and simply had not returned. It was a bit risky for the Romeros since they had vouched for Ida, but Mr. Romero had enough influence to get away with the lie; in wartime Manila, people disappeared frequently.

Ida and her mother quickly collected her remaining belongings at the YWCA, but getting out of Manila would be risky because the only official documentation Ida possessed stated she must remain there. When at the outskirts of the city Japanese sentries stopped their bus to inspect the passengers' documents, a crate of chickens fortuitously broke open, and in the ensuing commotion mother and daughter slipped into the group of passengers that had already been checked. Then they easily boarded a boat for Negros Occidental and their home sugar plantation, Hacienda Balandra.

Ida Mason had become an outlaw. Her light brown, freckled skin marked her mixed heritage, and most people in and around Cadiz knew that she had an American father. If the Japanese authorities, garrisoned about fifteen kilometers north of the hacienda, decided to check into her papers, she could be detained and reinterned or worse, so this deception created a perilous situation for her and her mother. As food supplies on the island dwindled, the Japanese raided nearby farms looking for food and for guerrillas; for Ida, living on the plantation "became a routine of hiding in ravines, along river banks or elsewhere" so that the soldiers would not see her. She feared not only the possibility of reinternment but also rape by Japanese soldiers, describing the periodic encounters between civilians and soldiers as "sometimes brutal."[33] She had heard about a fourteen-year-old farm girl from near Cadiz who walked to that city one day to shop, and on her way back Japanese soldiers detained her at a guardhouse, where they repeatedly raped her. Ida was determined that such a thing would not happen to her.

One day, Japanese soldiers came to the plantation and raided it. Ida and her mother escaped across a sugar field full of piercing cane stubble, ran down a steep river embankment, crossed the chilling water, and fled into the underbrush, where they hid for hours before venturing back to the house, which the soldiers had looted. When Ida realized that the soldiers had seen letters from her father, with his American return address written plainly on the envelopes, she and her mother knew they could never stay there again. They took refuge in a one-room shelter in a nearby ravine, where Ida whiled away the days knitting socks and shirts from string, but even this place was not safe for long. In early 1943, she sought a risky alternative—aided by the provincial governor, who provided information to the guerrillas, Ida acquired a set of forged identity papers that showed Spanish citizenship. She argued that this was not a "total lie but a partial truth," because her great-grandfather was Spanish and his wife was a mestiza.[34] These papers enabled Ida to travel to Bacolod, where she lived with some friends who owned a restaurant and worked part-time as a private tutor for the governor's children and as an assistant to a Russian who manufactured cosmetics. In her spare time she took classes in Japanese language and in typing.

In late 1943, Ida decided the time had come to leave Bacolod. The constant presence of Japanese soldiers caused her increasing strain, and when she received an offer to tutor the children of one of the guerrilla leaders, she accepted and left the city. Ida settled into an area called Casanova, where she tutored four of the children of Aurelio Locsin, the deputy governor of the resistance government, a position she enjoyed even if she did not feel entirely safe. One day in November, when the guerrillas rescued five survivors of a downed American Liberator bomber, Ida recalled that the flyers "received a royal welcome" from the guerrillas and were "surprised to find an American girl in the mountains." Despite the food shortage, a feast was held in honor of the airmen, complete with suckling pig and songs, and for Ida it was the first time she had ever heard the song "White Christmas." In February 1945, the guerrillas abandoned Casanova, so Ida spent two months with them walking through jungles, sometimes marching more than sixty kilometers per day over mountainous terrain. By the end of March they settled in Vallahermosa, which had been liberated by another band of guerrillas the previous November, and on March 31, Ida watched the Americans land on Negros.[35]

In early April, after Bacolod had been pacified, Ida made her way back to the city; along the way, American soldiers joined her, thrilled to find an American woman in the midst of the war-torn countryside. They walked with her for a while, and when they gave her the latest stateside news of President Roosevelt's death, Ida remembered that she "sat down on the ground and wept. It was like being told my father had died." By this time, recollections of her mother had dimmed, perhaps out of guilt for leaving her, so Ida clung more ardently to her father's nationality, which made her an American as well. The soldiers then offered Ida a ride the rest of the way to Bacolod in the truck; the day after she arrived in the city, she went to army headquarters and "reported as a U.S. citizen."[36] She told military authorities about her activities on Negros, and, after she filled out some forms, they gave her army rations to take home, which helped improve her health. After her arrival at the 28th Replacement Depot on Leyte in July, members of the Central Intelligence Corps (CIC) of the army questioned Ida, a requirement before repatriation to the United States. The CIC mainly gathered information about suspected collaborators and spies, but Ida found the repeated questioning tiring and intrusive. She wanted to forget most of what had recently happened to her; she wanted to go home to the United States.

On the night of August 6, 1945, as Ida watched a movie, word came over the loudspeaker of the atomic bombing of Hiroshima. Five days later, the twenty-two-year-old woman left Leyte on board the USS *General Andre W. Brewster* along with seventy-five other civilians, bound for the United States. While still on board, news came that the war in the Pacific had ended. "Our joy was boundless," Ida recalled.[37] After her life had been interrupted for almost four years, she was finally heading home to the place she had left when she was still a child.

Japanese officials at Santo Tomas released Ida Mason in September 1942 because they believed that, as a product of an interracial marriage, she held dual citizenship, and her Filipino citizenship, reflecting the country she was born in, superseded her American citizenship. As a Filipina, Ida was then entitled to her freedom under the Japanese Greater

East Asian Co-Prosperity Sphere. Even though she had been born in the Philippines and her looks favored her Filipino mother, even though most of her acquaintances in the Philippines were Filipinos, Spaniards, or mestizos, Ida rejected any notion of dual citizenship. She emphatically claimed that she was "born an American citizen," which made her solely American. Of her work with the guerrillas, she carefully explained that she never contributed to the "military units" of the resistance, since she was hired by the deputy governor of the civilian resistance as a tutor for his children. Nevertheless, Ida conceded that she "felt in a small way I was a part of [a] unit of people resisting and refusing to submit to [Japanese] occupying rule."[38] She did what she could to support the guerrillas while looking out for her own safety, creating new families of support as she went.

Yay Panlilio, born in Denver, Colorado, to an Irish father and a Filipina mother, was a citizen of the United States but considered the Philippines her adopted home and moved there when she was eighteen years old. While she carved out a career as a newspaper reporter, Yay married and then separated from Eduardo Panlilio after they had three children. Before the war started, Captain Ralph Keeler, assistant chief of Intelligence for the USAFFE, swore Yay in as an S-2 intelligence agent, but she continued her work as a reporter, passing along any information she believed useful to the military. When the Japanese occupied Manila in January 1942, Yay took a job with the Japanese-controlled KZRH radio station, where she passed on false information to enemy intelligence, broadcasting useful information to the USAFFE on Bataan and Corregidor using "triple talk," coded messages that sounded benign to the Japanese, who did not understand American nuances and slang.

By March, the Japanese caught on to Yay's true activities and issued an arrest order, but after finding a safe place for her children, she successfully escaped Manila by disguising herself in feminine attire. Yay customarily wore slacks and a kerchief over her short dark hair; to get out of the city she donned a dress and full makeup, and not even her friends recognized her. Furious at her various deceptions, the Japanese put a bounty on her head, issued a shoot-to-kill order, and made it known that they would seek out and hold her children hostage until she surrendered herself. Confident that the enemy could not find her children, she slipped out of Manila, only to contract malaria; while recovering, a band of guerrillas stumbled across her, leading to her involvement with Marcos "Marking" Villa Agustin and his men. Marking, an ex-boxer and former bus driver, organized a guerrilla unit based in the province nearest

Manila, the largest band on Luzon. An immediate attraction sparked between the two, with Yay quickly becoming his closest assistant and his lover, observing that "war was our marriage, the guerrillas our sons." Although their personal relationship was tumultuous—Marking was given to fits of jealous rage, and the two sometimes engaged in physical fights—Marking nevertheless relied on Yay to handle all of the unit's paperwork, and he also discussed with her his plans for guerrilla actions. Although he respected her intelligence and her advice, he resented her power and popularity with the guerrillas; as a result, Yay recalled, "Constantly, never-endingly, I was at his beck and call—forever 'on duty'; and now I was almost insane with it." It was only the fall of 1942, and she already had the responsibility for myriad fighters, saboteurs, propagandists, and spies.[39]

Although she carried a .32-caliber pistol, a souvenir of one of Marking's successful raids, Yay's expertise was organization, not combat, and the pistol was for her own personal safety. She kept endless records of the activities of the guerrillas, documentation that later could be turned over to the returning American forces so that the men could receive pay, official rank, and perhaps awards for bravery. She advised Marking and mothered the soldiers, tending them when they were sick, scolding them when they were impolite; experienced from her own children, she easily took on mothering others, presumably finding much comfort in this guerrilla family. High on Yay's list of priorities to teach her guerrilla sons was that all collaborators or Japanese captured and condemned by the guerrillas had to be executed quickly and mercifully. She rescinded this edict only once in late 1943, after an especially gruesome Japanese attack on the village of Talim, and she participated in the torture and execution of the local collaborators, unusual actions for a woman who typically abhorred violence. Some of Yay's aversion certainly stemmed from her occasionally brutal relationship with Marking; as often as Marking raged at her, slapped and punched her, she always forgave him after he apologized. She rationalized his actions as an expansion of the war and the nature of guerrilla warfare, but as soon as American forces landed in Luzon in early 1945, Yay finally decided she had had enough. She wanted a more normal family life now that the war was almost over, so she left Marking and took her children, whom she had successfully shielded from the Japanese, back to the United States. She hoped that, without her, Marking could confront his demons of masculine pride and warfare and conquer them by fighting on his own during the final days of the liberation of the Philippines.

Yay's situation was unusual for a woman of her time and place. Though other women aided the guerrilla forces during the war, Yay had military rank as a major, a carryover from her duties with Intelligence and a reflection of her importance to Marking. The guerrillas who fought with Marking had to accept the fact that their orders often came from a woman. The ones who stayed respected her position and developed a genuine affection for her. The young fighters, especially, called Yay "Mammy" because she not only gave them orders but also looked out for them, and although Yay acknowledged this part of their larger relationship, she once complained that she was "a mother with too damn many sons." She would only stretch traditional roles so far; when Yay found herself with too many sons, when she had had enough of war, she reclaimed a conventional family role. After she returned to her parents' home in Auburn, California, in early 1945, and after Marking's guerrillas were formally inducted into the U.S. Army, Yay received a "pledge" from the men still fighting: they named their regiment the "Yay Regiment." They intended to "honor our beloved guerrilla mother . . . who nursed us, comforted us, bawled us out, and loved us." Marking, feeling guilty about how he treated Yay, sent her a monthly allowance equivalent, he claimed, to a brigadier general's pay, and when the war in the Philippines ended, he came to California. After the couple married, Yay concluded that "then, all wars ended, we started home, to build the peace."[40]

The women who evaded capture by the Japanese braved rough living conditions and ill health in the hopes of remaining free until U.S. forces arrived to drive the Japanese away. These women believed that internment meant certain death, and since many of them had children, they refused to expose their young ones to the camps, preferring instead the uncertain freedoms of the jungles and mountains. Despite the lack of food, medicine, and shelter, the women refused to give up hope that help would arrive before the Japanese could catch up with them. In the end, some were successful and some were not, but almost every one of them survived because their months of freedom either prepared them for evacuation or shored them up for internment. Their dedication to staying out of the camps was not strictly selfish or even family-centered, since most of them did what they could to help the local population and also aided the guerrillas. Activity with the latter exhibited staunch bravery and patriotism, and a few American women went to great lengths to help the guerrillas and imprisoned Allies, risking their lives in the process. Some mixed-race women rejected Japan's Greater East Asia Co-Prosperity Sphere, because despite their darker skin, despite their partial Filipino lineage, their loyalties rested with the Americans. Other American women had even different reasons for evading and resisting the Japanese.

6

NATIONAL IDENTITY AND SUBVERSION OF THE ENEMY

"If I couldn't be an American, I'd be something else."

As difficult as life had been for women who hid in remote areas of the Philippines, at least two American women took a bolder risk to evade internment by taking advantage of Japanese definitions of nationality, creating new identities for themselves so that they could remain free to undermine Japanese authority. Margaret Utinsky, a Red Cross nurse who thwarted the Japanese in and around Manila, determined early on that "if I couldn't be an American, I'd be something else."[1] She and entertainer Claire Phillips forged documents to show their citizenship of an Axis or neutral country, which exempted them from internment according to Japanese rules, then used their freedom to help those incarcerated and to spy on the Japanese. For these two, staying out of internment represented their best chance for survival while also proving their patriotism and helping them avenge the deaths of their loved ones at the hands of the Japanese. Other American women remained outside the internment camps because they were married to men from Axis or neutral countries, and the Japanese believed that a wife's citizenship and national loyalty naturally followed her husband's. They also helped those in the prison camps, both civilian and military, but found much of their time taken up with keeping themselves and their families alive in enemy-occupied territory. The precarious position of these women not only exposed them to a variety of wartime dangers but also isolated them from the majority of American women in the South Pacific who spent the war years as internees. Despite this detachment, their stories generally corroborate each other without jeopardizing their star position.

SPIES AND SMUGGLERS

Two American women living in Manila, Claire Phillips and Margaret Utinsky, risked their lives during the war to aid the underground and harass the Japanese at every turn, constructing new national identities for themselves so that they could stay out of internment. Margaret established the highly effective smuggling network known as "Miss U," which specialized in aid to military prisoners, while Claire, who organized aid and passed information, became well-known in the underground by the code name "High Pockets," because she hid valuable information and supplies in her brassiere.

Claire Phillips, a divorced singer and entertainer with a young daughter, arrived in Manila in September 1941. She had been to the city years before with a touring company, never lost her love for it and the friends she left behind, and so returned despite rumors of war. Talented and attractive, she easily landed a well-paying singing job at the Alcazar Club, which enabled her to rent an apartment in the Dakota Apartments in the Ermita district and to hire two Filipina servants, one a cook and housekeeper, the other an amah for Dian. While singing at the Alcazar, Claire met and instantly fell in love with John (Phil) Phillips, a radioman for the USAFFE's 31st Infantry; the couple discussed a Christmas wedding, so wrapped up in each other that they ignored the changing world events around them.

The bombing of Pearl Harbor altered some of their plans, but Phil and Claire managed to slip out to a small town outside of Manila, where a village priest married them on Christmas Eve. By December 26, Phil had returned to his unit, and Claire, who remained outside the city with Dian and her amah, Lolita, aided civilians injured in the daily Japanese bombings, while Phil visited her as often as he could. When the Japanese moved into Manila the following week, Phil arranged for Claire and Dian to hide in the mountains with some Filipino friends for a couple of months until the Americans drove the Japanese from the island. After a few weeks, Claire grew uncomfortable with this arrangement, so she took Dian and Lolita across Japanese lines to Corregidor to find Phil, a long journey punctuated by frequent appearances of Japanese soldiers. When Claire encountered three American soldiers separated from their units, one of them, John Boone (who would later write the foreword to Claire's memoir), told her that the American and Filipino soldiers concealed in the mountains could form an effective guerrilla force if they had someone in Manila to send them food and supplies. He suggested that Claire be that person.

Foiled in her attempt to reach Corregidor and reassured that Dian was safe with other friends, Claire made her way back to Manila, dispirited by the USAFFE surrender and Phil's capture. Claire wished to help the guerrillas, but as a white woman, making her way around would be difficult since all of the Allied nationals had already been interned, so she had false Italian identity papers made up in the name of Dorothy Fuentes, making her the offspring of Italian parents, born in the Philippines. Italy was an Axis power, very few Italians lived in Manila, and Claire guessed that she would never run into a Japanese who spoke Italian. In addition to her papers, an influential Filipino, Judge Roxas, formally vouched for her identity with the Japanese authorities.

Claire laid a foundation for her guerrilla activities by first volunteering as a nurse in Remedios Hospital, run by Malate priests to care for sick Filipino soldiers, where she developed contacts among well-placed Filipinos. However, Claire needed money if she was going to supply useful items to the guerrillas, but she did not like relying too heavily on the kindness of her friends for increasingly scarce cash, so she took a job singing at a nightclub run by a German woman. Since the club catered to influential Japanese, Claire found herself in a perfect position to pick up information that would be useful to the guerrillas. She quickly realized that she could work more efficiently if she had her own club, unencumbered by an enemy boss scrutinizing her every move, and with the help of a Chinese businessman Claire opened up Club Tsubaki (named for the camellia flower) on October 15, 1942. Two Filipina entertainers from the German woman's nightclub defected to Claire's new establishment to help with her guerrilla activities.

Personal tragedy galvanized Claire into action when she learned that Phil had died in July of dysentery and malaria in Cabanatuan. Vowing to do whatever she could to prevent further needless deaths, Claire established her "High Pockets" network in January 1943, which sent supplies and information to the guerrillas in the hills and funneled food and supplies to military prisoners whenever possible. One of her special projects was helping the American prisoners at the Pasay Elementary School. Every day Japanese soldiers marched these men, underfed and nearly naked, to an airfield, where they labored under guard for twelve hours before being marched back to their makeshift barracks. Claire rented a house on the corner of Park Avenue and the National

Highway, where she could visually monitor these activities, and she and her compatriots found a way to bribe the guards to deliver bags of food to the American soldiers. She also devised a method by which bundles of food and clothing were left along the street for the soldiers to pick up as they walked back to their prison at the end of the day. On July 4, the most patriotic of American holidays, Claire and her helpers managed to make a thousand hamburger sandwiches to hand out to the men; when she saw "smiles on their gaunt faces" that day, that response alone provided "ample reward for our hard work."[2]

Claire's rewarding work was also dangerous; in late 1943, she realized that the Japanese were watching her nightclub and her activities. One day she sensed a trap when a Filipino whom she did not know presented her with a note supposedly from an American captain with the guerrillas, so she angrily sent the man away, shouting at him that as an Italian she did not care anything about the Americans. Her caution proved fortuitous—one of her nightclub workers then followed the Filipino outside and saw him with members of the Japanese Kempetai, the military police. While the incident prompted Claire to be more cautious in her dealings, she refused to give up her work, continuing to funnel information to the guerrillas, but she knew that her luck could not hold out indefinitely. In early 1944, Claire realized that her telephone was tapped; during the spring her network unraveled as the Japanese cracked down on the movements of civilians, the arrest of one of her operatives leading to the arrest of another. On the morning of May 23, 1944, four members of the Kempetai arrested Claire in the living quarters of her nightclub and took her to a nearby Japanese Administration Building.

The Japanese questioned Claire about her identity and about her activities as "High Pockets" because they suspected, but had no proof, that she was an American and a spy. During this first interrogation, the Kempetai kept Claire blindfolded. When she did not answer questions to their satisfaction, they slapped and punched her until she fell off of her chair. Back in her cell, trying to hold on to her secrets and her sanity, Claire received one ball of rice per day, sometimes accompanied by tea. After two weeks, the Japanese transferred her to Fort Santiago, the most infamous jail in Manila, but did not question her again until August. Then, over a period of several days, her jailers beat her with a bamboo rod, subjected her to the "water cure" by forcing water into her stomach and then stomping on it, and burned her with cigars. Claire, nearly broken from the abuse, provided her captors with a combination of truth and lies, anything to keep herself alive and her network safe. In September, the Japanese issued the ultimate threat: she would be executed unless she told everything she knew about her network. But for some reason, they did not follow through when they realized that she was not going to talk and instead transferred her to Bilibid prison to await sentencing for her crimes. She pleaded guilty and was sent to the Women's Correctional Institution located just outside of Manila, where she was to serve twelve years of hard labor, but American troops liberated the prison on February 10, 1945. Claire weighed ninety-five pounds, her hair came out in handfuls when she brushed it, and all of her teeth were loose, but she had survived and had avenged Phil's death by helping the Allied cause.

Margaret Doolin Utinsky, a Red Cross volunteer nurse in her early thirties, immediately decided to stay out of internment, claiming that she never liked being told what to do. She admitted that obeying Japanese orders "seemed like the sensible thing to do, but for the life of me I could not see what use I would be to myself or to anyone else cooped up."[3] More than anything, Margaret wanted to get to Bataan to find her husband, Jack, a civil engineer working for the government; once there, she could be useful—she could continue to nurse. She bided her time for ten weeks, sequestered in her apartment in the Ermita district of Manila, with Lee, her Chinese servant, as her sole companion and link to the outside; both carefully watched the movements of the Japanese.

After the fall of Corregidor in May 1942, Margaret determined she could safely go outside. The Japanese, she reasoned, believed that they had already interned all of the necessary enemy aliens and so would not pay any attention to a nondescript woman making her way through the streets. Still, she moved carefully, usually waiting until dark to go outside. First she visited Father Lalor at the Malate Convent, a friend of hers since the first days of the war, who told her that it was simply too dangerous for an American to be out on the streets of Manila, that the Japanese would surely pick her up. Margaret concluded that being able to aid the war effort was more crucial than the formalities of citizenship, reasoning that if "I couldn't be an American, I'd be something else."[4] Only in becoming "something else" could she express her American patriotism, function as a wife, and survive. She settled on being Lithuanian because Jack's family had come from a Baltic country, she knew that Kovno was a city in Lithuania, and best of all, Lithuania did not have a consulate in Manila. Margaret Utinsky became Rosena Utinsky, a single nurse born in Kovno, Lithuania, but raised in Canada, hence her perfect English and lack of Lithuanian. With the help of Lee and a Filipino friend, she had the necessary documents forged, then obtained a pass from the Japanese, which allowed her to move freely through Manila.

Next Margaret tried to get to Bataan, where Filipino doctors and nurses established hospitals and clinics to treat civilians—there she could be useful, but she also might find out what happened to Jack, her most pressing concern. Ironically, once she became Lithuanian, she found that Filipinos were wary of her because they did not know whose side she was on. They routinely rebuffed Margaret's offers of help until she renewed her acquaintance with another American woman named Elizabeth Kummer. Elizabeth remained uninterned because her husband, Max, was German, but people in Manila understood that he was not a Nazi, and during the war the Kummers did everything they could to support the Allies. The well-connected couple easily secured permission for "Rosena" Utinsky to join the medical corps on Bataan.

Although these doctors and nurses had permission to treat Filipino civilians, the Japanese forbade them to help the captured American soldiers, yet Margaret did so anyway, first easing their suffering, then questioning each about the whereabouts of her husband. She also hid escaped American soldiers in her Manila apartment and funneled supplies to the guerrillas. While Margaret worked in a rural clinic in Abucay, she made contact with some American military prisoners, arranging to deliver valuable medicine to them. When the prisoners moved to Camp O'Donnell, which housed seventeen hundred men, she went to nearby Capas and established her "Miss U" network to provide food, money, clothing, and medicine on a regular basis, smuggling supplies into the camp by ambulance with the help of uninterned civilians. Margaret also filled special requests ranging from repairing eyeglasses to securing oil paints.

In December 1942, the Japanese transferred the prisoners to Cabanatuan, a large military prison containing more than nine thousand men—many of them survivors of the Bataan death march—forcing Margaret to devise a new plan because of prison restrictions against sending supplies in by truck or ambulance. While making initial contacts with the men, Margaret found out that Jack had died there in August of tuberculosis and malnutrition, prompting her immediate resolve to prevent other prisoners from dying as he had. "Miss U" passed supplies to the thousand or so American soldiers who came out of the prison each day to work on the Japanese vegetable garden. Initially,

Margaret's operatives posed as peanut vendors; when the soldiers purchased peanuts, as the Japanese allowed, they found that their packages also contained hundreds of peso notes, enabling them to buy more food. Margaret then found a vendor named Maluto, who owned several stalls and who willingly passed food, clothing, and medicine free of charge to the soldiers when they came into the marketplace weekly to purchase supplies. Once again, she loaded trucks with supplies in Manila so her Filipino operatives could drive them to Cabanatuan to supply the local vendors. She worked frantically and tirelessly, knowing that her luck could not hold out indefinitely, that one day the Japanese would catch her.

That day came on September 28, 1944, in a Manila hospital where Margaret worked. The Japanese arrested her and took her to Fort Santiago, where they questioned her about her activities and her nationality, interrogating and torturing her for a month, but could not break her story. After signing a statement saying that she had been questioned but treated well, the Japanese released her. As soon as Margaret recovered, she resumed her "Miss U" activities but then fled Manila when she found out that the Japanese intended to pick her up again. When she headed to the guerrillas in the mountains, she had with her Dian, the daughter of Claire Phillips, who had already been arrested for her work as "High Pockets." Claire, who had sent for her daughter once she had established her nightclub, had managed to pass Dian on to friends for safekeeping while the Japanese held her, with Margaret the last person to take charge of the little girl. Margaret nursed for the guerrillas, plus she obsessively drafted a list of Japanese collaborators that quickly grew to thirty pages; after witnessing so much cruelty and destruction, she became overpowered with the desire to see these people punished.

On February 5, 1945, Margaret left the mountains with Dian and headed in the direction of the recently landed American army, encountering her first American soldiers while riding an old horse, "a skinny nag with a home-made saddle and no belly band," Dian sitting behind her, clutching her around the waist. Margaret was a startling sight: she wore a pair of men's shoes, a dress that had formerly been a pair of red curtains, a wide native hat, a gun belt, and socks knitted from string; her once brown hair was now gray; and her five-foot frame carried a meager eighty-five pounds. When she told one soldier of the Sixth Army what she had been doing in the mountains, he exclaimed, "Woman guerrilla? Goddam, what is this war coming to?" After Margaret patiently answered all of their questions, she had a few of her own, the first of which was about the length of women's skirts in the United States. By the time she and her military entourage reached the main body of American troops at Dinalupihan, the soldiers, many of whom had been aided by "Miss U," addressed Margaret as Lieutenant Utinsky. Upon her arrival in the city, she declined to take time off to rest and relax. Instead she worked with the Counter Intelligence Corps of the army to help track down spies and collaborators. For all of her efforts on behalf of the American military on Luzon, the U.S. government recognized Margaret Utinsky as a useful, patriotic woman and awarded her the Medal of Freedom in 1946.[5]

MARRIED WOMEN AND LEGAL EVASION

Life proved risky for these women who stayed out of internment illegally, especially if they were determined to aid the guerrillas, yet the terrain of the Philippines and their generally supportive people made this choice possible. In a city the size of Manila, Margaret and Claire could, with planning and daring, secure false papers and hope that they would not encounter anyone who knew them and would report them to the Japanese. Other women avoided internment because their husbands were either nationals of neutral countries or of countries within the Axis sphere. These women usually had two passports, one American and one from their husband's country; the latter kept them out of internment, the former guaranteed them good treatment when the American military reconquered the Pacific theater. In most cases, these women did not embrace their husband's nationality during the war years out of expediency or selfish motives of self-preservation. Those who remained outside of internment keenly felt the deprivations of war, but they also helped those in both civilian and military prisons, sometimes at the risk of their own lives, while always insisting in their autobiographies that this was something that they naturally had to do.

Emily Hahn, vivacious, adventurous, and dark-haired, earned a mining engineering degree at the University of Wisconsin in 1926 and eventually made her way to China to teach English in the 1930s. Emily's travels quenched her wanderlust while providing her with the means to earn a better living than she could in the Depression-ridden United States. Japan's war on China interrupted her teaching career in Shanghai—which she had enhanced by creating and publishing a successful periodical called *Candid Comment*—so she fled, settling in Hong Kong in 1941. Living in China also underscored Emily's rejection of traditional womanhood: she had no interest in marriage but was fascinated with Chinese culture. She made Chinese friends, unusual for most Caucasians, and perhaps her closest friend was Zau Sinmay, who worked at her magazine. In 1937, Sinmay proposed that he and Emily marry in order to protect *Candid Comment* from being seized by the Japanese, who might object that such a popular publication was owned and operated by a Caucasian woman. When his common-law wife expressed no objection, Emily agreed to Sinmay's proposal to safeguard her magazine, and she signed a paper in his lawyer's office making her his wife "according to Chinese law." Within a few years, Emily would be very grateful for having taken that step.[6]

As Emily moved from city to city at the end of the 1930s, Sinmay did not accompany her, although he did visit from time to time, and Emily continued to earn money by teaching English, working as a reporter, and writing the first of many books. During one of her initial visits to Hong Kong, she met Charles Boxer, a British army major and "Orientalist" expert on Japan, who sought her out because he was interested in her views about Japanese-occupied China. Emily, who felt an immediate attraction to the major, was dismayed when she later learned that he got married within a few days of that meeting.

Despite increasing Japanese military action in the Pacific, Emily ultimately refused to leave Hong Kong because she had fallen in love with Charles, who was part of her European social circle. Charles's wife had not adapted well to colonial life there, so the couple agreed to a trial separation—his wife went off to live in Australia—and Charles and Emily discreetly set up housekeeping. The European community did not recognize the legality of Emily's Shanghai marriage to Sinmay but accepted the special friendship between her and Charles as long as they did not flaunt it. However, in October 1941, Emily gave birth to their daughter, Carola; even though Emily had no interest in marriage, she had always longed to have children, so Charles acceded to her wishes. Charles's wife still refused to divorce him, the Europeans in Hong Kong were scandalized, but very soon more pressing matters captured everyone's attention.

Less than two months after Carola's birth, as Emily struggled with being an unapologetic unwed mother, the Japanese attacked Hong Kong, which fell on Christmas Day. While leading a charge against the enemy, Charles sustained a chest wound, which nearly claimed his life, plus another injury that left one of his arms permanently impaired;

despite the chaos of battle and invasion, Emily managed to help tend to him in the hospital. When she heard that the Japanese were rounding up Allied civilians for internment, she decided to stay out of camp, which she labeled "jail," so she could minister to Charles and be the best mother possible to Carola. During the first week of January 1942, Emily sought shelter in the Queen Mary Hospital, where she settled her daughter in a cot at the foot of a bed in the maternity ward, pretending to be a brand-new mother. When Japanese officers were not in the hospital checking up on the patients, Emily left Carola sleeping in her cot, visited the patients, and helped with whatever she could. She knew that this was not a permanent solution to staying out of internment, that the Japanese would eventually empty the hospital, but she remained there until another opportunity presented itself.[7]

When the Japanese finally ordered the removal of the maternity patients to Camp Stanley, Emily had to think fast. Convinced that Carola would not thrive there and worried that she would never be able to see Charles once she became an internee, she orchestrated a meeting with him to ask if he could get her and Carola exempted from camp. Charles's work as a Japan expert for the British army had brought him into routine contact with Japanese officials during the previous ten years, so he knew a lot of influential people, several of whom were currently stationed in Hong Kong overseeing the occupation. However, since it was wartime and the Japanese were the enemy, Charles refused to use his connections to ask them for any special treatment, even for Emily and Carola; in fact, he was appalled that Emily even asked him. When he stressed that her place was with the Allies, she informed him that most of the internees were British, that she had never been comfortable among them because they were "not my own people"—after years of living in China she felt more at ease with the Chinese and preferred to be with them during the war. Finally, Emily insisted that Carola would fare poorly in a camp and asked Charles if he had any objection to her remaining out of internment if she could find a legal way of doing so. For this request he gave his permission.[8]

Emily was not unique among American women who raised the issue of motherhood to exercise some control of their wartime circumstances. Margaret Sherk became pregnant with another man's child to ensure her survival in internment; Viola Winn successfully argued that her children would fare better in the mountains of Negros than in a camp. But as an American, Emily was unique in casting her identification with the Chinese; race apparently meant very little, as she preferred to take her chances on survival in an enemy-occupied city rather than the controlled environment of an internment camp with other Caucasians.

As the Japanese moved the last patients out of the Queen Mary Hospital, Emily boldly asked the officer in charge for permission to meet with a foreign affairs officer, telling him she knew that she could receive permission to remain outside the camp. When a Eurasian acquaintance asked Emily why she so adamantly resisted internment, she replied: "I just can't. I don't know why, exactly. I want to make a fight for it." Ultimately, Emily managed to "wriggle out" of internment by claiming her marriage to Sinmay, a Chinese citizen, because according to Japanese law the marriage made Emily Chinese as well, despite her American passport. Emily did not have a marriage certificate to prove the marriage, but luck was with her: on her way to the Foreign Affairs office, she ran into one of Sinmay's many relatives, a young nephew who amiably attested to the fact that Emily was indeed his "Auntie." Japanese authorities, whom Emily described as "mostly young, green, and bewildered," willingly believed her story; moreover, she recalled that the officer in charge "was pleased that an American girl should have married an Oriental." Emily then secured papers identifying her as the wife of a Chinese citizen, which allowed her to stay out of internment legally, though some highly placed Japanese officials understood her real situation. The Japanese consul, Mr. Kimura, knew Charles Boxer and his relationship with Emily, and during a brief but unnerving interview with Lieutenant Colonel Noma, head of the Hong Kong Kempetai, Emily admitted that while she was married to Sinmay, she was Charles's mistress and they had a child together. To her surprise, Noma found this all very funny, slapped her on the back, and let her go on her way.[9]

Emily's determination to stay out of internment centered on the welfare of Charles and Carola, an unconventional family by the standards of the time. Since the Japanese allowed British officers to receive food parcels, the extent of Charles's injury led Emily to believe that his life depended on her bringing him extra food. When she found out about other military prisoners who also needed help, she and a "draggletailed group of women whose men were locked up" arranged to take food packages to them as well, spending four days a week moving among four different camps. Each of these trips required a great deal of planning, because the Japanese imposed a host of complex rules; a minor infraction resulted in the rejection of a package, which meant the loss of time and money on behalf of the women, plus the men on the inside went hungry. By staying out of internment, Emily helped people other than herself and Carola to survive, which boosted her own morale on the days when she delivered food to Charles, because she usually managed to catch a glimpse of him while he walked in the outdoor recreation area. But the Japanese guards only allowed quick looks, and if the women attempted to shout at or even wave to the men, the guards stopped them with shouts, slaps, and occasionally unaimed bullets.[10]

Uninterned civilians, regardless of race or nationality, did not have an easy time in Hong Kong. When Emily left the hospital and returned to her apartment on May Road, she found that it had been taken over by a family of six Eurasians, so Emily and Carola moved in with them. Her association with them underscored her friendliness with the Chinese, which appeased Japanese authorities, plus she enjoyed the company of two other young women, also mothers of small children. Life was rough, because even with a roof over her head and a new family to provide her with psychological and emotional support, Emily had little money and few chances for earning any. The group could not afford to pay their utility bills, so electricity, gas, water, and the telephone were all cut off; food was expensive and scarce, yet Emily firmly believed that this situation was superior to internment.

Part of the tough times included staying away from the Japanese, as Emily worried about being picked up and taken to Camp Stanley, but she mostly fretted about sexual advances or attacks by Japanese soldiers. Emily and Irene, one of her apartment mates, walked daily to a local market to haggle for supplies for their household and for the prisoners, and while they mapped their route carefully, they could not always avoid Japanese troops. One day they ran into soldiers resting their horses at the roadside; a couple of them motioned that they would like to accompany the two women to town, ostensibly to help them carry their supplies back home. Emily nervously realized the soldiers were "looking for amusement," so she and Irene prudently laughed and gestured with them, but managed to get away without antagonizing them. Not long after that, Lieutenant Watanabe of the Kempetai began keeping close tabs on Emily to determine if she was involved in spying, smuggling, or any other activity that would prove she harbored "unfriendly feelings" toward the Japanese. He claimed he wanted to take English lessons, and even though Emily knew that he really sought information (he already spoke near-perfect English), she needed money and so agreed to tutor him. At their first meeting Watanabe asked if she was Eurasian, and when she quickly admitted that she was American, she noticed that Watanabe "did not look surprised." After a few weeks of tutorials plus some uncomfortable social engagements, he realized that Emily was not involved in anything suspicious and that he could not cultivate her sympathies for the Japanese cause, so he dropped his surveillance. Although partially amused at Watanabe's openly clumsy attempt to gather information, referring to him as her "own private spy," Emily was also understandably unnerved at being the object of a Japanese investigation.[11]

After a few months of unsettled life in her old apartment, the Japanese confiscated the building, so Emily and Carola, after bidding farewell to their Eurasian apartment mates, who managed to get into Free China, found an even more beat-up house to live in. According to Emily, this was when she and the rest of the Hong Kong civilians "settled down" during the Japanese occupation without even realizing it. She had adjusted by developing routines that made life seem normal again, including avoiding the Japanese as much as possible and bringing food to Charles as often as officials allowed. Most of Emily's friends were gone by 1943, either into internment camps or into Free China; her life became increasingly restricted and lonely, and Carola, growing quickly, learned pidgin English, something that particularly horrified Charles.[12]

Finally, Emily decided that the time had come to get out. She had refused the first opportunity of repatriation in 1942 because of Charles's health and because a Japanese official told her that she and Carola would have to go into Camp Stanley for a few weeks prior to repatriation. Nothing, not even the promise of being sent home, could induce her into camp. In the spring of 1942, Japan and the United States had agreed to an exchange of prisoners, with the Japanese allowing members of the State Department plus other nonpermanent American residents in Japan, Manchukuo, and occupied China—including journalists, employees of American businesses, missionaries, students, scholars, and researchers —to repatriate. Emily was surprised to find herself and Carola on that list, because according to Japanese officials she was Chinese, but she reasoned that her work as a journalist and the intervention of friends and family in the United States earned her a place. Still, when the exchange began in June 1942, Emily declined to take part because she could not leave Charles.

However, when rumors circulated that another repatriation ship would arrive in 1943, Charles encouraged her to take Carola back to the United States. His health had improved enough that he had been moved from the hospital to camp, conditions in Hong Kong had rapidly deteriorated, and, more ominously, the Japanese officials who knew and liked Emily and Charles encouraged Emily to get out now. They warned her that life would be tougher for noninterned Caucasians, that she might find both her liberty and life forfeit if she remained, so she finally agreed but insisted on seeing Charles one last time in the Argyle Street camp prison yard. The Japanese sentries made sure that Emily walked quickly along the prison walls, ordering her not to stare into the yard or call out to the men. Oblivious to adult rules, Carola stood up in the departing rickshaw, waved to Charles, and called out, "Daddy, bye-bye!" several times. To Emily's immense relief, the guards did not shoot at them.[13]

In September 1943, she and Carola joined the other repatriates on board the *Teia Maru* until they transferred to the *Gripsholm* at the Portuguese port of Lourenco Marques in Africa for the final leg of their journey to New York. When the ship finally docked in November, Army Intelligence questioned Emily for hours about why she had not been interned. Exhausted from the trip, she quickly grew tired of answering the same questions over and over again; Carola, now two years old, screamed and cried during the interrogation. Only after eight panels of Intelligence officers questioned Emily did they finally accept her explanation that she lied to stay out of internment because "the very idea of being herded behind barbed wire was revolting," that on the outside she could at least help the people on the inside. Her notions of patriotism, motherhood, and "wifely" duties required freedom of movement to ensure survival. It took months for Emily and Carola to adapt to life in the United States, an adjustment complicated by Emily's return as an unapologetic unwed mother, behavior still considered quite scandalous. But like Margaret Sherk with Jerry Sams, Emily believed that her love for Charles mitigated her behavior: true love superceded all else. When she read in a newspaper one day in 1944 of Charles's execution in Camp Stanley for espionage because he helped build a radio, she refused to believe it; her faith was not futile. Charles did indeed survive the war, the couple finally married in 1945, they raised a family, and Emily continued her writing career until her death in 1997.[14]

Gladys Savary stayed out of internment, spending her days helping the Santo Tomas internees and the military prisoners in and around Manila. She later described her activities as not "a story of valorous deeds or battles" but rather "just a tale of a woman, of me, who sort of muddled through it all and lived to carry on."[15] This modest statement masks the risks she took to provide food and information to Allied prisoners and attests to concepts of womanhood and duty: even though "just" women, she and others coped with the Japanese occupation, defying enemy orders to prove their patriotism, to prove that they were survivors.

Gladys Savary, born Gladys Slaughter in Nebraska, attended college in the 1920s but cut short her studies when her father died and her mother became ill. Following her mother's death, Gladys considered her family obligations fulfilled and headed off to Shanghai to visit some friends living there, a trip that whetted her appetite for travel and romance. When her money ran out, she returned to the United States and landed a job in Chicago promoting and coordinating publicity for the Chinese game of mah-jongg, quickly growing popular in America, which she had learned to play in Shanghai. While Gladys worked in Europe advertising the game, the company went bankrupt, so she remained in Paris studying the French language and culture with a tutor, who introduced her to Andre Savary, a young French engineer, and the two married.

The couple lived just outside of Paris for a time until Andre got work on an engineering project in Venezuela, staying there until 1929, when they moved to Culion, a small leper island in the Philippines, where Andre had a job setting up an electrical plant. The Savarys lived on the opposite side of the island from the leper colony, but Gladys routinely went to the settlement to drop off magazines and other treats for the lepers. She found her time in Culion quite "agreeable," but when the electrical plant was finished, the couple moved to Manila to consider their options. As they were having cocktails with some friends in 1932, they decided to open a French restaurant—although neither had any training in the restaurant business—and their small, homey enterprise attracted an influential clientele, quickly becoming a "huge success."[16]

The start of World War II in Europe signaled the beginning of the Savarys' difficulties. Leaving the restaurant in Andre's care in the spring of 1939, Gladys vacationed in Paris, courtesy of some money she had made playing the gold stock market. Although she found the city itself as lovely as ever, she discovered its people "uneasy, unhappy, and fearful. War was in the air, in the minds of everyone." Gladys fortuitously left Paris just before the war started, but shortly after arriving in New York she received a cable from Andre, informing her that he had been called to military service in Indochina. Realizing the important changes that this situation would make in their lives, Gladys quickly made arrangements to return to Manila but did not arrive until November, too late to see Andre off. She soon grew complacent about the likely role of the Philippines in the war, admitting she "became a convert to the popular theory that Japan wouldn't do any attacking of the Philippines because she could just walk into them in 1946 when Philippine independence would become effective." According to Gladys, the next two years before Pearl Harbor were "pleasant."[17]

This pleasant life unraveled during the second half of 1941. That summer the American military evacuated all of its dependents, and numerous civilian families booked passage on ships bound for the United States; in the fall, the remaining American and European women took up bandage rolling and first aid classes. The night before the attack on Pearl Harbor Gladys privately entertained some friends at the restaurant, including a recently promoted British admiral, who prophetically remarked upon parting, "Kids, that's the last fun we'll have together for a long, long time." After learning about Pearl Harbor the next morning, Gladys and her staff began tracking down food supplies to keep the restaurant going and to have enough for themselves. Gladys established a "private canteen" for the American soldiers who patrolled in her neighborhood—while on duty they received coffee and pastry, when they went off duty she gave them "something a bit stronger. Both seem to be appreciated, bless them."[18]

When the Japanese occupied Manila, Gladys remained within the safe confines of her restaurant, which fell into the same Japanese patrol zone as the Bay View Hotel, where some Allied nationals congregated. On January 4, she had her first direct contact with Japanese soldiers when a group of them, accompanied by an interpreter, came into the restaurant asking to use her stoves to cook their food. Gladys's Filipino employees took the opportunity to impress upon those soldiers that their employer was French, not American, as these loyal workers understood that it was "better not to be an American at this moment, a sad commentary on the things that be."[19] The next day, as people from the Bay View lined up in the heat of the day waiting for transport to internment, Gladys gave them cigarettes, beverages, and tinned meat, then prepared food packages for several American boarders who lived above her restaurant and were taken away later that night. Gladys expected to be taken along with her boarders since she possessed an American passport, but the Japanese interpreter helped secure her liberty because he had lived in Manila for years and knew and liked the Savarys. The interpreter insisted that since Andre Savary was French, according to Japanese law so was his wife, so they must be considered members of a friendly nation.

However, Helge Janson, the Swedish consul in Manila and a friend of the Savarys, warned Gladys that her "standing as French was pretty shaky" since many people knew that she had worked for the Free French Committee and knew that Andre fought with the Free French. Gladys decided to settle the question by calling the Vichy French consul. After she explained about her marriage, telling the consul that she had an American passport, he informed her that she had been registered with the French consulate in Manila in 1931 as the wife of a French national, and offered to issue her a French passport. She declined and instead asked for a certified copy of the registry entry, which functioned as her freedom pass throughout the war, although the Japanese felt free to pick her up for questioning every now and again.[20] As important as her freedom was to her, Gladys would not secure it with a passport from a foreign country, even if it was the country of her husband's birth.

Initially, Gladys regretted that she did not insist on internment, because she quickly realized the difficulties of life on the outside, thinking it was not "very smart to be out loose. I should be in camp where decisions would be made for me. I wouldn't be working any harder inside." She also felt that she had betrayed her country by staying out on a nationality loophole, but then she discovered that she could help the internees by using her restaurant contacts and Helge Janson's neutrality to procure food and other supplies for them. On January 14, Gladys "talked" herself into Santo Tomas to secure the release of an ailing friend, assessed the situation in the camp, and observed that the Japanese were not "caring much about the physical comfort of people."[21] If the Japanese refused to care, Gladys felt it was her duty to do so; therefore, nearly every morning she waited in the package line to deliver food and supplies to her friends inside, as well as the laundry she did for some of the internees.

Gladys also kept her restaurant open as a "center for the Americans" who managed to secure release passes from Santo Tomas: pregnant women, mothers with small children, the elderly, and the sick. These Americans made up what Gladys dubbed the Social Pariah Club and patronized the restaurant more for socializing opportunities than for the food, which was decidedly not up to its prewar quality. Camaraderie in these changing times proved vital; in retrospect, Gladys observed that the "first spring was a madhouse, but fun, in a way, compared to the rest of the war." Along with her visits to Santo Tomas and running the restaurant, she also passed messages between the American soldiers still fighting at Corregidor and their wives in Manila, and though this meant

involvement with the underground, Gladys considered the risk worthwhile. She kept very busy, maintained a positive attitude, and believed
that all of the Americans she knew were "full of hope, or pretended to
be. Really, up to the fall of Corregidor, there were people who believed
we had a chance, that the war would soon be finished—in our favor."[22]

That first spring also held myriad uncertainties as to whether Gladys
would be able to remain outside of internment. Just before the fall of
Bataan, the Japanese compelled all French citizens whose names did not
appear on the Vichy consul's roster to report to Santo Tomas for questioning, so Gladys, confidently dressed in her best clothes, went off to
meet her fate. She told the commandant that Andre was off with his
regiment—omitting that he fought for the Free French—and emphasized
that she was the American-born wife of a French citizen, pointing out
that she had been registered with the French consulate since her arrival
in Manila in 1931. The commandant then informed Gladys that she
could stay out of camp "since the conquered nationals were not entitled
to 'protective custody'" by the Japanese. Gladys asserted that she should
be interned because of her U.S. citizenship, but when the commandant
insisted that her marriage to Andre made her ineligible for Japanese
"protection," she went back to her restaurant, determined that as long
as she stayed free she would be "ready to drag a few red herrings across
the Nip path."[23]

In April, when the Japanese finally forced Gladys to turn her restaurant over to them, she felt relieved, because they had been pressuring
her to turn it into a nightclub for their soldiers plus routinely searched
it and the rooms above for evidence that Gladys either profiteered or
harbored enemy nationals. Just before the fall of Corregidor in May, the
Kempetai summoned her to Fort Santiago to answer questions about
one of her French tenants. Although they did not charge her with anything or even treat her roughly, the whole experience left her "with less
fear of the Japanese; they weren't so smart as I thought them. If I could
get away with all I had been doing, then there was no reason I couldn't
get away with more."[24]

Later in May, Gladys moved into a pair of rented houses on Zamora
Street in the Pasay district, then rented out some of the rooms to about
a dozen people who managed to secure temporary passes to stay out of
Santo Tomas. Even without the restaurant her life stayed busy. Americans who used to congregate at her restaurant now gathered at her
houses. In addition, Gladys still sent goods in to more than fifty people
in camp at least three times a week, boasting that she and her helpers

never missed a day. She described the effort that went into these endeavors as a "man-sized job": "The cook and I partially prepared the food the evening before. Reheating of roasts—or of steaks or chops, cooking of them—was done in the early morning. We got up about four-thirty for this, the cook and I. Salads and vegetables were prepared the night before, and desserts. We packed the food in four-tray containers . . . which fitted one above the other into a holder, with a handle. The laundry went out in huge tin pails with covers, as protection against the weather."[25]

Gladys never jeopardized her work for the package line by attempting to hide forbidden messages in the food or laundry containers, because she did not want to risk banishment from the line or another interrogation at Fort Santiago. She did carry notes and news and managed to smuggle money in and out; that the Japanese never nabbed her doing anything illegal Gladys credited to their own limited views about women. She believed that the Japanese had "so little regard for women that they never understood that women could do any harm"; consequently, it "was always the women and girls who made the best contacts with the military prisons." If they were caught, however, their gender did not accord them any special privileges; Gladys knew that the Japanese executed some of the women and girls they apprehended.[26]

During the spring and summer of 1943, Gladys and some of the other women in the Pasay district proved her theory about the effectiveness of women helping military prisoners. When the women saw the several hundred American soldiers billeted at the Pasay Elementary School who were forced to rebuild an airstrip at nearby Nichols Field, they found ways to make the prisoners' lives as comfortable as possible. From their large two-story house at the corner of Fernanda Rein and Park Avenue, American Dorothy Janson, her husband, Helge, and their two young sons observed the soldiers every day—barefoot and clad only in scanty shorts, marched to the airstrip each day, where they worked without rest and little food for twelve hours. Dorothy recalled that the first morning she woke up in the new house she heard a soft repetitive sound that she initially took for rain, but when she looked out of the window, she realized that the noise actually came from shuffling. As she watched the men, "a wave of nausea swept over me when I realized I was looking at Americans, American prisoners walking four abreast in a ragged formation, their heads bent to the rough surface of the road—emaciated, ragged, barefoot."[27] Helge, also appalled at what he saw, vowed that he and Dorothy would find a way to help these men.

First, the Jansons and Gladys concealed food and money in some loose bricks in the school building, confident that the prisoners would find the items. When Dorothy and Gladys saw that the Japanese guards allowed the prisoners to buy food at a local shop, they convinced the owner to let them make the items for the prisoners to purchase. The women made rice cakes, called *bibinkas*, that were chock full of meat, eggs, and sometimes money, and Dorothy recalled that the shop owner also made some with extra ingredients supplied by the neighborhood women. Gladys downplayed the importance of these activities, claiming that the women "could do little that way," yet she acknowledged that they passed along several hundred of these fortified cakes per day to the Americans. Eventually, an elderly American woman named Mrs. Norton secured permission from the Japanese to bring in food, clothing, and medicine to the military prisoners, a concession that encouraged the women to push for as much as they could get, which Gladys labeled "small beginnings toward prisoner relief."[28]

Soon civilians in the district formed a committee that in November 1943 was recognized by the Japanese as the Neutral Welfare Committee, headed by Helge Janson and functioning under the auspices of the International YMCA. However, the new organization found itself tangled in red tape and protocol issues, many of which concerned the Red Cross. Technically, the YMCA provides recreation only while the Red Cross furnishes food, but the Jansons knew that the military prisoners needed food and medicine the most. Working with Red Cross officials, the Jansons, Gladys, and others collected donations of food, medicine, and money from companies and individuals to achieve their goal. Dorothy's responsibilities centered on secretarial work, keeping painstakingly accurate accounts of which items went to each camp and documenting the Neutral Welfare Committee's supply shipments to seven military prison camps in the Manila area during December 1943. At the end of the month, Japanese authorities ordered the committee shut down, claiming a severe food shortage in Manila, but this order was loosely enforced, so the committee continued its work, constantly dealing with the whims of the Japanese military. In April 1944, the Japanese allowed the committee to make weekly deliveries of milk and eggs into Santo Tomas to supplement the children's diets; then, according to Dorothy, on June 7, the day after the Allies launched their successful Normandy invasion in Europe, the Japanese "brusquely advised" Helge to cease all activities. The Neutral Welfare Committee was out of business.[29]

While Gladys and Dorothy spent much of their "free" time helping those imprisoned, they knew of another group of American women who managed to stay out of internment, but in this rare instance their motives appear to be selfish. These young women, none of whom has apparently written an autobiography, lived nearby on Cuneta Street and spent their time entertaining Japanese officers. Of this ostensible collaboration, Gladys commented that, while it really was not any of her business, the behavior of the women did seem "slightly scandalous" and meant "loss of face for Americans in general." Dorothy had known some of these Cuneta Street women prior to the war; while she did not condone their behavior, she believed that they at least did not spy for the Japanese. She could just tolerate the fraternization, perhaps passing it off as youthful indiscretion, but could not abide the thought that these women were totally disregarding patriotic American womanhood by drinking, flirting, and passing valuable information to the enemy. When a list was drawn up for the second repatriation on board the *Gripsholm* in the fall of 1943, the names of all the "Cuneta Cuties," as Gladys and Dorothy referred to them, were on it. Gladys described a cartoon about the repatriation ship, which showed a group of aged and sick people staring longingly at a vessel called the *Puta Maru* as attractive young women walked up the gangplank. Gladys, declining to explain the meaning of puta, found it a "good joke, slightly vulgar, but we all laughed."[30] Americans could always find humor in any situation.

Humor gave way to boredom and then near-starvation when the Japanese military took control of the civilian camps in early 1944, shut down the package line at Santo Tomas, revoked almost all of the passes from the camp, and forced most of Gladys's tenants to reenter internment. Since she had little to do besides read and tend her garden, she also established a kindergarten for the children in the neighborhood, something that allowed her to feel useful. Yet her relative inactivity led her to develop a guilty conscience over her various "comforts": a private home, freedom to move about in Manila, and an adequate food supply. After September 21, 1944, when American forces began bombing Manila as a prelude to invasion, Gladys, living so close to Nichols Airfield, began spending her days responding to air raid sirens by hiding herself and her pupils in a well-padded nook under her stairway. The next month officers of the Japanese navy took over her rented houses, and, unable to find suitable accommodations on such short notice, she moved in with the Jansons. Gladys and Dorothy, proud Americans now virtually assured of victory, could scarcely contain their glee at the advances of the Americans, especially the invasion of Leyte in October. Helge had to be more circumspect since he functioned as the representative of a neutral country, and Gladys recalled that she and Dorothy "gave him some bad moments . . . in our rash exuberance."[31]

Anxious for war news, Gladys and the Jansons listened to the newly established Voice of Freedom from Leyte even though the Japanese forbade it. As the war moved into its final months, they all worried about what would happen to Manila when the Japanese finally made their last stand, watching furtively as Japanese troops laid mines and other traps throughout the city, strategies designed to delay the American advance. Helge's position as the representative of a neutral country afforded his household protection from confiscation or looting by the Japanese, but the rest of Manila exploded in chaos. The Kempetai picked up more and more civilians for questioning, many of whom simply disappeared; they even picked up and interrogated Helge several times but always released him. Those last months of the war prior to the arrival of the Americans were emotional ones. Gladys found that Dorothy often got "teary round the lashes," but Gladys did not cry; in fact, she claimed that she had "shed very few tears these last three years, and mostly of rage. We can shed a few of joy soon."[32]

Danger and fear came sooner than the tears of joy. During January and the early days of February 1945, Manilans remained in the midst of a hot war zone as the Japanese set fire to entire sections of the city, determinedly pursuing a scorched earth policy. Several times Japanese soldiers threw lighted paper over the wall surrounding the Janson home, so Gladys and the Jansons dug ditches in the front garden to contain any fires that might spread. The rapid repeats of machine guns could be heard from everywhere, tanks rumbled down the streets, and mobs of Japanese and Filipinos looted everything that they possibly could, including roofs and bathroom fixtures. Gladys could no longer safely leave her small enclave. When the Japanese cut off water, gas, and electricity, she and the Jansons spent more and more of their time in the air raid shelter. On February 10, they heard a battle between the Japanese and the guerrillas rage just outside their wall that frightened them so much they all made their wills and prepared to evacuate the house should the skirmish push through. Gladys heard so much noise that she could not "distinguish between Japanese gunfire, American gunfire, shells, bombs, 22's, soixante-quinzes, or demolition explosions," but she admitted that she could recognize "a real rifle bullet if it is near enough to me."[33]

Despite the fierce battle, the group did not evacuate their home, and they watched with relief and awe as American troops from the 11th Airborne arrived the next day. After hearing excited shouts from a neighbor that there were American soldiers on Park Avenue, Gladys and Dorothy rushed out to see what they had longed for these three years. But when they saw yellow-skinned soldiers wearing strange uniforms, they turned to run back toward the house, convinced that these were in fact Japanese soldiers. The strange-looking soldiers then hailed the women, "Hey you, are youse Americans?" Gladys and Dorothy paused and looked back again, and Gladys rejoiced that "it isn't Japs. It's Brooklyn!" Deprived of American newspapers and magazines during the war, the women had never seen paratroopers' uniforms, nor did they know that a new antimalaria drug called Atabrine turned complexions yellow.[34] While the battle for Manila continued, American troops secured the Pasay district, making Gladys and the Jansons safe. Although the Jansons survived with their family intact, Gladys became one of the millions of war widows—she was unable to find out exactly what happened to Andre in Indochina; he never returned home.

While Gladys and Dorothy did everything in their power to help those imprisoned, another American woman found life in Japanese-occupied Manila so difficult that she could only manage to keep herself and her family alive and well. Sofia De Mos Adamson stayed out of internment because of her husband's nationality, but, unlike Gladys and Dorothy, she spent her days primarily ensuring her own survival and that of her family. Aiding those less fortunate or expressing patriotism took a decided backseat. Sofia arrived in Manila with her new husband, George Adamson, a Greek national, in May 1939. George's family ran the Adamson School of Industrial Chemistry, which specialized in training Filipinos in how to set up small industries that required chemical knowledge such as soap making or tanning, and George served as the dean of the College of Engineering. The school ensured the family a place in the upper echelon of Manila society, entitling Sofia to a whirl of nighttime social activities, but during the day she used her UCLA training to develop and teach a variety of education courses at the school. In October 1941, her life changed direction when two friends from the USAFFE convinced her to take a civilian clerk position with the army, arguing that it was Sofia's patriotic duty, "that able American women on the staff would release enlisted men from office work for service in the field." Sofia willingly gave up her teaching job, which she had found too strenuous, to work half days for the USAFFE at Fort

Santiago, later used by the Japanese for interrogation, torture, and imprisonment of their enemies.[35]

Despite her daily interaction with the military, Sofia was unprepared for Pearl Harbor and the subsequent swift, stunning victories of the Japanese. She and George decided that the safest thing to do was to stay in their flat in the Michel Apartments, because they believed that their fifth-floor residence served as a good protection against flying debris from bombs. The couple remained virtually sequestered there for the first weeks of the war, enjoying occasional visits from members of George's family and from Sofia's mother, who, along with Sofia's stepfather, had arrived shortly before the war, opening a candy store to earn a living. So during the first days of the war Sofia drew comfort and support from her mother, husband, and in-laws. In mid-December, the USAFFE reassigned Sofia and six other civilian clerks to Sternberg General Hospital, where officers believed the women would be safe; the soldiers Sofia worked with at Fort Santiago went off to Bataan. As both Christmas and the Japanese approached at the end of December 1941, Sofia's mother, concerned for her safety, tried to convince her to quit her job and stay home, but Sofia refused, telling her mother that to do so "would be desertion. Even if we're not doing anything but ducking bombs, I've got to stay with my job!"[36]

However, by New Year's Day 1942, as Manilans waited anxiously for the Japanese to arrive, the Adamsons' friends began to recombine into large family units for better protection, gazing with incomprehension as looters took advantage of the chaos, carrying off anything they could from private homes and businesses. On January 2, when the Japanese occupied Manila, the streets fell eerily silent; no one dared go out. A resident of the Michel Apartments advised George to hide Sofia somewhere in the apartment when the Japanese arrived, to show them only his Greek passport, and to simply say that he had a wife since, according to Japanese law, Sofia was Greek. The Adamsons took this advice, then watched from their window as the Japanese took their American neighbors away in a truck, leaving Sofia relieved that the Japanese allowed her mother to stay out of internment to care for her elderly, ill husband.

Sofia's uninterned life was not trouble-free. Like Gladys Savary, the Japanese scrutinized her citizenship, and at the end of April 1942, they summoned Sofia to their headquarters to prove that she was married to a Greek citizen. Armed with a marriage certificate from the Greek Orthodox Church plus a phony certificate with the forged signature of the Archbishop of Athenagoras created by her mother, Sofia managed to convince her questioner that she was entitled to an exemption from internment. Soon, however, the Japanese required all "Third Party Enemy Aliens" to report to the Bay View Hotel for registration; when George reported as ordered, officials told him that he and Sofia were to each pack one piece of luggage and go to Santo Tomas the next day. Instead of interning them, however, the Japanese issued the couple red armbands identifying them as Greek citizens and instructed them to come back again the following month, but Japanese officials never pursued the matter further.[37]

With the Adamsons' position outside of internment more secure, they planned their survival in the occupied city. Sofia's mother began to make and sell cornmeal muffins, while George figured out a way to easily grind corn into flour that he and Sofia bagged and sold as "Royal Corn Meal," a popular commodity since white flour had all but vanished from Manila. After several months, when the corn supply disappeared as well, the Adamsons rented out their grinding equipment to anyone who needed to grind up food staples such as coffee and rice, with the couple taking a portion of the items in payment, thereby assuring themselves a constant supply of foodstuffs. Sofia emphasized that they dealt fairly with their customers so they would not be accused of profiteering, a crime that could land them in Fort Santiago. The business ensured the survival of the family by providing them with food, but they also used it to help the military prisoners—when the Japanese brought corn to be ground for the prisoners, the Adamsons mixed in extra vitamins and hid vials of medicine in the sacks. In addition to helping with the grinding, Sofia established a school for children of the Third Party Enemy Aliens, where she taught English grammar and composition, mathematics, and algebra to the older children, plus shorthand as a specialty course. Sofia especially appreciated this work, because she "desperately needed" something to keep her mind occupied, admitting that the "money was welcome, too."[38]

The Adamsons did not work as selflessly as Gladys Savary and Dorothy and Helge Janson to help the American prisoners, but they helped when they could, suffering more severely at the end of the war despite their close family ties. George's relatives lived in Manila and worked at the Adamson School, so during the war they pooled their efforts and resources to make sure that the entire family survived. Mother-daughter closeness became emotional and stressful when Sofia's mother fell ill with breast cancer, quickly succumbing, and while adjusting to that loss, the rest of Sofia's life began to change as well. As American forces battled their way into Manila in February 1945, Sofia and George did not find a safe place to hide. Sofia first sustained a deep shoulder laceration plus multiple shrapnel wounds on her arms and back, and a sniper's bullet grazed George's thigh as he attempted to find help; during a bombing raid Sofia broke her leg, and George received a serious neck wound. On February 15, as the two waited for medical attention, American troops reached their neighborhood, so Sofia finally pulled out the army dog tag that she had hidden in her shirt pocket, the tag issued to her when she took the clerical job with the USAFFE in October 1941. She showed it to one of the soldiers who, upon reading it, shouted, "There's an American girl here. We've got to get her out of here."[39] He arranged for the couple's immediate evacuation first to an aid station, then on to the 54th Field Hospital. Sofia, who weighed seventy-five pounds at this time, spent a month there before transferring to yet another hospital, where she remained until she and George were repatriated to the United States in April.

American women sought out and exploited loopholes in Japanese regulations regarding definitions of nationality, loopholes they used to stay out of internment so they could aid the war effort, provide comfort to Allied prisoners, or better ensure their families' survival. Claire Phillips and Margaret Utinsky, bold, purposeful, and angered at the loss of their beloved husbands, falsified identity papers so they could stay out of Santo Tomas and spy on the Japanese and help military prisoners. Gladys Savary and Dorothy Janson used their spousal exemptions to send food and supplies to military and civilian prisoners, sometimes breaking established Japanese rules, while Sofia Adamson used her exemption to keep her family alive and well but still did what she could to help the prisoners. All of these women at times flouted Japanese regulations, risking punishment and internment in order to do what they thought was right. They drew strength from their identity as Americans even if they could best express their patriotism by denying or obscuring their nationality in order to participate in actions that would best reveal it. A deep love for family was intertwined with the patriotism of these women; they did whatever was necessary to help the loved ones in their immediate family and in their adoptive family of guerrillas and prisoners. Their planning, hard work, and suffering eventually paid off when they were liberated.

7

RESCUE AND ITS AFTERMATH

"Some day the Americans will come."

Every evening while interned in Baguio, Ethel Herold and her daughter, Betsy, ended their goodnights to each other with the confident statement, "Some day the Americans will come."[1] No matter how difficult or boring their day had been they never forgot to reinforce this hope to each other before they drifted off into a sleep that would prepare them for another day of captivity under the Japanese. The Herold women's simple statement encouraged them to believe that maybe the next day would be their last as prisoners, that tomorrow would be the day American troops would finally arrive to liberate them.

The final months of internment proved critical for the Americans in terms of survival, liberation meant exhilaration and danger because of escalating warfare, while freedom required thoughtful consideration of the immediate future. After years of negotiating traditional norms of womanhood and motherhood to meet the realities of internment, American women faced going home to friends and family who might not understand the reasons for those alterations. For some of these women, writing their stories provided the necessary explanations and helped them develop a perspective on their wartime experiences.

THE LIBERATION OF SANTO TOMAS

General Douglas MacArthur was determined to liberate Luzon as the U.S. military cut a bloody swath through the South Pacific, toward Formosa and then Japan. In a July 1944 meeting at Pearl Harbor, when Admiral Chester Nimitz suggested that perhaps Luzon was not a military necessity and that other areas in the Philippines could be secured more easily, MacArthur lectured President Roosevelt and Nimitz for three hours on the "moral and strategic reasons for proceeding with the conquest of Luzon." MacArthur, unable to save Luzon at the beginning of the war and evacuating to Australia as the USAFFE prepared to surrender, needed to atone. The liberation of Luzon began with the battle for Leyte on October 20, 1944, which provided MacArthur the opportunity for his "I have returned!" statement, and the fight continued, fullblown and ruthless, over the next few months. From Leyte, where the Japanese lost most of their air and sea power, MacArthur invaded Mindoro, laid airstrips, then set his sights on Luzon. By late January 1945, the 37th Division and the 1st Cavalry were racing toward Manila for one of the most horrific battles of the Pacific theater. Intelligence reports informed MacArthur of the necessity of liberating the military and civilian prisoners in the area since they were in poor health, plus rumors abounded that the Japanese intended to massacre them before American troops arrived.[2]

Indeed, the last months of captivity proved especially difficult for the internees, both physically and emotionally. By the end of 1944, most Santo Tomas internees had used up all of their extra food provisions, so the camp kitchen had to feed more people than ever at a time when food was scarce on Luzon. Anything available was poor in quality and astronomically expensive; to make matters worse, in mid-November the Japanese twice cut the internees' rice ration. Around this time Frieda Magnuson signed a promissory note for one thousand American dollars to purchase, through outside contacts, two kilos of rice, one kilo of brown sugar, and two kilos of mongo beans. One of the camp doctors told her that her husband, Chet, suffering from beriberi, would die without this extra food and that she needed the extra strength to take care of her two young daughters. The doctor told Frieda to divide up the food between herself and Chet, since the girls seemed healthy enough to get along without it. Frieda, who considered herself a good and devoted mother, found this task so difficult that she and Chet waited until their daughters fell asleep before they ate "an infinitesimal amount of the ambrosia."[3]

Tressa Roka, who had a daily bird's-eye view of the effects of malnutrition because of her hospital work, recorded each ration cut in her diary as well as the daily death tolls. On December 10, 1944, she observed a "peculiar though understandable mania" that developed in Santo Tomas: men, women, and even children spent hours each day exchanging and copying recipes. If they could not eat food, they could talk about it and plan it, which Tressa found counterproductive, "the cruelest form of torture," firmly believing that the Japanese intended to starve the internees to death.[4]

Beginning in November 1944, actions of Japanese officials in Santo Tomas appeared both bizarre and threatening: increased raids of living quarters, confiscation of contraband money hoarded to purchase food, punishment of anyone caught looking at American planes, and refusal to hand out new Red Cross parcels rumored to have arrived. Then, without warning, on January 5, 1945, the Japanese arrested three men of the Executive Committee—Carroll Grinnell, Alfred Duggleby, and C. L. Larson—and took them out of camp. Officials refused to say what the men were charged with or where they had been taken, causing the internees to fear, unfortunately correctly, that the men would be executed. Two days later, the Japanese prepared to pull out of the camp, to leave it unguarded when the American troops finally reached it, in order to prevent innocent bloodshed. Tressa watched with anticipation as they "packed food and other supplies into trucks. They burned papers and barked last-minute orders to subordinates." But at the last minute they changed their minds and stayed, determined to fight to the bitter end for control of Luzon, leaving Santo Tomas internees caught in the middle.[5]

Everyone knew it was just a matter of time before the Americans arrived, but the final month of waiting proved excruciating, as they feared they would be dead before liberation. On January 21, Japanese officials decreed that all internees, except for the bedridden, had to attend the twice-daily roll call in person, further sapping their strength. Enforced roll call also put the internees in a vulnerable position, because while grouped together, the Japanese could easily open fire and kill them. And by this time, tempers were short; internees sniped at each other, and family members fought more frequently. Elizabeth Vaughan had been a prolific diarist throughout the war, but as conditions rapidly deteriorated her entries became brief and sporadic. On New Year's Day 1945, she wrote a short, heartbreaking account of internees who swept up rice that had spilled out onto the road from a broken sack; a few hours later children were "still gathering a few grains mixed in sand." Nothing vaguely resembling food could be wasted because it meant life.[6]

Emily Van Sickle recalled that February 3, 1945, started off like most other days, with one peculiar exception: American planes continually flew over Santo Tomas but without bombing or strafing. At about seven o'clock that night, Emily heard gunfire outside of the camp walls; at first she paid no attention because guards often shot at real or imagined threats on the outside. But soon it became evident that the shots were not sporadic; they were sustained and then intensified. Internees, hoping to find out what was going on, dashed around the campus as rumors flew, but Emily's husband, Van, instructed her to stay in their shanty until he brought news. When she heard shouts that the Japanese had left the camp and the Americans had arrived, she left the shanty to see for herself, running right into Van, who told her it was all true, that he had just talked to an American soldier. Emily found that her "joyful thoughts were too turbulent for articulation" at that point; she watched in stunned silence as the 1st Cavalry took over Santo Tomas.[7]

Tressa Roka clearly remembered the frenzied activity during the early evening of February 3. In the midst of a dazzling sunset, American planes flew low over the camp, so low that the internees could see the pilots in their cockpits, one of whom threw out a pair of goggles containing the message, "Roll out the barrel, Christmas will be either today or tomorrow!" Denny Williams remembered that the message "went around the camp like electricity"; when she heard all of the noise, she had a feeling that liberation had come. For the next several hours, Tressa and her fiancé, Catesy, joined in with the other internees who "watched, waited, prayed, and listened with trembling excitement" to everything going on in and around the camp. Then Tressa noticed that the sky lit up "like a giant Christmas tree" from flares, and Denny watched in awe as the 1st Cavalry's "metallic monster tore through the sawali fence." Even as Tressa saw the soldiers arrive, she could not quite believe that this finally meant liberation: "Not until we saw the American flag draped over the lead tank did we really believe that, at last, the realization of a beautiful dream had materialized." For Denny liberation was "like Christmas and the Fourth of July on the same day."[8]

Although some of the Japanese surrendered immediately, more than sixty fled to the Education Building, taking over the second floor and holding about two hundred hostages, mostly men and boys. Emily and Van went back to their shanty, where they spent a pleasantly sleepless night discussing the courageous, self-assured American soldiers, while the "realization of our sudden freedom flooded away all weariness." Early the next morning American troops ordered the Van Sickles and other shanty-dwellers to move to the Main Building for safety; since the Japanese still occupied the Education Building, the American military predicted a fight to get them out and wanted as few casualties as possible. The Japanese finally agreed to leave the building on February 5, when the Americans allowed them to depart unmolested from the campus with their side arms, a concession that outraged most of the internees. But the enemy did not go unpunished: Filipino guerrillas tracked and killed them in Manila.[9]

The food situation immediately improved as the former internees raided the Japanese warehouse for additional rations the very night American troops arrived. The day after liberation the American military sent in trucks filled with food and other supplies, and Alice Bryant marveled that the army "came equipped for everything," especially brooms, which she described "as symbolic to me as the Stars and Stripes." Although these cleaning luxuries dazzled Alice, she and others delighted in the improved and increased amounts of food. The day after liberation the camp kitchen served a "Star Spangled Luncheon" of kidney bean stew followed by a "Star Spangled Dinner" of soy bean stew, prompting Emily Van Sickle to point out that the "old army chow that G.I.s loathed tasted like ambrosia to us." Frieda Magnuson's attention immediately focused on food after the 1st Cavalry occupied the camp; she and Chet cooked the remainder of their rice, their friends the Karrers brought over their last can of corned beef, and they all shared this bounty. Despite this abundance, Frieda's first question to an American soldier was: "What [d]o you think we will have for breakfast?" She recalled that even as American troops fired at the Japanese in the Education Building, the internees set up cook fires and "feasted" on into the night.[10]

As safe as Emily Van Sickle felt with the presence of the 1st Cavalry, she was astonished to find out that Santo Tomas was the only free section of Manila, and Alice Bryant admitted that the internees initially did not understand how daring a rescue the 1st Cavalry had mounted. With Manila still securely in enemy hands, seven hundred members of the 1st Cavalry, joined by the "wildest looking" guerrillas, sped down from the Lingayen Gulf, skirted the Japanese, and took the camp guards by surprise. The American military believed that this maneuver was the only way of saving the lives of the internees, because if the Japanese had had advance knowledge of the Americans' arrival, they would have slaughtered the inmates. Outside the camp walls, the battle for Manila continued, as some twenty thousand Japanese troops burned entire sections of the city and massacred thousands of civilians. According to Alice, the Japanese went through Manila "blowing up bridges and buildings, setting fire to [allegedly] inflammable houses and machine gunning people of all nationalities who ran out of them."[11]

One of the more notable events of the days immediately following liberation was a visit by General MacArthur on February 7. Such a huge crowd gathered that Frieda Magnuson hoisted her daughter, Susan, on her shoulders so that the little girl could see him, watching together as MacArthur stood on the steps of the Main Building to announce, "I have returned!" Denny Williams, who found the whole spectacle "wonderful to watch," recalled that the huge cheer from the crowd that greeted the general was only "silenced by an enemy shell bursting nearby."[12] During his short speech he promised that he would come back the next day for a flag-raising ceremony, but according to Frieda this did not occur until February 27, and MacArthur did not attend. Nevertheless, most of the internees found it touching that he came to the camp to personally check on their welfare.

After three years without overseas correspondence, liberation meant that internees could finally send and receive mail, so Emily Van Sickle spent a few days getting caught up on world and home news. The Red Cross brought in bundles of letters the day MacArthur visited, most of which had been written back in October when the invasion of the Philippines began, and Emily eagerly read and then wrote letters home. Alice Bryant claimed that the only thing she was "keenly interested in" besides food was mail. She received a variety of letters, the most important of which came from her brother, who informed her that her daughter Imogene was thriving in the United States, and she dashed off some in response, which the Red Cross mailed out that very evening.[13]

In the midst of such basic human comforts as food, mail, and news, Emily expressed astonishment at Santo Tomas's transformation from a civilian internment camp to a military one, with soldiers and military equipment everywhere. Internees had to learn a new vocabulary to get along in this altered environment—Frieda Magnuson recalled that the soldiers found it "amusing" that the internees had never heard the term "G.I." Tressa Roka could not get enough of just looking at the soldiers, thinking how "wonderful those boys looked to us! Their presence acted as a heady wine and we couldn't seem to get our fill." Young single girls, especially, welcomed these healthy men, and quick courtships ensued. The women also delighted in the courteous way that the soldiers treated the internees; according to Alice Bryant, "Our own mothers could not have been more kind and gentle to us than were the soldiers." She viewed liberation in terms of a large family reunion, something that benefited both the internees and the soldiers: "In rescuing us from our isolation they [the soldiers] had redeemed a part of Uncle Sam's family. After months of loneliness and nostalgia in a foreign jungle, they seemed back among their relatives; and the American women and children around them gave them the impression of really being at home."[14]

In addition to these positive changes, the internees had to get used to living in a hot war zone, because on February 7, the Japanese began heavy shelling of Santo Tomas and its surroundings. Casualties in the Main Building ran especially high: fifteen internees who had struggled through almost three years of captivity lost their lives the first morning of the shelling, and another ninety were wounded. Before the battle ended, thirty-two internees died, with about two hundred wounded. Little Susan Magnuson, napping in a room in that building, was one of the first injured, suffering a shrapnel graze on her rear end plus, more seriously, shell shock. Her sister, Karen, was hospitalized with dysentery and their father, Chet, with beriberi. Karen and Chet managed to transfer to an outside hospital, while Frieda and Susan, the healthiest Magnusons, remained in the camp dodging bullets and bombs. Alice Bryant had a few close calls with falling concrete from the roof of the Main Building but secured a safe place in the corner of one of the women's bathrooms, which served as her refuge during shelling. The Van Sickles, huddled in an air raid shelter they constructed, eventually decided to take their chances inside the Main Building, now overcrowded with other former shanty dwellers. Emily, sickened by all of the new food she had been eating over the past few days, had to restrict her intake to liquids, a real frustration in the face of longed-for delicacies, but her system readjusted itself within days. Her problem was common to the majority of internees: faced with an abundance of food, their bodies rebelled and then adapted; many put on twenty pounds within three weeks.

Van, however, got sicker throughout February. Despite the improved food he did not gain weight, suffered from asthma, then developed heat exhaustion, so the Van Sickles were among the first sent home, leaving Manila by plane on March 9 to head for Leyte, where they boarded a ship for the United States. The couple settled in New Martinsville, West Virginia, but Van never fully recovered from the health problems that developed during internment and died in 1954. Emily subsequently moved to Washington, D.C., where she took a job at American University, eventually writing a memoir of the war years. Internment taught her "that no nation or race holds a monopoly on virtue; that all individuals of all races and nations can be valiant or cowardly, kind or cruel, just or grossly unjust; that evil triumphs when just men grow weak and complacent." Emily also learned never to take freedom for granted and offered up hope "that the whole world may some day truly live in peace."[15]

Elizabeth Vaughan and her children, Clay and Beth, were also among that first repatriation group because of the young ages of the children. A widow now that her husband, Jim, lay buried with hundreds of others in a military prison graveyard, Elizabeth weighed ninety pounds and had to be careful of what she ate. When the family arrived on Leyte to wait for transportation home, Beth suffered from a centipede sting and Clay from a vaccination fever, but the children spent most of their time frolicking with the soldiers. Before departing on March 18, Elizabeth recorded in her diary, without additional comment, that she had to sign a promissory note for the cost of their passage home. The Vaughans arrived in San Francisco on April 8; after visiting and recuperating with family members in California and Georgia, Elizabeth decided it was time to get on with her life. Always an untraditional woman for her time, she knew she had to support herself and the children, so she enrolled in the Ph.D. program in sociology at the University of North Carolina, where she wrote a dissertation based on her camp experiences. Elizabeth, who never remarried, taught sociology at the college level until 1957, when advanced breast cancer forced her into early retirement; she died that year.

Tressa Roka and Catesy decided to stay in Manila—despite military advice to leave—because Catesy believed that he could rebuild what he lost during the war. He went to work for the army, using his prewar contacts to supply much-needed pharmaceuticals to the Philippines, plus he attempted to reestablish his own drug company. During the month after liberation, Tressa tracked down her ever-hopeful suitor, Mr. Nagy, to repay him for his kindness while she was interned. She found the elderly Hungarian gentleman in a hospital suffering from tuberculosis; she did what she could to help him until he died a peaceful death later in the spring. Tressa spent the rest of her time trying to find a new home, eventually managing to find a house that she and Catesy arranged to share with another man. Housing was scarce in Manila, so Tressa felt lucky to find a place even in a section of the city considered marginally acceptable; several times after they moved in, Tressa had to chase away soldiers and sailors who mistook the residence for a house of prostitution.

Tressa's long-delayed wedding finally took place on June 24, 1945, when an army chaplain married her and Catesy inside the ruins of a local church. Tressa wore a housecoat made with "yards and yards of fragile ivy-colored Peiping gauze shot with a delicate bamboo pattern over peach taffeta" that she had purchased in China in 1940 and kept carefully preserved under her bed in Santo Tomas. The newlyweds opted to honeymoon in the United States, but because of a shortage of transportation, they sailed on separate ships. In retrospect, Tressa claimed that she and Catesy "do not regret our three years of internment," because they both managed to totally recover from the health problems they developed in camp. She believed that internment brought the two of them closer together, caused them to "appreciate the little things in life" like a loaf of bread and a glass of milk, but most of all, "made us appreciate our freedom, our blessed freedom that we all take for granted."[16]

As the Bryants left Manila on April 9, 1945, Alice eagerly anticipated their reunion with their daughter, Imogene, but she also worried about her husband, who contracted pneumonia in March; even with the help of sulfa drugs and penicillin it took him a month to recover. Because of William's ill health, the couple traveled back to the United States on what they were told was a hospital ship but was, according to Alice, a Norwegian freighter with some special berths. As happy as she felt at the thought of seeing her daughter, she regretted leaving the Philippines, which had been her home for so long; to her, repatriation did not mark a "proper ending" to her life there—she always had the nagging feeling of unfinished business. The Bryants arrived in San Francisco on May 14, thirteen-year-old Imogene met them later in Los Angeles, and the reunited family traveled to Seattle to the home of Alice's father to begin their postwar life.[17]

Writing her memoir within two years after her return home, Alice expressed a general tone of forgiveness. She had no long-term ill effects from the war but had missed several years of her daughter's life and needed to catch up on those; when they met again in Los Angeles, Imogene was a "lovely daughter," whom Alice did not recognize. In the end, despite the deprivations of internment, Alice proclaimed a strict separation between civilian and military, observing that she had experienced a "rather peaceful war. . . . I did not have to fight, I did not have to hate."[18]

The Magnusons had to wait a bit longer for repatriation because, even though they had two young daughters, the family stayed basically healthy and so had no pressing reason to leave. In May 1945, they traveled on a converted troop transport, the SS *John Lykes*, with four hundred former internees plus troops. To Frieda, finally visiting family in Washington and Oregon "was all wonderful but somehow seemed unreal. The real us were back in Manila with our soldiers and fellow internees." The family settled in a rented ranch house in Los Altos, California, Chet went back to work in San Francisco, and they lived much like other middle-class families, counting ration coupons and waiting for the end of the war. For a time, though, they were "celebrities wherever we went," with various local groups asking Frieda to speak about her experiences. When the war finally ended, the Magnusons moved to San Francisco, but their troubles were not over: Chet developed hepatitis and then had a nervous breakdown, and Susan and Karen remained "nervous" children for a few years. Frieda, who did not admit to any ills, spent most of her time taking care of her family and tracking down the one household item she longed for—an automatic washing machine—which she finally bought in 1947. She fell back into the suburban wife and mother roles as if internment had never happened. The following year Chet's company transferred him to Peru, and he uprooted the entire family again, because separation seemed unthinkable after everything they had been through. Looking back on her experiences, Frieda concluded that "the ability to cope comes forth when needed and . . . there are more good people than bad (we are all a mixture of both) in this world."[19]

Denny Williams worked her way through the first days of liberation. Casualties mounted because of heavy Japanese shelling, so she went back to the hospital to help, which provided support during a dark period of uncertainty as she tried to get word of her imprisoned husband, Bill. Shortly after liberation, Mann Yancey, one of Denny's in-laws, tracked her down, bringing the unwelcome news that when the 6th Rangers emancipated Cabanatuan on January 30, they found it empty. He told Denny that the prisoners had probably been transferred to Bilibid Prison, and if so, Bill was undoubtedly there, but with the battle still raging Denny knew that it would be awhile before she could find out. So she worked. A new army doctor suggested that she "slack off" since she had done so much while in ill health, losing more than sixty pounds during the war, but Denny told him that she and the rest of the nurses were "too keyed up, too happy. Why, we wouldn't know what to do with ourselves." As she nursed both civilians and soldiers, trying to keep busy without losing sight of her priorities, she asked each of the soldiers if they had encountered a man named Bill Williams. None had.[20]

Dr. Richard Whitely brought additional, inconclusive news a few days later. Whitely, a surgeon and survivor of the Bataan death march who had been imprisoned in Cabanatuan with Bill, told Denny that Bill had been transferred out of Cabanatuan sometime before last Christmas, sent to either Formosa or Tokyo. Because of this information, Denny finally began looking forward to going home to wait for word of the release of the remainder of American prisoners. On February 11, 1945, she learned that the army nurses were to be flown home, a service not accorded to the civilians, and Lieutenant Nola Forrest, in charge of the replacement nurses, informed the sixty-seven captured nurses that each would receive a promotion, a Presidential Citation, and the Bronze Star. Denny felt proud and happy about these awards, but her concern about Bill overshadowed everything else; she felt "no grief" over leaving Santo Tomas. Her hopes for the future shattered when she learned that Bill had died on board the Japanese prisoner-of-war ship *Encura Maru* on January 9, 1945, when American bombers hit it while anchored in the Formosa harbor, making him one of over four thousand Allied prisoners who perished in an unmarked "hell ship." Denny continued her nursing career with the army, retiring as a lieutenant colonel, and eventually wrote a book about her wartime experiences, which did not end with messages of kindness and optimism for humanity. Denny, who never married again, died after a lengthy illness in 1997.[21]

THE DRAMATIC LOS BANOS RESCUE

In Los Banos, liberation did not come for more than two weeks after the Americans secured Santo Tomas, but the Japanese actually pulled out of the camp for a week beginning on January 7, 1945, because they believed in an imminent American invasion. Margaret Sherk and Jerry Sams, who had been sharing living quarters since Margaret's last serious illness just before Christmas, awoke that morning to loud shouts from other internees, cheering that the Japanese had retreated. Jerry, a crack radio technician responsible for hiding a contraband radio in camp, brought the device out into the open so that everyone could listen to news broadcasts from KGEI in San Francisco. At six o'clock that morning, the internees convened a camp meeting, first playing "The Star Spangled Banner," then raising an American flag above the barracks. For Margaret, the words to the national anthem had "never been so significant, and the flag which had been kept hidden somewhere has never looked so proud or meant so much." As they waited for the American military, internee officials decided to allot double rations to everyone with food looted from the guards' quarters, and for the next six days the internees ate amounts of food they had only dreamed of. Their euphoria was short-lived—instead of graciously welcoming their liberators, the internees watched with heavy hearts as their captors returned, presumably to make their final stand against the American military.[22]

During the next few weeks, the internees subsisted one step from death by starvation as Japanese camp officials, humiliated by their abrupt departure and return, took their frustrations out on the internees by doing nothing to ease their hunger. Dorothy Still, close to collapse from a lack of food and from working her hospital night shift, realized one evening that she could not detect her breathing or her heartbeat. She thought this "pleasant feeling" was death, but it turned out to be either a dream or wishful thinking, because her heart began beating again. Margaret Sherk, also fatigued and starving, observed that internees ingested anything remotely edible in an attempt to stave off the gnawing hunger: pigweed, papaya trees, green bananas and banana skins, slugs (which she "could [never] have eaten under any circumstances"), and cats and dogs. According to Grace Nash, "Slow starvation cannot be described. To be understood it must be felt." Almost everyone's conversation revolved around food, food they remembered from better times, food they dreamed of eating once again, and Grace recalled that at bedtime her sons, Stan and Gale, only wanted to hear stories about food. Children no longer played. Margaret forbade her son, David, to play because it took too much energy, and she "could not stand having him watch every bite of food I put in my mouth." As of February 21, the internees' daily food ration consisted of a handful of unhusked rice per person; through the camp fence they saw trees laden with bananas but knew the Japanese guards would shoot them if they tried to snatch the life-sustaining fruit. Estimating that their average daily caloric intake had fallen below nine hundred calories, Grace speculated whether any of them could live for much longer. Virtually all movement in the camp ceased.[23]

Recognizing the desperate situation, Margaret Sherk and Jerry Sams decided to tempt fate and, with their children, hop the fence and take their chances evading the Japanese until they could reach American troops. They figured that even if they got shot while going over the fence, that kind of quick death was better than slow starvation. After the couple laid their plans, Jerry contracted bacillary dysentery, which delayed their breakout; on February 21, they made their final plans. Concerned that young Gerry Ann would cry as they went over the fence, Margaret arranged a sedative shot for her, which sent the baby into a two-hour crying jag, causing the family to again postpone their departure. Margaret did not think that she and Jerry had "ever, together, felt as lost and hopeless as we did that night." Nothing seemed to be going well, but the following day two American P-38s flew low over the camp and bombed and strafed nearby, which Margaret took as "proof positive" that liberation was not long off.[24]

Grace Nash awoke in the early morning of February 23 to the smell of smoke. Weak with hunger, she rose slowly and carefully; as she reached for her housecoat, she heard the deafening sound of planes flying low overhead. When she got outside, she saw American troops parachuting out of their planes, appearing to Grace as "Greek gods coming from heaven!" The Nashes opened up their last tin of meat in celebration as they watched the 11th Airborne take over the camp. Dorothy Still, preparing to go off her hospital night shift when she heard all the commotion outside, heard machine guns and assumed the worst: "Oh, dear God! They're going to kill us!" Instead she saw American tanks effortlessly break through the sawali fence that surrounded the camp, then spotted soldiers parachuting out of American C-47s: the Americans had finally arrived. Margaret Sherk woke that morning with the realization that her daughter, Gerry Ann, now thirteen months old, had spent her entire short life as a prisoner. Margaret and Jerry heard a lot of shouting outside, and just after he went out the door, he called back to Margaret to come and see what she later described as "the most beautiful sight I shall ever witness"—members of the 11th Airborne floating down out of the sky. One of the planes had "This is your liberation" painted across its side; "As if we needed to be told," Margaret commented.[25]

Events moved quickly that morning. The paratroopers had taken the Japanese by surprise, managing to kill all of them as they performed their morning exercises, their weapons conveniently propped up against a barracks. Dorothy Still, carrying the infant she had been tending to in the hospital, went outside to greet the Americans. As she casually chatted with them and showed off the baby, the soldiers stuffed her uniform pockets with Hershey bars and cigarettes, which she promptly took into the hospital to share with the others. Overall there was little time for socializing; the internees had to be moved quickly to a safe place because the surrounding territory was not secure. Jerry Sams, conscious of the dangers of the situation, predicted that the camp would be evacuated within two hours, but after scarcely an hour Margaret Sherk saw "a long, long line of the most wonderful-looking American boys," who shouted at the internees to get ready to move. The paratroopers directed the scurrying inmates to the amphibious tractors that had come crashing through the front fence of the camp, and Margaret felt "most inadequate" because she needed help climbing into one of the vehicles, but she never looked back as the camp burned behind them. Grace Nash carefully packed up her two violins, put the rest of her possessions in one small suitcase, gathered her children, urged her husband, Ralph, to hurry, and they all raced for a tank. As the mobilized camp headed toward Laguna de Bay, Japanese troops opened fire, yet the American military managed to get everyone safely across the bay to Muntinglupa, where the liberated internees remained at the new Bilibid Prison Farm for six weeks.[26]

Reveling in their liberation, the former Los Banos internees ate, read mail from home, and caught up on the war news. They contended with the disturbing rumor that the Japanese had intended to kill everyone on the day of the liberation, a rumor that most internees took as unquestioned fact. Imogene Carlson recalled that one of the married missionary women who read Japanese happened upon an order from the Japanese military authorizing the execution of all of the inmates during morning roll call on February 23. Internee officials managed to smuggle this information out of camp to General MacArthur's forces and to the guerrillas, who solicited volunteers to perform the rescue. The unconfirmed rumor spread quickly, causing great consternation, but since the internees were now safe and free, they concentrated on the more immediate concern of eating. Surrounded by an abundance of food at New Bilibid yet conscious of their malnourished state, Grace Nash and her family carefully monitored their intake, but freedom offset their food difficulties, and Grace watched contentedly as her boys started acting like boys again. The resourceful Gale and Stan quickly attached themselves to American soldiers, who generously provided them with gum and chocolate.[27]

In April 1945, the Nash family finally left the Philippines on the SS *Eberle*, a trip that proved eventful—they encountered a typhoon and also had to outrun two Japanese submarines—but they arrived safely in California on May 2. Grace's main concern at that point was getting to Cleveland to see her dying father, but civilian travel within the United States was restricted in favor of the military. She finally booked a flight with Roy, the child her stateside family did not know about, but the reunion on May 7 did not go as anticipated. Grace feared that she had lost all emotion, that she was nothing but an "empty shell," and that even though she came home, she was still in prison because she could not shake the experiences of the previous thirty-eight months.[28]

Adjustment took time after the Nashes moved in with Grace's sister, Mabel, and her family in Cleveland: the family avoided crowds and standing in line, and Gale and Stan inspected the refrigerator frequently each day just to make sure it had food in it. Roy, who knew nothing of peacetime life, required assurance that all the meat he ate was dog, because that was the only kind he ever remembered. In September, Gale and Stan entered school, Ralph took a job designing buses, Grace went back to her violin, and they moved into their own house in December. As adults, Stan and Gale became professors, and Roy became a wood and masonry craftsman; they each married and had their own children. In 1960, Grace finally gave up the violin because of arthritis, and several years later she and Ralph retired to Scottsdale, Arizona, but continued to teach, write, and travel. In the 1980s, they toured China, Japan, and the Philippines, where they went back to the site of Los Banos only to find the land now used as pasture for carabao. But a plaque in their honor still stands, reading in part, "Within these grounds up to three thousand Americans and other nationals of the free world were interned by the Japanese military, suffering great physical privation and national humiliation."[29]

There is little bitterness in Grace's recollections of the war years. She summed up their experiences by explaining that while none of her family outwardly showed any negative signs of internment, "inwardly not a day goes by that our thoughts and actions are not in some way affected by what we have lived through, and for each of us our need to live—to LIVE TO THE FULLEST—NEVER STOPS!"[30]

In Muntinlupa, Margaret Sherk realized that she was "really among Americans again" because of the smell of food, especially bread. But now, with the expectation that her family would disown her—adultery and giving birth to another man's child were not light transgressions—she had to write to her mother to explain the circumstances of Gerry Ann's birth. After about a week of tense freedom, expecting a reproachful letter from home, Margaret was dealt two huge personal blows. An acquaintance from Santo Tomas, Bob Merrill, told her that Bob Sherk died in October 1944 while en route to Japan on the *Meiyo Maru* when American planes bombed the ship. Margaret believed that her husband's tragic death would always be her "cross to bear" in life, that her guilty conscience over her relationship with Jerry could only have been eased had Bob survived the war and made a new life for himself. The next day Margaret learned that her younger brother, Edward, had also been killed in the war.[31]

While waiting in Leyte for their spot on a homeward-bound ship, Margaret admitted that for every day that went by without a letter from home, she had "too much time to dread going home and having no one to welcome me." In April she, Jerry, and the children finally sailed for the United States, landing in San Francisco after an uneventful monthlong journey. Margaret's worries about her family proved to be unfounded; her mother, aunt, and two brothers were waiting for her at the pier, making her understand that "the fatted calf would be killed for me," that her family welcomed her home.[32]

Once home, Margaret quickly regained her health, and her dreams came true when Jerry's wife granted him a divorce, enabling the couple to marry on January 26, 1946. Jerry already had a communications job with the navy, so the Samses settled into a comfortable middle-class suburban life and had two more children. Margaret, a busy housewife, took time to craft a memoir of her experiences, which proved to be "wonderful therapy" for her, as it helped her to work out her beliefs about true love, to make sense of internment and the choices she made. After Jerry retired in 1972, the couple moved to a ranch near Chicago Park, California, where they still lived at the time of this writing, as devoted to each other as they were during the trying times of internment. David served in the navy twice and then retired, and Gerry Ann, a college graduate, grew up to be a substitute teacher.[33]

Dorothy Still marveled at the advances in medical technology in New Bilibid, where she worked with an army doctor. She found disposable needles and intravenous tubing most intriguing but was disturbed to watch as these once-used items were actually thrown away; such actions seemed wasteful and violated her camp mentality. Dorothy and the other navy nurses stayed in New Bilibid until, relieved by a group of fresh army nurses, they moved into Santo Tomas before being flown to Leyte, then boarded a C-47 cargo plane to island-hop their way to the United States. Back home in California, Dorothy found adjustment difficult because she missed the closeness she had enjoyed with the nurses in Los Banos. She spent most of her time giving talks about her experiences and participating in publicity shots for the navy, but she felt "insignificant and unworthy" because she had "simply sat the war out"; she did not see herself as a good symbol for the Navy Nurse Corps. Finally, in 1946 Dorothy left the navy, got married, had three children, and settled into a comfortable postwar life. After her husband's death, she returned to work in the health care field, and when her children had all grown, she became reacquainted with a man she knew from Los

Banos, a man she had loved but did not get involved with at the time because he was married. But by then both had lost their spouses, making it possible for the two of them to finally marry.[34]

THE SAGA OF THE BAGUIO INTERNEES

The Japanese, anticipating an American invasion from northern Luzon, dismantled Camp Holmes in late December 1944, transferring the internees to Bilibid Prison in Manila, a massive migration requiring ten army trucks and two separate caravans to carry all of the prisoners and their possessions. As she traveled through Baguio with her family, Natalie Crouter felt like an "immigrant woman, my hair tied in a kerchief, sitting high on top of the mattress, surrounded by bags, pots, cans, and boxes." Packed into a small truck with thirty-five internees plus a few guards, Betty Foley described the tedious, jolting ride over bombed-out roads as "like being on a subway in rush hour." After Ethel Herold carefully packed all of her family's items that the Japanese allowed her to take, she hid in her bosom her few remaining items of value: family papers, money, jewelry, and the American flag that the women had secretly worked on. Ethel observed that by this time she was "so flat chested that the flag . . . made me stick out a bit pre-warish," but however it made her look, she never dreamed of leaving without that flag. The trip, which started at eight o'clock in the morning and involved several unloadings and reloadings along the way, finally finished with roll call in Bilibid at one o'clock the following morning.[35]

Fern Harrington was part of the second wave of internees sent to Bilibid; as her caravan moved south, she registered astonishment that the Japanese had allotted trucks for their transport, noting that during the enemy's move to the north, it had commandeered every kind of vehicle it could find. Considering how the Japanese had treated the internees over the past three years, that during their first transfer from Camp John Hay to Camp Holmes the internees had to walk, she "marveled that the Japanese were so generous with us." Judy Skogerboe found the transportation a mixed blessing, since it was so haphazardly packed with people and possessions that people tied themselves together with rope to keep from being pitched off as the vehicles lurched over holes in the roads and swayed with sharp turns.[36]

Even before the war started, Bilibid Prison, a former Spanish jail sometimes referred to as Old Bilibid, had been declared unfit for human habitation. Nevertheless, the Japanese used it first to house sick American military prisoners, then the Baguio internees. In addition to its natural deterioration, both Japanese and American bombers had damaged portions of it, making conditions there terribly filthy. The internees had to get settled in all over again, using their limited strength to make this new place habitable. Judy Skogerboe described the squalid conditions: "We had to sleep on the dirty cement floor with rats and mice running about. Of course, mosquitoes and flies and bedbugs were ever present. The latrine was a more serious problem." Ethel Herold succinctly referred to Bilibid as "the filthiest hole I have ever seen," so the prisoners set to work with what they had, which was next to nothing. When the Foleys arrived, they felt exhausted and their few possessions had not yet been delivered, but Betty recalled that organization was second nature by now, and no matter how tired, internees immediately began to order their new living space.[37]

The renewed fighting in Manila meant that internees had an even more difficult time securing food, which proved devastating and dangerous for the already malnourished prisoners. Initially, the Japanese allotted what Betty Foley referred to as "Jap army rice," clean, unhusked, and the "best rice we had to eat," but when that supply quickly ran out it was replaced with an inferior grade of corn occasionally supplemented with bits of fish or beans. Ethel Herold, along with about fifty other women, valiantly tried to make something edible out of the vegetables that the Japanese brought in, foodstuffs that "looked like the sweepings of a filthy dirty market floor." They picked through the mess to find pieces that were "not too rotten to boil," tedious efforts that yielded one tablespoon per person of unrecognizable boiled greens. Betty guessed that the internees received about seven hundred calories per day, barely enough to keep their hearts beating and their brains functioning. During the third week of January 1945, with starvation imminent, Natalie Crouter wondered, "How much longer will we have to stagger on, eating corn mush and tough green stalks?" Fern Harrington acknowledged that the moldy mush that passed for food put them on the brink of starvation. By the end of January, her legs and fingers were swollen with beriberi, her entire body ached, and she found breathing difficult, yet she noted incredulously that she was "among the healthiest" in Bilibid. Fern did not accuse the Japanese of deliberately trying to starve them, reasoning that the increased fighting on Luzon made food scarce, and Natalie concurred, observing that there "is no doubt that it is heroic for a Japanese to get supplies at all in these times."[38]

There is little doubt, though, that while these internees were close to starving to death, Japanese troops had enough energy to fight, so adequate food was available from somewhere. The Japanese simply did not pass it on to their prisoners. Despite all of her hard work and determination, Ethel Herold watched helplessly as her children and husband suffered with boils, complications of malnutrition. When Elmer had to get up at least eight times a night to urinate, one of the camp doctors told Ethel that when a person's body begins dehydrating this way, it is a sure sign of starvation. The actual trip to the toilet at night proved hazardous, for there were no lights, the facility was rickety, and there were too many people and belongings shoved into too small a space. After Elmer almost fell through a hole in the floor one night, Ethel insisted that he use a "tinkle" can rather than make the repeated trips to the toilet. For her, these were the worst weeks of the entire war, because there was nothing to life but basic survival: "Our aim now was to keep body and soul together."[39]

On February 3, 1945, Natalie and Jerry Crouter's eighteenth wedding anniversary, the family celebrated by opening their next-to-last can of SPAM for dinner, then heard shots fired outside of the building. Their son, Fred, who dashed off to investigate, returned claiming to have seen an American tank. The Herolds, sitting on their bunk when they heard all of the noise, peeked through a crack in the boarded-up window to see American tanks. At first they thought that these were captured tanks but then noticed the "men on them were huge, with strange helmets, and dark uniforms. Japs could not be that big, they must be Americans." The two tanks, part of the 1st Cavalry headed toward Santo Tomas, became separated from the rest and ended up at the back wall of Bilibid. Fern Harrington heard one of the tank soldiers pop the hatch, look around, and yell, "Hell, Harvey, we're on the wrong street!" and according to Fern, "Never had profanity sounded so beautiful." Amidst all of the gunfire, chaos, and jubilation, all Ethel Herold could think was "THE AMERICANS HAD COME."[40]

But the Japanese, determined to lay waste to Manila if necessary, refused to give up without a fight and stationed themselves on the roof of the main building, armed with machine guns, rifles, and Molotov cocktails. The internees took shelter inside the prison building as the battle raged outside, eating whatever food they could find and discussing their impending freedom. The next day the Japanese, finally convinced of the futility of the Bilibid situation, issued an official release to the prisoners and left the compound. Natalie Crouter recalled that when the last Japanese official departed, all of the internees cheered, held up the pieced-together American flag Ethel Herold smuggled in, and sang "The Star Spangled Banner" and "God Bless America." Fern Harrington remembered that the internees became so emotional that they could not even finish the first verse of the national anthem. Natalie went to Jerry and their daughter, June, and they sat together "with tears running down our cheeks for quite a long while, not saying anything." For Betty Foley, February 4 would always be her family's Fourth of July, a very special independence day.[41]

The American troops who moved into Bilibid on February 5, bringing cigarettes, food, and chewing gum, had, to Natalie Crouter, "such an American look; above all, secure and well fed." She recounted a meeting she had with an officer from Massachusetts eager to visit with someone from his home state; like other soldiers, he had been fighting in the Pacific for about two years without seeing any nonmilitary Caucasians. He confessed to Natalie that at times the soldiers had been discouraged and dispirited with their progress, but "when we came in here and found you people prisoners in these walls—found you women and children—then we knew what it was all for and that it was worth it!" Ethel Herold, who relished the tea she could now drink, especially since it came with white sugar, watched incredulously as the soldiers casually threw away the once-used tea leaves. Still unaccustomed to bounty, she knew that those leaves "could have lasted us weeks." When Judy Skogerboe ate her first real American breakfast—oatmeal laced with milk and sugar—she noticed that the army sergeant who served the food abruptly went back into the kitchen, where he cried because he could not believe "Americans could be so happy and grateful for a bowl of oatmeal."[42]

Although liberated, the Crouters' troubles were far from over, because both Natalie and Jerry were ill and because they worried about Nida and Ismael Bacani, who were still in Baguio. The Crouters ate carefully and supplemented their diet with vitamins, while a friend of theirs who had more freedom of movement promised to go to Baguio to find out about their former servants. By mid-February, Natalie had become so debilitated that she had to dictate her diary entries to her daughter, June; her uneven recovery actually took years. On March 15, the family left Bilibid on the first leg of their trip back to the United States, causing Natalie to comment that despite everything they had been through in the past three years, leaving "gave us a certain nostalgia. We had found a brotherhood in these years." However, a tinge of bitterness went along with that nostalgia. Natalie became infuriated that Jerry, along with the other liberated internees, had to sign a promissory note to cover the cost of their passage back to the United States, $275 apiece. The following week, when the Counter Intelligence Corp of the Army required Natalie to turn over all of the "notes" that made up her diary, she told the officer who confiscated them: "It means nothing to you, everything to me, for it is all I've saved. It is three years of suffering and experience, and I want to keep it for my children's children."[43] She was right to be concerned about the fate of her literary labors because it would be a year and a half before Natalie could get her diary back. She was also right about the historical value of the laboriously written document, a testament to a little known event.

After Natalie arrived in the United States on April 21, for the first time in eighteen years, she filled her days with hot baths, shopping, eating, and drinking in the sights of California. On May 1, the family arrived back home in Boston. While Natalie was hospitalized for three months for a variety of starvation-related ailments, she received a letter from Nida Bacani, who informed her that she was ill and that Ismael had died during the war, a victim of forced labor for the Japanese. When Jerry Crouter took a job with the U.S. War Shipping Administration, which sent him to Washington, D.C., and Manila, Natalie and the children moved to Cleveland, Ohio, to live with her divorced sister. There Natalie became involved with liberal politics and joined the Women's International League for Peace and Freedom. Jerry, unable to totally regain his health, died in 1951. Both of the children grew up to be solid and useful citizens in Natalie's eyes: June became a social worker, and Fred taught high school history. Mindful of her debt to Nida, Natalie sent her money for years to try to repay the woman for all she had done to help the Crouters during the war. Natalie also visited Nida in the Philippines several times before Nida died in 1979; Natalie lived until 1984, long enough to see her diary in print.

Fern Harrington quickly began to regain her health while still in Manila, but she remembered that "boredom replaced anxiety as we waited for an opportunity to return to the States," even though the army provided the former internees with magazines and a radio to help pass the time. She traveled around when it was allowed, visiting an evacuation hospital along with her friend Cleo Morrison in an attempt to cheer up injured soldiers. In mid-March, the two women moved into Santo Tomas to await repatriation. On April 8, they began their journey home on the SS *Eberle*, which made a brief stop in Honolulu, providing FBI agents the opportunity to interview all of the passengers and confiscate their written material, so Fern reluctantly turned over her diary. When the ship landed in Los Angeles on May 2, the Red Cross stepped in to help the former internees adjust to their surroundings, giving Fern and Cleo each about $130 to buy clothes and other necessities. Fern was elated that the May Store provided her with a personal shopper, then presented her to the president of the company after she had selected a new outfit; being a missionary did not overwhelm her feminine impulses.

Fern traveled on to Kansas City, Missouri, while Cleo went home to Texas. For a short time Fern was a local celebrity in her home rural farming community; everyone knew that she had been a prisoner of the Japanese, so whenever she went into town, people pointed at her and whispered. Although she felt happy to be home, she knew she had to make plans for the future, but this effort proved difficult: "For more than three years I had longed for freedom more than anything else. Now that I had freedom, I was scared of the responsibility it entailed." Ultimately deciding to continue her missionary work, she went to Yale University's College of Oriental Studies because she wanted to learn the Chinese language better in preparation for her next assignment. Her subsequent missionary work took her to China, then back to the Philippines, and she even visited Japan in 1957. In 1976, Fern married a retired sociology professor, Herbert Miles. Overall, Fern believed that "in the crucible of adversity during internment, the positive Christian influence was largely responsible for the transformation of a motley group of frightened, frustrated, and mutually hostile persons into a caring, sharing, loving community in captivity." Best of all, the internees "have been able to forgive and forget."[44]

Judy Skogerboe sailed home on the same ship with Fern, and although she asserted her relief that her wartime ordeal had ended, she also expressed apprehension about returning to the United States. She tried to convince herself that she was happy about leaving the Philippines, but she was not: "I was afraid to leave the unreal life of the past three and a half years that had become my consuming reality. I sensed an involuntary cringing from resuming normal life in America." The trip back to the United States was difficult because of overcrowding on the ship, the lack of air conditioning, and growing tensions among the passengers. When the ship finally docked in Los Angeles and a waiting Red Cross volunteer offered Judy some coffee and donuts, the "dam of emotion broke"—Judy had dreamed of these simple things for years, and now she was almost too overwhelmed to enjoy them. Her feelings were perhaps best exemplified by a comment made by three-year-old Billy Gray, whose missionary father had died in Baguio from torture by the Japanese. Judy spent her first night in Los Angeles with Billy, his mother, Marian, and another friend, and as they settled in, Billy asked if they could now go look for his father. When Marian gently reminded Billy that his father was in heaven, Billy replied, "Yes, but this is heaven, isn't it?" A few days later Judy rejoined her family in Minneapolis, married the fiancé who had waited for her, and continued her missionary work. Judy summed up her experiences with the observation that the "ugliness of war is that it distorts our moral judgments and impairs our vision. Feelings prevail over reason and right thinking. In any conflict, no side is totally evil and the other completely good."[45]

Betty Foley had health worries upon liberation. On February 5, as the military evacuated Bilibid because of increased fighting in the area, she had to manage everything because both her husband, Rupert, and her son, Michael, were very ill. As she and the others headed for the temporary refuge of the Sixth Army Headquarters, the Filipinos in the streets cheered them, helping Betty feel "like conquering heroes rather than the bedraggled refugees we were." Within six weeks, everyone recovered enough to travel, so the Foleys went home. Although Betty enjoyed being back in the United States, indulging in "such common-place things as sheets, hot tub baths, and privacy," she and Rupert longed to get back to the Philippines. Betty had been born and raised there, she married and gave birth to Michael there, and her brother, Jim Halsema, stayed in the Philippines after the liberation of Bilibid. Although she returned to Baguio only for periodic visits, she frequently gave public talks about her wartime experiences until her sudden death in 1997.[46]

The Herolds remained in Manila until March 10, when Ethel finally "cut the apron strings," allowing Billy to fly to Leyte, then board a troop ship that had additional space for six single men. After more than three years of unusually close family togetherness, she felt sorry for herself as she sent her son "off FROM war," leaving her wondering how mothers felt when they sent their sons "off TO war." Five days later she, Elmer, and Betsy flew to Leyte, where they waited for about a month for a ship for home; after arriving in the United States on May 9, they journeyed on to join Billy, who was with relatives in Missoula, Montana. Billy and Betsy finished high school there, while Ethel edited her diary, which she viewed as a valuable legacy to her family, and by 1948, Ethel and Elmer, eager to go where they could be the most useful and where they felt the most comfortable, returned to the Philippines. Their children vacationed there when possible. Ethel worked on her diary again, typing it, expanding on abbreviations, adding updates, always insisting that this effort was not a way for her to work out her wartime experiences; rather, it helped to ease the loneliness of being without Billy and Betsy. A sensible down-to-earth woman, Ethel spent the rest of her life doing for others, despite her failing eyesight and the more devastating loss of Elmer in 1971. Upon her death in 1988, she was buried next to her beloved husband in a cemetery near Potosi, Wisconsin.[47]

THE LAST OF THE LIBERATED

If the fighting in the Philippines proved difficult for American troops, it was even more bitter and prolonged in other Japanese-occupied areas of the Pacific theater. In the spring of 1945, when the Americans in the Philippines were being sent home, Agnes Keith still fought for survival on Borneo, a struggle that continued for an additional six months. The Japanese enforced long work hours on their female captives, requiring them to work in the fields growing food for the army and making the women so desperate for nourishment that they ate raw tapioca root as they labored. The appearance of Allied planes cheered them, but after seeing the winged signs of hope every day for six weeks with no change in their own situation, they began to take the planes for granted and accepted that liberation was still far off. Agnes remembered that the women "ceased expecting release. We ceased expecting. We just existed."[48] In August, exhausted and dispirited, she admitted that she knew for certain the Allies would be victorious, but she did not know when or if she would be alive to see it.

On August 15, 1945, as the Kuching prisoners marked their third-year anniversary in the compound, rumors of an armistice between the Japanese and the Allies circulated during the half-hour visit Colonel Suga allowed between husbands and wives. Although Harry brought this information, prompted by the atomic bombings of Hiroshima and Nagasaki, Agnes at first dismissed it as another hopeful rumor, telling him, "I'll believe the war is over when I see American sailors in Kuching Square!" But she could not fail to notice that the mood in the compound had changed—she heard singing from the Allied soldiers, hopeful ditties including "Yankee Doodle Dandy" plus a camp favorite, "They'll Be Coming Up the River When They Come." When the Japanese guards began to kill and eat their chickens, Agnes realized they would not be around much longer, but Japanese officials resolutely denied the rumors of peace.[49]

Five days later, Allied planes dropped leaflets announcing the defeat of the Japanese and advising the prisoners to wait for liberation, as the Allies had difficulty reaching Kuching because of its particular geographic location and because of protracted Japanese resistance. Colonel Suga ominously informed Agnes that the battle for Borneo continued, that "the battle for supremacy would be held over our captive bodies." But on August 24, he abruptly ordered the women to assemble at 4:00 o'clock in the afternoon in the camp chapel, a clear signal to Agnes that the situation had changed in the captives' favor. While waiting for him to appear, she observed the women sitting with her: "We had stood a great deal. When the Japs cut our rations, we had laughed. When they sent us to work in the fields we had laughed. When they cut off the water, and we carried it from wells, we had laughed. When we were hungry, ill, tired, we had laughed. But now, if this promise of peace was one final joke—we could not laugh!"[50]

It was not a joke. Suga announced that peace had come, but liberation for the prisoners was a delicate matter since some Japanese troops still refused to surrender; he advised them to be patient and wait. Soon Allied planes parachuted food supplies into the camp. The women, now reflexively ingenious, not only gleefully swept up the longed-for food but also refashioned the parachutes into much-needed clothing for themselves and their children. Suga hosted a farewell party on September 3, which most, but not all, of the prisoners attended. Agnes went to the party and drank whiskey with her former captors even though she recognized that sitting with the Japanese as guests and wishing each other well was a "perversion of every instinct." Australian forces took over Kuching on September 11 at 5:03 P.M., and American sailors moved in as well, so according to her own criteria Agnes had to believe that liberation occurred. Harry, Agnes, and George stood together as a bedraggled, war-weary family with the rest of the prisoners as Brigadier General Eastick of the 9th Australian Division informed them that they were finally free. Agnes adored the soldiers and the freedom that they brought: "They were for that time a part of all goodness and virtue, a part of all love. They brought us liberty and freedom, and something even greater—belief again in the decency of men."[51]

The Keiths were among the first of the released prisoners to be evacuated, receiving top priority because both Agnes and Harry suffered from severe malaria and because of George's young age. As sick as she was, Agnes vowed that whatever happened as they packed up to go, she would not leave her diary behind; she bundled together all of the notes she had made, and Harry put the parcel in his luggage so that Agnes could focus her attention on George. The military flew the family to a rest camp at Labuan, where Agnes began her long recuperation by eating fresh fruits and vegetables. She learned that most of the Japanese officers and guards from Kuching were dead, either from meeting with "accidents" or by their own hand; Colonel Suga, her admirer and erstwhile protector, committed suicide. After five days in the rest camp, the Keiths boarded a plane bound for Manila, the first part of their journey back to the United States.

Agnes, too ill to revel in her freedom because of problems associated with malnutrition, pessimistically believed that she and Harry would never be able to regain their prewar health. Beyond these medical problems, Agnes also had emotional and intellectual ones to deal with, especially the hatred she detected all around her. She listened to people of different nationalities and races snipe at each other on board the ship that took them home; she endured condescension and hostility from the American navy, which had been part of their liberation team. Agnes observed that "love of country flourished, while love of humanity withered." She rejected the idea that the Allies had fought the war "to retaliate in kind for the actions which we condemned. But war brutalizes all whom it touches; if it did not do so it could not be endured."[52]

If the war brutalized Agnes Keith, she successfully hid any manifestations of it. She admitted that during internment she had become "hard, cold, tough," qualities necessary to stay alive and to function as a normal mother, but after liberation she became, according to her son, George, "just an old softie again." It took three years before Agnes's health problems cleared up, the most persistent of which were long-term injuries from the vicious beating she received after reporting the attempted rape. Six months after liberation, Harry returned to his job on Borneo, while Agnes and George went to British Columbia so that Agnes could recuperate further before they joined him. By this time George had regained his health, so he spent his days just like other little boys his age, roller-skating, riding a scooter, and shooting marbles. Agnes continued to accompany Harry around the world to each of his successive jobs, writing books about nearly every place that they lived.

Of her wartime experiences, Agnes concluded that "when we work as hard in peacetime to make this world decent to live in, as in wartime we work to kill, the world will be decent, and the causes for which men fight will be gone."[53]

Darlene Deibler encountered similar harsh conditions and terrors during the first months of 1945 as the Allies conducted daily bombing raids close to Kampili on Celebes. Darlene and the other women dug air raid trenches to hide in; soon they spent nearly every night crammed into these trenches as the raids increased. In July, an American plane flew so low over the camp that Darlene could see the pilot, so she knew that he realized he had found a camp of women and children. A couple of days later more planes arrived, this time delivering both hope and devastation: first the planes dropped chocolate bars, canned food, and leaflets, and then the bombing began, leaving the entire prison camp in flames. Several of the prisoners sustained injuries; one little boy later died from complications of a severed leg. The Japanese moved the inmates to a hastily constructed camp just across a rice paddy, one secluded under heavy jungle growth and invisible from the air. Darlene, originally optimistic after being located by the Allies, did not understand why the camp had been targeted for destruction: "Was it to destroy a work force used by the Japanese, or were we just expendable?"[54]

In August, the Japanese allowed the women some unexpected "luxuries." With the sewing room in the schoolhouse repaired after the July bombings, Darlene expected that the women would be put to work making new uniforms for the soldiers; instead, fabric arrived, enough to make a new dress for each woman in camp. The material was thin and cheap but made of bright colors, causing Darlene to welcome this treat even though she observed that the women "looked like cadaverous spiders draped in sheer, colorful webs." Next the Japanese delivered a pile of white canvas tennis shoes, leaving the women and children scrambling to grab two shoes of the same size. This sudden generosity, coupled with the increased presence of Japanese officials moving in and out of the camp, made Darlene wonder what they had in mind next for the prisoners. The women speculated that liberation must be near, that the Japanese wanted them to look decent when the Allies arrived, but August ended and freedom had not come.[55]

In early September, Commandant Yamaji assembled the women and children to inform them of the Japanese surrender, which put the area under the jurisdiction of the Australian Army of Occupation, and announced that the former prisoners would be transferred to Macassar as soon as adequate housing could be arranged. No wild victory celebration ensued. Darlene recalled that there "was not even a conquering soldier in sight who had come to set us free, whom we could thank, whose hands we could kiss and wet with our tears of gladness," so the women had a "silent celebration of tears." Given her strong religious beliefs, it is unlikely that she would have paid exclusive homage to a soldier; for Darlene, God had brought about liberation. The next day she was called into camp headquarters to assist with translations between the Australians and Japanese to facilitate the transfer of authority and to begin evacuating the prisoners. Darlene then wanted to learn more about her husband Russell's death and to visit his grave before she left Celebes. A Dutchman, Dr. Goedbloed, tracked her down and told her that he had attended Russell during his fatal bout with dysentery in August 1943 and that his dying thoughts had been of her. After receiving this news, Darlene finally felt a sense of peace; a few days later, she managed to visit Russell's grave in Pare Pare.[56]

Following her encounter with the Dutch doctor, Darlene ran into an American naval officer who asked her what she needed, telling her that he would arrange an air drop of food and other necessities for the women and children while they waited for evacuation. According to Darlene, one of the most sought-after items from the drop was SPAM, because the women had had little meat since the beginning of the war; they considered the canned meat hybrid a "succulent" delicacy. Darlene spent her last days on Celebes praying, eating, and trying to make herself presentable for her trip back to the United States—her religious dedication did not make her unaware that she had lost her natural good looks. A striking dark-haired beauty when she had arrived eight years before as a young missionary bride, Darlene Deibler was now a twenty-six-year old widow with snow-white hair, who wore ill-fitting borrowed clothes over her eighty-pound frame. After the *Klipfontein* docked in Seattle, Washington, in November 1945, Darlene made her way to Oakland, California, where her parents lived. As she watched the scenery from her train seat, she remembered feeling like Rip Van Winkle because the United States had changed so much since she had left.[57]

Darlene spent the next two years regaining her strength. She also spoke to groups about her ordeal on Celebes, which likely influenced her decision to return to missionary work despite the advice of friends and family to take more time to recuperate. Friends arranged an introduction to Gerald Rose, a young missionary well acquainted with Russell Deibler's work in New Guinea and who also had an assignment there. Darlene and Jerry Rose married in April 1948; the following year they traveled to New Guinea to begin their work, eventually raising two children, Bruce and Brian. The family remained there until 1978, when Darlene and Jerry moved to the Australian outback to continue their ministry. Darlene maintained a characteristically religious interpretation of all of her years in the Netherlands Indies: "Viewing those eight years from this far side, I marvel at the wisdom and love of our God, Who controls the curtains of the stage on which the drama of our lives is played; His hand draws aside the curtains of events only far enough for us to view one sequence at a time."[58]

Endurance, ingenuity, hard work, and faith ensured the survival of these interned American women. No matter how difficult life became—despite starvation, repeated illnesses, and exposure to warfare—they never stopped believing that the U.S. military would rescue them, that some day the Americans would come. Their faith and dedication paid off as American forces swept through the Pacific theater, routing out the Japanese and liberating the islands previously held by the enemy. The worst of times ended with freedom, and some women turned to autobiography to make sense of their experiences and to explain to family, friends, and outsiders how they survived their ordeals while maintaining their identities as American women.

CONCLUSION

"[We] muddled through it all and lived to carry on."

Nearly ten years after the war, Gladys Savary described her generous, sometimes dangerous work of aiding military prisoners as "just a tale of a woman, of me, who sort of muddled through it all and lived to carry on," denying that hers was "a story of valorous deeds or battles."[1] Taking these statements at face value, she obviously believed that war was men's business, that in wartime men planned and executed strategies, took bold action, and fought heroically. Yet as American women in the South Pacific "muddled through," they suffered as much as soldiers and had their lives transformed as much as any soldier, ultimately proving that they were survivors. Even though they had not expected war to tear apart their comfortable colonial lives, they rose to the occasion and drew from their inner reserves to protect themselves and their families.

American women's reliance on concepts of womanhood, which highlighted marriage, motherhood, and family, guaranteed their survival in a hostile, uncertain, and, at times, violent environment. In late 1941, Grace Nash and Agnes Newton Keith chose family unity and refused to leave the South Pacific despite growing threats from the Japanese, because as wives and mothers they believed it was their duty to stay with their husbands, to keep the family together. During the Japanese attack and advance, women coped with fears of rape by their conquerors; fortunately for them, these fears were unrealized, as the Japanese usually targeted Asian women for sexual abuse. After internment, Natalie Crouter, Ethel Herold, and Emily Van Sickle continued their wifely roles; despite restrictions on commingling, despite separate sleeping quarters, they maintained a semblance of a normal marriage because their husbands remained close by.

Although married couples continually tried to find ways around the ban on commingling and to set up family living spaces, most apparently restricted physical contact. Hugs, kisses, and other petting were acceptable, but sexual intercourse represented danger, because it might lead to pregnancy, which posed health risks for mother and child plus angered the Japanese. For these women, companionship was the most important component of marriage and courtship under wartime circumstances. Yet to Grace Nash and several others, pregnancy remained a natural by-product of marriage, war or not, and they maneuvered through various deprivations to give birth to healthy babies. Margaret Sherk, fearful of her chances for survival and hopelessly in love with Jerry Sams, got pregnant as an expression of love and to make sure that Jerry continued to help and protect her and David. While all of these women agreed about the importance of love, marriage, and family, there was no consensus about the appropriate actions to maintain them.

Women, whether interned or not, also attempted to retain their standards of femininity by paying attention to wardrobe, hairstyles, and cosmetics. Tressa Roka—young, attractive, and engaged—understood the value of such things, both as morale boosters and as ways to attract men. Viola Winn, as she hid with her children in the mountainous regions of Negros, lamented the loss of fine summer dresses, hosiery, and a regularly scheduled appointment with a hairstylist. At the end of the war, even missionary women, including Fern Harrington and Darlene Deibler, expressed concern over their appearance after years of deprivation; devotion to God did not preclude a predilection for feminine finery. Natalie Crouter, however, found women's attention to fashion silly and impractical, while Agnes Keith capitalized on her fellow internees' love of fashion to swap pieces of her expensive wardrobe for food and medicine for George. Clearly, these women did not agree on the function of feminine style during wartime.

Organization and work were crucial to survival, since Japanese authorities assumed little responsibility for the well-being of their captives. Internees established quasi governments dominated by men, with representatives, committees, and even voting; while women took the backseat in these activities, they did vote, occasionally served on committees, and in Baguio had their own Women's Committee. The Baguio internees even debated the appropriateness of women's participation in these political matters, as Natalie Crouter and her faction pushed for universal suffrage rather than women voting only on Women's Committee issues. Discussion of the democratic political process abounded, with the men resisting universal suffrage until the Japanese military took over Camp Holmes and ordered all adults to vote for their repre-

sentatives. Though interned women took an interest in voting and politics, their overall low level of participation indicates that family concerns took precedence plus illustrates a belief that in wartime, these
were men's issues.

Accustomed to a domestic life dominated by servants, these women
quickly (but not always happily) gave up their privileged colonial
lifestyles, pitching in with cooking, cleaning, and various other chores,
former routine household activities that would now help guarantee
their survival. Ethel Herold abandoned womanly niceties, barking out
orders to her fellow female internees to make sure they knew what
needed to be done and when, for by her standards, a good woman willingly contributed her skills for the common good. Agnes Keith and
Darlene Deibler also faced forced labor for the Japanese—Agnes toil-
ing in a garden, Darlene tending a piggery—both working as hard as
men, encouraged by Japanese bayonets and the determination to stay
alive. Any semblance of genteel colonial life had been discarded in
favor of survival.

Assistance from the local population also proved crucial to survival,
as many Filipinos and other Asians, generally suspicious of Japanese
intentions, did what they could to help the interned and evading Americans. The prewar racial boundaries were therefore upset, with Americans relying on support from the people they once ruled over, sometimes
receiving welcomed aid, sometimes being taken advantage of. Natalie
Crouter, who could count on the loyalty of the Bacanis, celebrated the
humanity of the reversed situation, claiming that the altered relationship was "like breathing to me, the realization of one's dependence on
another," that "all [were] friends in adversity."[2] But Tressa Roka and
Grace Nash learned early in the war that Filipino allegiance was not
absolute—their former servants stole from them while they were interned. Women in hiding faced similar uncertainties, as they never knew
which Filipinos could be trusted to help them evade the Japanese. The
Winns and Lindholms, however, trapped on Negros, found the Filipinos supportive and helpful, enabling them to survive until the rescue
submarines arrived.

As mothers, many of these women feared that people who did not
fully understand their situation would label them bad mothers. They
had not protected their children from harm by evacuating them from
the Pacific theater, they could only protect them so much from the
Japanese, and some had to function as single mothers, thereby depriving their children of a traditional family life. Margaret Sherk and Eliza-

beth Vaughan negotiated internment without the love and support of their spouses, ultimately managing to pull their families through, albeit using different strategies. Margaret challenged prevailing notions of womanhood with her infidelity, while Elizabeth persevered to keep her family together by acting as the model good wife and mother. Agnes Keith endured one of the harshest internments without the daily help of her husband, yet she created the illusion for George that she was powerful and managed to pull him through. Women who evaded internment also had a difficult time even though they had the aid of their husbands. Crude living conditions and rapid removes from the enemy—such as those Viola Winn faced—made their daily chores tougher and challenged their abilities to keep their children safe and unscarred by terror; only the safe deliverance of their children would prove that they were good mothers.[3]

Despite their sometimes harrowing wartime experiences, few of these women admitted to any long-lasting problems for themselves or their children. Frieda Magnuson acknowledged that her two daughters exhibited nervous problems, but only for a while, and Frieda claimed that her own readjustment went smoothly. However, women certainly were not unaffected by their adventures; they did not block out the war years or deny them in an attempt to forget. Some, including Betty Foley and Dorothy Still, gave public talks about internment, and others drew on their wartime experiences to positively shape their postwar lives. Natalie Crouter and Ethel Herold devoted themselves to their families, but because of the war they could not shut out the rest of the world—they had to make it better for their children. Natalie, despite her persistent ill health, became an active supporter of the Women's International League of Peace and Freedom, and about a year after liberation, Ethel, along with Elmer, returned to Baguio to help the Filipinos rebuild their country. Natalie and Ethel, despite their different views of community during internment, realized the importance of helping to shape a new world. Elizabeth Vaughan, widowed with two children, turned to academia to make sense of what happened to her family and to explain to others the unintended consequences of war, using her career to bring the lessons of war and community to another generation of Americans. Emily Hahn and Agnes Keith also combined family responsibilities with their professions: as working mothers, they continued to write about the world they traveled in. The war affected all of these women, yet their basic commitments to family and country remained.

Legal definitions of citizenship enabled some women to stay out of internment, loopholes they capitalized on to guarantee their own survival and to help others. Gladys Savary, married to a Frenchman, was not entitled to "protective custody" by the Japanese, so she used her freedom to aid military prisoners in Manila. Trapped in Hong Kong, Emily Hahn claimed her Chinese marriage to Zau Sinmay to keep her out of Camp Stanley so that she could better care for her young daughter, provide extra food for her imprisoned lover, and organize food deliveries to the various military prison camps. Marriage to a Greek national kept Sofia Adamson free in Manila, but helping others came second to ensuring her own survival and that of her immediate family. For these women, family concerns intertwined with charitable activities, with some women more willing to focus on the former.

Claire Phillips and Margaret Utinsky, separated from their husbands, created new national identities to stay out of Santo Tomas and help the USAFFE prisoners and the guerrillas. For them, being a loyal American and a good wife meant doing anything they could to support their country's cause, especially since it was one their husbands fought for. This subterfuge jeopardized their lives, but they drew from their inner resources to avenge their husbands' deaths, to survive torture, and to withstand the war. A few Filipina Americans avoided internment because the Japanese emphasized their Filipina nationality, assuming Asian solidarity over Caucasian "oppressors," but Dorothy Dore, Ida Dolphin, and Yay Panlilio, accentuating their American identity, cast their loyalty with the Allied cause and aided the USAFFE in any way possible.

National identity supported American women as they braved internment or evasion. The Baguio internees' postwar description of what it meant to be an American indeed held true: these women relied on keeping their minds and bodies occupied with learning, work, and leisure activity; they adapted their needs to their surroundings; they implemented democratic governing structures; they kept their families together; and they occasionally laughed about their situation. This positive attitude was made possible, in large part, by their hope that someday the Americans would rescue them. Missionary women, not surprisingly, incorporated influences of God and faith with national identity and patriotism. Darlene Deibler, surrounded mostly by Dutch nationals, was acutely aware of her nationality but repeatedly focused on the power of prayer rather than the power of the military; while living among a group of predominantly secular Americans, Fern Harrington credited rescue to

God's providence. For these women, the U.S. triumph was just a matter of time, but God guided the victory.

Although Gladys Savary modestly downplayed her activities in Manila, insisting she simply muddled through the war, the fact that she wrote a memoir about those activities shows their importance to her, that she perceived herself as a valuable contributor to the war effort. Gladys claimed a starring role in prisoner relief not to gain glory but to explain what good American women do in such situations. The "star" role figures significantly in all of these autobiographies. Gladys was one of a few authors who acknowledged the crucial participation of another woman (Dorothy Janson), while the others glossed over their relationships or contacts with other women. Given the relatively small size of the internment camps and the length of confinement, the women must have known each other or at least known of each other, but for these authors, people outside their own family—or in the case of the nurses, their own group—only had a fleeting importance. Natalie Crouter criticized Ethel Herold (and gave her and everyone else in Baguio a pseudonym) at many points in her diary, but Ethel hardly mentioned Natalie in hers. Emphasis on the self highlighted women's individual capacity for survival, making their stories truly their own.

Several of these women expressed positive interpretations of their wartime experiences, further emphasizing their "star" role and their ability to triumph over adversity. They not only survived, but they learned a larger life lesson from their war days: Grace Nash learned to live life to the fullest, Fern Harrington celebrated the community of internment and focused on forgiveness, Tressa Roka discovered the value of freedom. Although others were thankful for their survival, they could not embrace forgiveness or tolerance. Denny Williams and Elizabeth Vaughan, widowed because of the war, offered no soothing statements; Dorothy Still, frustrated in her postwar navy career, felt guilty that internment did not allow her to significantly contribute to the war effort.

These women used their stories as a way of explaining, justifying, and documenting their actions, motives not wholly unconscious. Natalie Crouter, Agnes Keith, and Fern Harrington all resisted having their diaries confiscated by the American military, with Natalie telling an officer, "It means nothing to you, everything to me, for it is all I've saved. It is three years of suffering and experience, and I want to keep it for my children's children."[4] She understood the historical importance of her diary as documentary evidence of the war years and also claimed it as family history, something a mother hands down to her children. For Natalie, larger world events were inextricably linked with her personal life, and she wanted her diary preserved as proof of what she had been through. Certainly Agnes, as a professional writer, understood the value of her diary and intended to refashion it for the general reading public. Out of all of these war stories, only her book, *Three Came Home*, was a best-seller, to this day still in print, plus Hollywood turned it into a movie in 1950. Through her book and the movie, Agnes's story reached a wide audience, showing that she had been a devoted wife and mother, maintained faith in an American victory, worked hard for survival, and triumphed over the adversities of war and internment. Still, the public may be left with the impression that Agnes was one of a handful of women in this situation rather than one of thousands.

The published and unpublished autobiographies of these women compel a rethinking of how people remember World War II, since war generally emphasizes men and battles. If public memory is, as John Bodnar explains, "a body of beliefs and ideas about the past that help a public or society understand both its past, present, and by implication, its future," then these autobiographies may have been unsettling in the postwar years.[5] The seemingly ordinary women who negotiated those difficult years implied that their success lay in the strength of their womanhood, a realization at odds with the postwar emphasis on domesticity as the prescriptive norm for American women. Published wartime stories of the abilities of women to work hard, think quickly, and survive would have increased anxiety over changing gender roles during a time when Americans wanted to believe in traditional male-female roles, in the "Mom and apple pie" the soldiers had fought for. Rosie the Riveter, the stereotypical World War II female factory worker, ideally turned in her goggles and hard hat at the end of the war and once again donned an apron, becoming the June Cleaver of the 1950s. According to the norms of womanhood, Rosie gladly made the change because riveting was men's work, something she took up only to bring home her husband, brother, or father more quickly from the war.

This stereotype was only a cheerful façade, however, since scholars have recently shown that women in the 1950s were not June Cleaver: many steadily moved back into the workplace, others became active in a variety of social and political causes, and some joined the countercultural Beat movement. World War II accelerated the constantly changing roles of women in American society, a wartime trend that can be traced to the founding of the United States. Following the American

Revolution, women became Republican Mothers, embodiments of virtue and intellect who would raise model sons to take part in the new government. In the aftermath of the Civil War and their involvement with organizations such as the Sanitary Commission, northern white women further pushed at the boundaries of domesticity and embraced the entire community as their home, making themselves a major force in benevolent work. Women's wide-ranging participation in World War I—from factory workers to nurses to telephone "Hello Girls"—finally secured them a constitutional amendment guaranteeing their right to vote.[6] Wars enabled women not only to show their patriotism but also to demonstrate that they could think as intelligently and work as hard as men; therefore, in the postwar periods women gradually gained an increasing public presence and the right to make more choices about their lives. These changes, however, sparked public debates over the "proper" roles of women, provoking unease about altering gender roles. In this climate, men's wartime memoirs would be better received, because war is traditionally within the masculine sphere.

Not until the 1980s and 1990s, after the resurgence of feminism and the establishment of women's studies programs, after the harsh lessons learned from Vietnam, did more of women's wartime autobiographies find their way into print. Feminists pushed for changes in gender roles and for women's rights, while scholars of women's studies turned their attention to the broader meanings of war, both groups (plus much of the American public) influenced by televised scenes of the devastating effects of war on the Vietnamese people and countryside. Clearly, war no longer simply meant soldiers and battlefields; it involved home and family and required women's participation. After fifty or more years, Americans, reflecting on the tangled web of Vietnam, began to realize that American women, as much as men, must have had a variety of experiences during World War II, including spying, assisting guerrillas and prisoners of war, evading the enemy, and surviving internment. The autobiographies used in this book show how American women in the South Pacific acquitted themselves through various wartime trials, not by Gladys Savary's self-deprecating claim of muddling through, but as Agnes Newton Keith asserted: by fighting with everything they had.

NOTES

INTRODUCTION

1. Natalie Crouter, *Forbidden Diary: A Record of Wartime Internment, 1941–1945*, ed. and with an introduction by Lynn Z. Bloom (New York: Burt Franklin, 1980), 103.

2. Standard works on American women during World War II include Karen Anderson, *Wartime Women* (Westport, CT: Greenwood Press, 1981), and Susan M. Hartmann, *The Homefront and Beyond* (Boston: Twayne Publishers, 1982).

3. The exact number is unknown, ranging anywhere from 7,500 to 14,000. Currently, the Center for Civilian Internee Rights in Miami Beach, Florida, a group fighting for compensation and an apology from the Japanese government, puts the number closer to 14,000.

4. Excerpts of the 1929 Geneva Convention are in E. Bartlett Kerr, *Surrender and Survival: The Experience of American POWs in the Pacific, 1941–1945* (New York: William Morrow, 1985), 329–34. For a discussion of internees and prisoners of war, see Shirley Castelnuovo, "Internment and the Rules of War," *Oral History Review* 19 (Spring/Fall 1991): 115–20. Although some Allied civilians were returned to their home countries, the Japanese and U.S. governments had diplomatic and military difficulties organizing repatriation. For the most complete account, see P. Scott Corbett, *Quiet Passages: The Exchanges of Civilians Between the United States and Japan During the Second World War* (Kent, OH: Kent State University Press, 1987).

5. Agnes Newton Keith, *Three Came Home* (New York: MacFadden-Bartell, 1965), 252; Marilyn Lake, "Female Desires: The Meaning of World War II," in *Feminism and History*, ed. Joan Wallach Scott (New York: Oxford University Press, 1996), 436; introduction to Margaret Randolph Higonnet et al., eds., *Behind the Lines: Gender and the Two World Wars* (New Haven: Yale University Press, 1987), 1; Victoria Bynum, *Unruly Women: The Politics of Social and Sexual Control in the Old South* (Chapel Hill: University of North Carolina Press, 1992), 111.

6. Gail Bederman, *Manliness and Civilization: A Cultural History of Gender and Race in the United States, 1880–1917* (Chicago: University of Chicago Press, 1995), 7. Bederman's concern is with men and constructions of manliness, but this approach is applicable to women as well. The most influential article on gender remains Joan Wallach Scott's "Gender: A Useful Category of Historical Analysis," in *Feminism and History*, ed. Scott (New York: Oxford University Press, 1996), 152–80.

7. The classic example of a study of nineteenth-century women is Nancy F. Cott, *The Bonds of Womanhood: "Woman's Sphere" in New England, 1780–1835* (New Haven: Yale University Press, 1977). The idea of womanhood did cut across the nineteenth and twentieth centuries according to Priscilla Murolo, *The Common Ground of Womanhood: Class, Gender, and Working Girls' Clubs, 1884–1928* (Urbana: University of Illinois Press, 1997). In her overview of American women's history, Mary P. Ryan evidently finds the term "womanhood" appropriate for all centuries, as indicated in her title, *Womanhood in America: From Colonial Times to the Present,* 2d ed. (New York: New Viewpoints, 1979). A perusal of the *Reader's Guide to Periodical Literature* for 1929–1941 shows no separate category for "womanhood" and no articles with that word in the titles, suggesting that as a referential term it had fallen into disuse. Yet a telling tie to tradition remained: the "woman" category in the *Reader's Guide* contains a "see also" list, which, for the above same years, included "housewives," "marriage," "mothers," and "wives."

8. On scientific motherhood see Rima D. Apple, "Constructing Mothers: Scientific Motherhood in the Nineteenth and Twentieth Centuries," in *Mothers and Motherhood: Readings in American History,* ed. Apple and Janet Golden (Columbus: Ohio State University Press, 1997), 90–110. On scientific motherhood and the permissive era, see Sharon Hays, *The Cultural Contradictions of Motherhood* (New Haven: Yale University Press, 1996), chap. 2. For an explanation of bad mothers, see Molly Ladd-Taylor and Lauri Umansky, introduction to *"Bad" Mothers: The Politics of Blame in Twentieth-Century America,* ed. Ladd-Taylor and Umansky (New York: New York University Press, 1998), 3.

9. See Linda K. Kerber, *Women of the Republic: Intellect and Ideology in Revolutionary America* (New York: W. W. Norton, 1980), chaps. 7–9; Mary Beth Norton, *Liberty's Daughters: The Revolutionary Experience of American Women, 1750–1800* (Boston: Little, Brown, 1980), chap. 9; Hays, chap. 2.

10. Lynn Z. Bloom, "Reunion and Reinterpretation: Group Biography in Process," *Biography* 13 (Summer 1990): 229.

11. See John W. Dower, *War Without Mercy: Race and Power in the Pacific War* (New York: Pantheon Books, 1986), 102–4.

12. Sidonie Smith, *A Poetics of Women's Autobiography: Marginality and the Fictions of Self-Representation* (Bloomington: Indiana University Press, 1987), 19.

13. Lynn Z. Bloom, "Escaping Voices: Women's South Pacific Internment Diaries and Memoirs," *Mosaic* 23 (Summer 1990): 101–12; Lynn Z. Bloom, "Women's War Stories: The Legacy of South Pacific Internment," in *Visions of War: World War II in Popular Literature and Culture,* ed. M. Paul Holsinger and Mary Ann Schofield (Bowling Green, OH: Bowling Green State University Popular Press, 1992), 66–77.

14. See n. 2 above for a basic historiography on American women and World War II. Brief coverage of internment can be found in H. W. Brands, *Bound to Empire: The United States and the Philippines* (New York: Oxford University Press, 1992), 211–12, and Stanley Karnow, *In Our Image: America's Empire in the Philippines* (New York: Random House, 1989), 305–6. On Jewish women in Nazi concentration camps, see "Prologue: Women and the Holocaust," in Carol Rittner and John K. Roth, eds., *Different Voices: Women and the Holocaust* (New York: Paragon House, 1993), 2–3. On Japanese-American women, see Valerie Matsumoto, "Japanese American Women During World War II," in *Unequal Sisters: A Multi-Cultural Reader in U.S. Women's His-*

tory, 2d ed., ed. Vicki L. Ruiz and Ellen Carol DuBois (New York: Routledge, 1994), 436–49.

15. The prewar years are discussed only to set the stage for wartime activities. It is beyond the scope of this book to explore the complex race, class, and gender issues of the American presence in the Pacific Rim up until 1941.

1. WOMEN'S DUTY AND THE DECISION TO STAY IN THE PACIFIC

1. Agnes Newton Keith, *Three Came Home* (New York: MacFadden-Bartell, 1965), 24.

2. Keith, 24.

3. Critiques of benevolent assimilation can be found, for example, in Vincente L. Rafael, "White Love: Surveillance and Nationalist Resistance in the U.S. Colonization of the Philippines," in *Cultures of United States Imperialism,* ed. Amy Kaplan and Donald E. Pease (Durham: Duke University Press, 1993), 185. While there is a burgeoning historiography on European women and empire, there is little on American women and empire, a topic that merits its own full-length study and is outside the scope of this book. On European women, see, for instance, Kumari Jayawardena, *The White Woman's Other Burden: Western Women and South Asia During British Rule* (New York: Routledge, 1995), and Julia Clancy-Smith and Frances Gouda, ed., *Domesticating the Empire: Race, Gender, and Family Life in French and Dutch Colonialism* (Charlottesville: University Press of Virginia, 1998). Jayawardena's book does contain some information about American women.

4. Jane Hunter, *The Gospel of Gentility: American Women Missionaries in Turn-of-the-Century China* (New Haven: Yale University Press, 1984), xiii; Kenton J. Clymer, *Protestant Missionaries in the Philippines, 1898–1916: An Inquiry into the American Colonial Mentality* (Urbana: University of Illinois Press, 1986), 5.

5. Hunter, 182.

6. H. W. Brands, *Bound to Empire: The United States and the Philippines* (New York: Oxford University Press, 1992), 72.

7. Clymer, 18–20.

8. Anne C. Kwantes, *Presbyterian Missionaries in the Philippines: Conduits of Social Change, 1899–1910* (Quezon City, PI: New Day, 1989), 130–35.

9. Darlene Deibler Rose, *Evidence Not Seen: A Woman's Miraculous Faith in the Jungles of World War II* (New York: HarperSanFrancisco, 1988). I refer to the women by the names they used during the war years; to avoid confusion and excess words to distinguish between husbands and wives, I refer to the internees and evaders by their first names.

10. Stanley Karnow, *In Our Image: America's Empire in the Philippines* (New York: Random House, 1989), 201–2.

11. "Advice to the American Teachers in the Provinces," in *Tales of American Teachers in the Philippines,* ed. Geronima T. Pecson and Maria Racelis (Manila: Carmelo and Bauerman, 1959), 123; Alice M. Kelly, "The Bua School— A Few Personal Notes," in *Tales of American Teachers in the Philippines,* 78; Brands, 71.

12. Quoted in Karnow, 205.

13. Mary H. Fee, *A Woman's Impressions of the Philippines* (Chicago: A.C. McClurg, 1910), 86, 115, 247.

14. Caroline S. Shunk, *An Army Woman in the Philippines* (Kansas City, MO: Franklin Hudson, 1914), 59–60, 175.

15. Margaret Tayler Yates, *"Via Government Transport"* (Manila: Philippine Education Co., 1926), 1, 75, back page (unnumbered).

16. Elizabeth Vaughan, *The Ordeal of Elizabeth Vaughan: A Wartime Diary of the Philippines*, ed. Carol M. Petillo (Athens: University of Georgia Press, 1985); transcript of interview with Betsy McCreary by Rita Cumming Knox in possession of the author, 1 March 1992, 4.

17. Florence Horn, *Orphans of the Pacific: The Philippines* (New York: Reynal and Hitchcock, 1941), 90.

18. Dorothy Dore Dowlen, unpublished manuscript in possession of the author, 26 (a published version of this wartime memoir of a young woman in the Philippines is forthcoming from McFarland and Company Publishers, Jefferson, NC).

19. Natalie Crouter, *Forbidden Diary: A Record of Wartime Internment, 1941–1945*, ed. and with an introduction by Lynn Z. Bloom (New York: Burt Franklin, 1980), xiv–xvi.

20. Margaret Sams, *Forbidden Family: A Wartime Memoir of the Philippines, 1941–1945*, ed. and with an introduction by Lynn Z. Bloom (Madison: University of Wisconsin Press, 1989), 39.

21. Alice Franklin Bryant, *The Sun Was Darkened* (Boston: Chapman and Grimes, 1947), 20, 22.

22. Bryant, 23–24.

23. Frieda Magnuson, *Out in '45, If We're Still Alive* (Sisters, OR: The One-Book Company, 1984), 32.

24. John W. Dower, *War Without Mercy: Race and Power in the Pacific War* (New York: Pantheon Books, 1986), 102–4. Brian McAllister Linn challenges this assumption, arguing that U.S. military planners knew the Japanese would be a formidable force in the Pacific. However, the women in this book were not of the same opinion. See Linn's *Guardians of Empire: The U.S. Army and the Pacific, 1902–1940* (Chapel Hill: University of North Carolina Press, 1997), 177.

25. These issues are covered in Ronald H. Spector, *Eagle Against the Sun: The American War with Japan* (New York: Free Press, 1985), 55–56; Brands, 174–75; Linn, chap. 7.

26. Fern Harrington Miles, *Captive Community: Life in a Japanese Internment Camp, 1941–1945* (Jefferson City, TN: Mossy Creek Press, 1987), vii.

27. Judy Hyland, *In the Shadow of the Rising Sun* (Minneapolis: Augsburg Publishing House, 1984), 9.

28. Peter R. Wygle, "References Regarding Actions Which Affected American Civilians in the Far East at the Approach of WWII" (unpublished paper, n.d.), 2; Brands, 180–81.

29. Spector, 68–69.

30. Quoted in Lewis E. Gleeck Jr., *The Manila Americans, 1901–1964* (Manila: Carmelo and Bauermann, 1977), 238; Helen N. Brush to author, 19 December 1995.

31. Frederic H. Stevens, *Santo Tomas Internment Camp, 1942–1945* (Limited private edition: Frederic H. Stevens, 1946), 2–3.

32. Stevens, 5.

33. Sams, 48; Sams to author, telephone interview on 18 January 1996.

34. Magnuson, 32.

35. Grace C. Nash, *That We Might Live* (Scottsdale, AZ: Shano Publishers, 1984), 15–16.

36. Bryant, 12–13.

37. Keith, 30–31.

38. Betty Foley, "Jap Jail Birds," 1945–46, 1, unpublished paper in possession of the author; Betty Foley to author, 8 February 1996; Keith, 44.

39. On the Japanese in China, see Dower, 43. Dower points out that the death total is controversial; Crouter, 1; Sams, 49; Sams to author, telephone interview on 18 January 1996.

40. Gwen Dew, *Prisoner of the Japs* (New York: Alfred A. Knopf, 1943), 5–6.

41. Dew, 17.

42. Tressa R. Cates, *The Drainpipe Diary* (New York: Vantage Press, 1957), 9.

43. Nash, 21; Vaughan, 3; Bryant, 9–10.

44. Helen N. Brush to author, 19 December 1995; Sams, 49.

45. Spector, 107.

46. Magnuson, 36; Nash, 22–23.

47. Crouter, 3.

48. Vaughan, 5; Bryant, 36–37.

49. Keith, 33.

50. Rose, 38.

51. Bryant, 36.

52. Sams, 56–57.

53. Josephine B. Hanning, "Years to Remember: The Diaries of Josephine B. Hanning, Santo Tomas Internment Camp, Manila, Philippines, January 1942–November 1943," comp. Mike Hanning, unpublished diary in possession of the author, c. 1989, 2.

54. Keith, 35, 38.

55. Keith, 41.

56. Keith, 43.

57. Dew, 100, 103.

58. Dew, 105, 108.

59. Vaughan, 10.

60. Vaughan, 17, 32.

61. Vaughan, 47–48.

62. Bryant, 44.

63. Hanning, 2.

64. Sams, 58.

65. Nash, 31; Cates, 32.

66. Rose, 45.

67. See Dan P. Calica and Nelia Sancho, eds., *War Crimes on Asian Women; Military Sexual Slavery by Japan During World War II: The Case of the Filipino Comfort Women* ([Manila?]: Task Force on Filipina Victims of Military Sexual Slavery by Japan; Asian Women Human Rights Council–Philippine Section, 1993); George Hicks, *The Comfort Women: Japan's Brutal Regime of Enforced Prostitution in the Second World War* (New York: W.W. Norton, 1995).

68. For a full account of this event, see Catherine Kenny, *Captives: Australian Army Nurses in Japanese Prison Camps* (St. Lucia, AUS: University of Queensland Press, 1986), 29–36.

69. Dew, 137; Kenny corroborated Dew's contemporary account.

70. Dew, 136.

71. Vaughan, 30–31; Nash, 53; Bryant, 122.

72. Keith, 47. On the racial views of the Japanese, see Dower, chaps. 8 and 9.

2. THE STRUGGLE TO ORGANIZE

1. Josephine B. Hanning, "Years to Remember: The Diaries of Josephine B. Hanning, Santo Tomas Internment Camp, Manila, Philippines, January 1942–November 1943," comp. Mike Hanning, unpublished diary in possession of the author, c. 1989, 8.

2. These numbers were determined by the Center for Civilian Internee Rights and published in its January 1997 newsletter. The organization concludes that 4,749 Americans were held by the Nazis and 13,996 by the Japanese.

3. Bureau of Publicity, Department of General Affairs, Japanese Military Administration, *The Official Journal of the Japanese Military Administration* (Manila: Nichi Nichi Shimbun Sha, n.d.), 1:3, 3:17.

4. For a general history of the Santo Tomas Internment Camp, see A. V. H. Hartendorp, *The Santo Tomas Story*, ed. Frank H. Golay (New York: McGraw-Hill, 1964).

5. Emily Van Sickle, *The Iron Gates of Santo Tomas: The Firsthand Account of an American Couple Interned by the Japanese in Manila, 1942–1945* (Chicago: Academy Chicago Publishers, 1992), 16, 17, 19.

6. Grace C. Nash, *That We Might Live* (Scottsdale, AZ: Shano Publishers, 1984), 34.

7. Tressa R. Cates, *The Drainpipe Diary* (New York: Vantage Press, 1957), 7, 11.

8. Natalie Crouter, *Forbidden Diary: A Record of Wartime Internment, 1941–1945*, ed. and with an introduction by Lynn Z. Bloom (New York: Burt Franklin, 1980), 9.

9. Elizabeth Vaughan, *The Ordeal of Elizabeth Vaughan: A Wartime Diary of the Philippines*, ed. and with an introduction by Carol M. Petillo (Athens: University of Georgia Press, 1985), 102.

10. Margaret Sams, *Forbidden Family: A Wartime Memoir of the Philippines, 1941–1945*, ed. and with an introduction by Lynn Z. Bloom (Madison: University of Wisconsin Press, 1989), 59, 62.

11. Sams, 108.

12. Agnes Newton Keith, *Three Came Home* (New York: MacFadden-Bartell, 1965), 47–48.

13. Darlene Deibler Rose, *Evidence Not Seen: A Woman's Miraculous Faith in the Jungles of World War II* (New York: HarperSanFrancisco, 1988), 61–62, 69.

14. Keith, 97.

15. Hanning, 3.

16. Van Sickle, 55.

17. Hartendorp, 83. This brief summary of camp elections and politics comes from both Hartendorp and Frederic H. Stevens, *Santo Tomas Internment Camp, 1942–1945* (Limited private edition: Frederic H. Stevens, 1946).

18. Van Sickle, 138; Cates, 39.

19. Van Sickle, 139; Sams, 149.

20. Ethel Thomas Herold, "World War II Diary, December 7, 1941 to May 9, 1945," unpublished manuscript in possession of the author, 36, 59.

21. Betsy Herold Heimke to author, 31 January 1996.

22. Fern Harrington Miles, *Captive Community: Life in a Japanese Internment Camp, 1941–1945* (Jefferson City, TN: Mossy Creek Press, 1987), 39.
23. Herold, 92.
24. Crouter, 81, 144, 149.
25. Crouter, 153, 156.
26. Miles, 98–99.
27. Miles, 99; Crouter, 290, 293.
28. Keith, 93.
29. Keith, 147–148.
30. Rose, 69.
31. Rose, 69.
32. Rose, 181.
33. Hanning, 3; Vaughan, 213.
34. Cates, 38; Van Sickle, 29, 197; Nash, 39.
35. Van Sickle, 23; Cates, 43; Nash, 39.
36. For a discussion of Filipino resistance and collaboration, see H. W. Brands, *Bound to Empire: The United States and the Philippines* (New York: Oxford University Press, 1992), 198–204.
37. Cates, 134; Nash, 46.
38. Sams, 69.
39. Cates, 202.
40. Miles, 38.
41. Miles, 38; Herold, 134, 287.
42. Crouter, 19, 27.
43. Crouter, 48–49.
44. Crouter, 186–87.
45. Keith, 61.
46. Keith, 198.
47. Herold, 310; Vaughan, 150. Such reactions were not unique to Americans, as women of other nationalities expressed similar patriotic fervor.
48. Crouter, 51–52.
49. Crouter, 96; Vaughan, 179.
50. Crouter, 265; Vaughan, 259; Cates, 194.
51. Keith, 170–71.
52. Hanning, 11; Herold, 312; Cates, 63.
53. Crouter, 103.
54. Bryant, 124; Herold, 299.
55. Van Sickle, 242–43.
56. Crouter, 388.
57. Herold, 238.
58. Keith, 63.
59. Hanning, 28–29.
60. Keith, 96, 98.
61. Miles, 61–71.

3. WORK AND WOMANHOOD IN INTERNMENT

1. Natalie Crouter, *Forbidden Diary: A Record of Wartime Internment, 1941–1945*, ed. and with an introduction by Lynn Z. Bloom (New York: Burt Franklin, 1980), 54.

2. Frederic H. Stevens, *Santo Tomas Internment Camp, 1942–1945* (Limited private edition: Frederic H. Stevens, 1946), 24; Frieda Magnuson, *Out in '45, If We're Still Alive* (Sisters, OR: The One-Book Company, 1984), 52; Emily Van Sickle, *The Iron Gates of Santo Tomas: The Firsthand Account of an American Couple Interned by the Japanese in Manila, 1942–1945* (Chicago: Academy Chicago Publishers, 1992), 134.

3. Ethel Thomas Herold, "World War II Diary, December 7, 1941 to May 9, 1945," unpublished manuscript in possession of the author, 44, 46.

4. Herold, 95, 254.

5. Crouter, 20, 60, 107.

6. Herold, 44; Crouter, 54, 81.

7. Margaret Sams, *Forbidden Family: A Wartime Memoir of the Philippines, 1941–1945*, ed. and with an introduction by Lynn Z. Bloom (Madison: University of Wisconsin Press, 1989), 88; Crouter, 191; Betty Foley, "Jap Jail Birds," 1945–1946, unpublished manuscript in possession of the author, 8.

8. Elizabeth Vaughan, *The Ordeal of Elizabeth Vaughn: A Wartime Diary of the Philippines*, ed. and with an introduction by Carol M. Petillo (Athens: University of Georgia Press, 1985), 98; Alice Franklin Bryant, *The Sun Was Darkened* (Boston: Chapman and Grimes, 1947), 126.

9. Crouter, 25.

10. Vaughan, 125.

11. Herold, 48; Crouter, 43; Foley, 8.

12. Bryant, 155–57.

13. Tressa R. Cates, *The Drainpipe Diary* (New York: Vantage Press, 1957), 147.

14. Vaughan, 148, 189; Van Sickle, 29.

15. Magnuson, 54.

16. Vaughan, 148; Sams, 87, 94.

17. Herold, 63.

18. Herold, 249.

19. Cates, 38–41, 195.

20. For a more detailed discussion of the treatment of military prisoners of war, see Ronald H. Spector, *Eagle Against the Sun: The American War with Japan* (New York: Free Press, 1985), chap. 18, and John W. Dower, *War Without Mercy: Race and Power in the Pacific War* (New York: Pantheon Books, 1986), chap. 3. On the military nurses, see Elizabeth M. Norman and Sharon Eifried, "How Did They All Survive? An Analysis of American Nurses' Experiences in Japanese Prisoner-of-War Camps," *Nursing History Review* 3 (1995): 108. On the Guam nurses who were captured but repatriated, see "Nurses As Prisoners," *The Oak Leaf* [Oakland, CA], 9 April 1943, photocopy of article in Navy Nurse POW File, Navy Bureau of Medicine and Surgery, Washington, D.C.; Joan R. Atchison, "The U.S. Navy Nurse Corps Involvement in Military Conflicts: Past and Present" (M.S. thesis, University of Maryland, 1991).

21. Dorothy Still Danner, *What a Way to Spend a War: Navy Nurse POWs in the Philippines* (Annapolis, MD: Naval Institute Press, 1995), 80–81, 98.

22. Rose Rieper Meier, interview by Maj. Margaret Lauer, 12 March 1984, 1, transcript, and Ethel Blaine Millet, interview by Maj. Patricia Rikli, 9 April 1983, 13, transcript, both in Army Nurse Corps Oral History Program, U.S. Army Center of Military History, Washington, D.C.

23. Denny Williams, *To The Angels* (San Francisco: Denson Press, 1985), 12.

24. Williams, 61–62.

25. Minnie Breese Stubbs, interview by Peg Baskerfield, 9 April 1983, 14, transcript, Army Nurse Corps Oral History Program, U.S. Army Center of Military History, Washington, D.C.; Williams, 91, 96; Millet, 17.

26. Gladys Ann Mealer Giles, interview by Maj. Dena A. Norton, 9 April 1983, 20, transcript, and Inez Moore, interview by Col. Connie Slewitzke, April [?] 1986, 26, transcript, both in Army Nurse Corps Oral History Program, U.S. Army Center of Military History, Washington, D.C.; Williams, 97.

27. Madeline M. Ullom, "The Philippines Assignment: Some Aspects of the Army Nurse Corps in the Philippine Islands, 1940–45," unpublished manuscript, 92, Army Nurse Corps, U.S. Army Center of Military History, Washington, D.C.; Edith Shacklette Haynes, interview by Maj. Susan McMarlin, 9 April 1983, 15, transcript; Earlyn Black Harding, interview by Col. Marilee Tollefson, 9 April 1982, 15, transcript; Helen M. Nestor, interview by Maj. Thomas Beeman, 9 April 1983, 4–5, transcript, all in Army Nurse Corps Oral History Program, U.S. Army Center of Military History, Washington, D.C.

28. Sallie Durrett Farmer, interview by Mary B. Knight, 25 May 1984, 12, transcript, Army Nurse Corps Oral History Program, U.S. Army Center of Military History, Washington, D.C.

29. Hattie R. Brantley, interview by Judith R. Petsetki, 9 April 1983, 23, transcript, Army Nurse Corps Oral History Program, U.S. Army Center of Military History, Washington, D.C.

30. Williams, 123, 125; Haynes, 16.

31. Danner, 104.

32. Geneva Jenkins, interview by Lt. Col. Joyce Johnson Bowles and Lt. Col. Karen Sollinberger-Vinson, 3 April 1983, 13–14, transcript, Army Nurse Corps Oral History Program, U.S. Army Center of Military History, Washington, D.C.

33. Williams, 143.

34. Jenkins, 17; Nestor, 21; Mildred Dalton Manning, interview by Lt. Col. Ruth Mobley, 11 April 1984, 14, transcript, Army Nurse Corps Oral History Program, U.S. Army Center of Military History, Washington, D.C.; Millet, 19.

35. Mary Rose Harrington Nelson, interview by Maj. Donna Owen, 23 April 1983, 19, transcript, Army Nurse Corps Oral History Program, U.S. Army Center of Military History, Washington, D.C.; Danner, 176.

36. Untitled song by anonymous author, Navy Nurse POW File, Navy Bureau of Medicine and Surgery, Washington, D.C.

37. Williams, 146.

38. Crouter, 38.

39. Sams, 88.

40. Foley, 8.

41. Van Sickle, 44, 183; Sams, 70.

42. Cates, 160–61.

43. Bryant, 154.

44. Van Sickle, 65.

45. Van Sickle, 188.

46. Van Sickle, 230–31; Cates, 231.

47. On the military situation in 1944, see Spector, chaps. 17 and 19; Herold, 315, 320.

48. Bryant, 126; Vaughan, 233; Van Sickle, 25.

49. Cates, 39; Bryant, 192–93.

50. Vaughan, 113; Grace C. Nash, *That We Might Live* (Scottsdale, AZ: Shano Publishers, 1984),156–59.

51. Crouter, 123; Vaughan, 251.

52. Crouter, 45.

53. Cates, 232, 214.

54. Agnes Newton Keith, *Three Came Home* (New York: MacFadden-Bartell, 1965), 57.

55. Keith, 115–16.

56. Keith, 192.

57. Keith, 196.

58. Keith, 213.

59. Darlene Deibler Rose, *Evidence Not Seen: A Woman's Miraculous Faith in the Jungles of World War II* (New York: HarperSanFrancisco, 1988), 88, 187.

4. ROMANCE, MARRIAGE, AND FAMILY LIFE DURING THE WAR

1. Margaret Sams, *Forbidden Family: A Wartime Memoir of the Philippines, 1941–1945*, ed. and with an introduction by Lynn Z. Bloom (Madison: University of Wisconsin Press, 1989), 80.

2. Sams, 77–78. For an overview of American women and beauty, see Lois W. Banner, *American Beauty* (Chicago: University of Chicago Press, 1983), chap. 13.

3. Josephine B. Hanning, "Years to Remember: The Diaries of Josephine B. Hanning, Santo Tomas Internment Camp, Manila, Philippines, January 1942–November 1943," comp. Mike Hanning, unpublished diary in possession of the author, c. 1989, 7–8, 34–36.

4. Elizabeth Vaughan, *The Ordeal of Elizabeth Vaughan: A Wartime Diary of the Philippines*, ed. and with an introduction by Carol M. Petillo (Athens: University of Georgia Press, 1985), 128.

5. Hanning, 32–34; Vaughan, 273.

6. Vaughan, 171, 215; Emily Van Sickle, *The Iron Gates of Santo Tomas: The Firsthand Account of an American Couple Interned by the Japanese in Manila, 1942–1945* (Chicago: Academy Chicago Publishers, 1992), 59; Vaughan, 232.

7. Sams, 63; Vaughan, 171.

8. Fern Harrington Miles, *Captive Community: Life in a Japanese Internment Camp, 1941–1945* (Jefferson City, TN: Mossy Creek Press, 1987), 60; Natalie Crouter, *Forbidden Diary: A Record of Wartime Internment, 1941–1945*, ed. and with an introduction by Lynn Z. Bloom (New York: Burt Franklin, 1980), 36.

9. Miles, 116–17.

10. Crouter, 267, 269.

11. Van Sickle, 80; Tressa R. Cates, *The Drainpipe Diary* (New York: Vantage Press, 1957), 106–07.

12. Cates, 157.

13. Van Sickle, 74; Cates, 129.

14. Cates, 64.

15. Cates, 224.

16. Crouter, 18, 29, 33.

17. Agnes Newton Keith, *Three Came Home* (New York: MacFadden-Bartell, 1965), 135, 137.

18. Keith, 104–6.

19. Ethel Thomas Herold, "World War II Diary, December 7, 1941 to May 9, 1945," unpublished manuscript in possession of the author, 316.

20. Sams, 103.
21. Crouter, 76.
22. Sams, 110–11. Lynn Bloom explores these interpretive issues in her introduction to Sams's book; see especially p. x.
23. Crouter, 70; Van Sickle, 117.
24. Crouter, 78.
25. Crouter, 58; Vaughan, 155–56.
26. Cates, 37, 42.
27. Cates, 123.
28. Sams, 55, 99, 102–3.
29. Charlotte Brussolo to author, telephone interview, 24 October 1996.
30. Crouter, 21, 111, 123.
31. Vaughan, 101.
32. Herold, 60; Keith, 64–66.
33. Keith, 117–18.
34. Hanning, 36.
35. Hanning, 36; Van Sickle, 142.
36. Hanning, 38–39.
37. Van Sickle, 143–44.
38. Grace C. Nash, *That We Might Live* (Scottsdale, AZ: Shano Publishers, 1984), 40.
39. Crouter, 21, 61, 84, 111; Herold, 77.
40. Crouter, 148.
41. Hanning, 16, 25, 55–56.
42. Cates, 55.
43. Crouter, 43, 99; Herold, 143–44; Miles, 126.
44. Herold, 49, 53.
45. Herold, 132, 202; Crouter, 109.
46. Crouter, 121, 265; Keith, 187–88.
47. Herold, 152, 165, 167, 204.
48. Van Sickle, 50.
49. Crouter, 43, 95; Cates, 157.
50. Crouter, 191, 297.
51. Crouter, 299.
52. Crouter, 300, 327, 389; Herold, 296.
53. Van Sickle, 200.
54. Miles, 129–30; Herold, 293–94; Crouter, 417.
55. Crouter, 110; Vaughan, 105; Cates, 242–43.
56. Keith, 88, 90.
57. Herold, 168.
58. Van Sickle, 102; Crouter, 245, 293; Herold, 272.
59. Hanning, 23.
60. Sams, 135.
61. Sams, 141, 154.
62. Sams, 196, 218, 221.
63. Sams, 234–36.
64. Keith, 127.
65. Keith, 132.
66. Keith, 137–38.
67. Herold, 55–56.
68. Herold, 56.
69. Keith, 119.

5. EVADING INTERNMENT

1. Abby R. Jacobs, *We Did Not Surrender* (Manila: Privately printed, 1986), 53.

2. Viola S. Winn, *The Escape* (Wheaton, IL: Tyndale House Publishers, 1975), 5.

3. Jacobs, 7.

4. James and Ethel Chapman, *Escape to the Hills* (Lancaster, PA: Jaques Cattell Press, 1947), 13.

5. Jacobs, 10, 14.

6. Winn, 18.

7. Winn, 40–41.

8. Chapman, 23.

9. Chapman, 23.

10. Winn, 31, 35.

11. Jacobs, 18, 20.

12. Chapman, 35; Scott A. Mills, *Stranded in the Philippines: Missionary Professor Organizes Resistance to Japanese* (Quezon City, PI: New Day, 1994), 11.

13. Mills, 13.

14. Winn, 55.

15. Jacobs, 60.

16. Winn, 85–86.

17. Jacobs, 68.

18. Paul R. Lindholm, *Shadows from the Rising Sun: An American Family's Saga During the Japanese Occupation of the Philippines* (Quezon City, PI: New Day, 1978), 75–76; Jacobs, 72. Clara Lindholm wrote a couple of the chapters of Paul's book.

19. Jacobs, 80, 86.

20. For a detailed description of Villamor's activities, see Caridad Aldecoa-Rodriguez, *Negros Oriental from American Rule to the Present: A History*, vol. 2 (Tokyo and Dumaguete City, PI: Toyota Foundation and the Provincial Government of Negros Oriental, 1989), 90–96.

21. Chapman, 154; Mills, 93.

22. Chapman, 156–57.

23. Winn, 152.

24. Chapman, 161.

25. Chapman, 182.

26. Jacobs, 127.

27. Jacobs, 134; Mills, 124.

28. Winn, 179; Lindholm, 117.

29. Lindholm, 122.

30. Winn, 191, 211.

31. Dorothy Dore Dowlen, unpublished manuscript in possession of the author, 81, 83 (a published version of this wartime memoir of a young woman in the Philippines is forthcoming from McFarland and Company Publishers, Jefferson, NC).

32. Dowlen, 181–182.

33. Ida Rowe Dolphin, *Life on Hold* (Fairfield, WA: Ye Galleon Press, 1992), 79.

34. Dolphin, 95.

35. Dolphin, 119; Aldecoa-Rodriguez, 144.

36. Dolphin, 130–31.
37. Dolphin, 143.
38. Ida Rowe Dolphin to author, 7 May 1996.
39. Yay Panlilio, *The Crucible: An Autobiography by "Colonel Yay"* (New York: MacMillan, 1950), 22, 62.
40. Panlilio, 137, 337, 348.

6. NATIONAL IDENTITY AND SUBVERSION OF THE ENEMY

1. Margaret Utinsky, *"Miss U"* (San Antonio, TX: Naylor, 1948), 14.
2. Claire Phillips and Myron B. Goldsmith, *Manila Espionage* (Portland, OR: Binfords and Mort, 1947), 129.
3. Utinsky, 1.
4. Utinsky, 14.
5. Utinsky, 148–49, 151. Margaret's activities are described in H. Furnas, "Miss U," *Collier's*, 5 January 1946, 34; corroboration of her lieutenant rank and wartime activities can be found in "Lt. Margaret Utinksy—Bill Reimbursing Her for Supplies She Furnished Americans Behind Jap Lines," *New York Times*, 3 July 1946, 25:2. Her Medal of Freedom is discussed in Vern L. Bullough et al., eds., *American Nursing: A Biographical Dictionary* (New York: Garland, 1988), 326. Claire Phillips provided an overview of her wartime experiences in "I Was an American Spy," *American Mercury*, May 1945, 592–98, in which she admitted that her "High Pockets" network was part of the larger "Group U" headed by "Madame Unidsky," clearly a reference to Margaret's "Miss U." The books of both women are littered with names and photographs of American soldiers who aided their networks, men who corroborated their stories; Gen. Jonathan Wainwright wrote the foreword to Margaret's book.
6. Emily Hahn, *China to Me* (Boston: Beacon Press, 1988), 57. This memoir was originally published in 1944, while the war was still going on.
7. Emily Hahn, *Hong Kong Holiday* (New York: Doubleday, 1946), 78.
8. Hahn, *China to Me*, 312.
9. Hahn, *Hong Kong Holiday*, 103; Emily Hahn, *Times and Places* (New York: Thomas Y. Crowell, 1970), 283, 286; Hahn, *China to Me*, 310.
10. Hahn, *Times and Places*, 286.
11. Hahn, *Hong Kong Holiday*, 135, 161, 163, 174.
12. Hahn, *Hong Kong Holiday*, 211.
13. Hahn, *Hong Kong Holiday*, 274.
14. Hahn, *Times and Places*, 286.
15. Gladys Savary, *Outside the Walls* (New York: Vantage Press, 1954), 1.
16. Savary, 9–11.
17. Savary, 13.
18. Savary, 16, 18.
19. Savary, 30.
20. Savary, 35–36.
21. Savary, 38–39.
22. Savary, 46, 50–51.
23. Savary, 52.
24. Savary, 72.
25. Savary, 73.
26. Savary, 75.

27. Dorothy Janson, "Prisoners of War and the YMCA," *American Historical Collection* [n.d.]: 18.

28. Savary, 90–93.

29. Janson, 23–24.

30. Savary, 107–8.

31. Savary, 134.

32. Savary, 145.

33. Savary, 174.

34. Savary, 175.

35. Sofia Adamson, *Gods Angels Pearls and Roses* (El Monte, CA: American International Publishing, 1982), 128–29.

36. Adamson, 140.

37. Adamson, 157–58.

38. Adamson, 163.

39. Adamson, 202.

7. RESCUE AND ITS AFTERMATH

1. Ethel Thomas Herold, "World War II Diary, December 7, 1941, to May 9, 1945," unpublished manuscript in possession of the author, 310.

2. Ronald H. Spector, *Eagle Against the Sun: The American War with Japan* (New York: Free Press, 1985), 418. On MacArthur's liberation of the Philippines, see, for example, Spector, chap. 22; M. Hamlin Cannon, *Leyte: The Return to the Philippines* (Washington, DC: Office of the Chief of Military History, 1954); William Manchester, *American Ceasar: Douglas MacArthur, 1880–1964* (Boston: Little Brown, 1978).

3. Frieda Magnuson, *Out in '45, If We're Still Alive* (Sisters, OR: The One-Book Company, 1984), 67.

4. Tressa R. Cates, *The Drainpipe Diary* (New York: Vantage Press, 1957), 233–34.

5. Cates, 239–40.

6. Elizabeth Vaughan, *The Ordeal of Elizabeth Vaughan: A Wartime Diary of the Philippines*, ed. and with an introduction by Carol M. Petillo (Athens: University of Georgia Press, 1985), 299.

7. Emily Van Sickle, *The Iron Gates of Santo Tomas: The Firsthand Account of an American Couple Interned by the Japanese in Manila, 1942–1945* (Chicago: Academy Chicago Publishers, 1992), 314.

8. Cates, 245–46; Denny Williams, *To The Angels* (San Francisco: Denson Press, 1985), 200–202. Internees do not agree on the exact wording of that message, if it even existed. Some recalled that it said Christmas was coming, others that Santa Claus was coming.

9. Van Sickle, 316.

10. Alice Franklin Bryant, *The Sun Was Darkened* (Boston: Chapman and Grimes, 1947), 215, 227; Van Sickle, 320; Magnuson, 71.

11. Bryant, 218.

12. Magnuson, 73; Williams, 218–19.

13. Bryant, 230.

14. Magnuson, 73; Cates, 247; Bryant, 216–17.

15. Van Sickle, 341.

16. Cates, 270, 272.

17. Bryant, 249.

18. Bryant, 249, 261.

19. Magnuson, 83–85, 133.

20. Williams, 211.

21. Williams, 221. Maude D. Williams died on 27 April 1997. Her obituary lists her husband's date of death as 14 December 1944. For information on the Japanese prisoner-of-war ships, see Spector, 400.

22. Margaret Sams, *Forbidden Family: A Wartime Memoir of the Philippines, 1941–1945*, ed. and with an introduction by Lynn Z. Bloom (Madison: University of Wisconsin Press, 1989), 256.

23. Dorothy Still Danner, *What a Way to Spend a War: Navy Nurse POWs in the Philippines* (Annapolis, MD: Naval Institute Press, 1995), 193; Sams, 244, 271; Grace C. Nash, *That We Might Live* (Scottsdale, AZ: Shano Publishers, 1984), 207–8.

24. Sams, 276, 278.

25. Nash, 215; Danner, 194; Sams, 278. See also Edward M. Flanagan Jr., *The Los Banos Raid: The 11th Airborne Jumps at Dawn* (Novato, CA: Presidio, 1986).

26. Sams, 280–81.

27. Imogene Carlson, *American Family Interned* (Cebu City, PI: Cebu Christian Mission, 1979), 147.

28. Nash, 231–32.

29. Nash, reproduction on back cover.

30. Nash, 241.

31. Sams, 283, 286.

32. Sams, 295, 299.

33. Sams, 307.

34. Danner, 211.

35. Natalie Crouter, *Forbidden Diary: A Record of Wartime Internment, 1941–1945*, ed. and with an introduction by Lynn Z. Bloom (New York: Burt Franklin, 1980), 434; Betty Foley, "Jap Jail Birds," 1945–1946, unpublished paper in possession of the author, 9; Herold, 345.

36. Fern Harrington Miles, *Captive Community: Life in a Japanese Internment Camp, 1941–1945* (Jefferson City, TN: Mossy Creek Press, 1987), 152; Judy Hyland, *In the Shadow of the Rising Sun* (Minneapolis: Augsburg Publishing House, 1984), 94.

37. Hyland, 97; Herold, 354.

38. Foley, 10; Herold, 357; Crouter, 457, Miles, 159.

39. Herold, 361.

40. Herold, 365–66; Miles, 161.

41. Crouter, 470–71.

42. Crouter, 474; Herold, 370; Hyland, 110.

43. Crouter, 498, 505.

44. Miles, 184, 189, 191.

45. Hyland, 113, 117–19.

46. Foley, 11–12.

47. Herold, 409.

48. Agnes Newton Keith, *Three Came Home* (New York: MacFadden-Bartell, 1965), 208.

49. Keith, 209.

50. Keith, 211, 213.

51. Keith, 218, 228–29.

52. Keith, 247.

53. Keith, 250, 254.

54. Darlene Deibler Rose, *Evidence Not Seen: A Woman's Miraculous Faith in the Jungles of World War II* (New York: HarperSanFrancisco, 1988), 178.

55. Rose, 184.

56. Rose, 187.

57. Rose, 195.

58. Rose, 221.

CONCLUSION

1. Gladys Savary, *Outside the Walls* (New York: Vantage Press, 1954), 1.

2. Natalie Crouter, *Forbidden Diary: A Record of Wartime Internment, 1941–1945*, ed. and with an introduction by Lynn Z. Bloom (New York: Burt Franklin, 1980), 48–49.

3. To date, there has been no comprehensive study of the effects of internment on the children, but memoirs are beginning to surface. See, for instance, Peter R. Wygle, *Surviving a Japanese P.O.W. Camp: Father and Son Endure Internment in Manila During World War II* (Ventura, CA: Pathfinder Publishing, 1991).

4. Crouter, 505.

5. John E. Bodnar, *Remaking America: Public Memory, Commemoration, and Patriotism in the Twentieth Century* (Princeton: Princeton University Press, 1992), 15.

6. On women in the post–World War II period, see Joanne Meyerowitz, ed., *Not June Cleaver: Women and Gender in Postwar America, 1945–1960* (Philadelphia: Temple University Press, 1994). Republican Motherhood is discussed in Linda K. Kerber, *Women of the Republic: Intellect and Ideology in Revolutionary America* (New York: W.W. Norton, 1980); changes in the lives of northern white women after the Civil War are covered in Elizabeth D. Leonard, *Yankee Women: Gender Battles in the Civil War* (New York: W.W. Norton, 1994); and the push for woman suffrage is recounted in Eleanor Flexner, *Century of Struggle: The Woman's Rights Movement in the United States* (New York: Atheneum, 1971).

SELECTED BIBLIOGRAPHY

PUBLISHED PRIMARY SOURCES

Adamson, Sofia. *Gods Angels Pearls and Roses.* El Monte, CA: American International Publishing, 1982.

"Advice to the American Teachers in the Provinces." In *Tales of American Teachers in the Philippines*, ed. Geronima T. Pecson and Maria Racelis, 123–30. Manila: Carmelo and Bauerman, 1959.

Bryant, Alice Franklin. *The Sun Was Darkened.* Boston: Chapman and Grimes, 1947.

Carlson, Imogene. *American Family Interned.* Cebu City, PI: Cebu Christian Mission, 1979.

Cates, Tressa R. *The Drainpipe Diary.* New York: Vantage Press, 1957.

Chapman, James, and Ethel Chapman. *Escape to the Hills.* Lancaster, PA: Jaques Cattell Press, 1947.

Crouter, Natalie. *Forbidden Diary: A Record of Wartime Internment, 1941–1945*, Edited and with an introduction by Lynn Z. Bloom. New York: Burt Franklin, 1980.

Danner, Dorothy Still. *What a Way to Spend a War: Navy Nurse POWs in the Philippines.* Annapolis, MD: Naval Institute Press, 1995.

Dew, Gwen. *Prisoner of the Japs.* New York: Alfred A. Knopf, 1943.

Dolphin, Ida Rowe. *Life on Hold.* Fairfield, WA: Ye Galleon Press, 1992.

Fee, Mary H. *A Woman's Impressions of the Philippines.* Chicago: A. C. McClurg, 1910.

Hahn, Emily. *China to Me.* Boston: Beacon Press, 1988.

———. *Hong Kong Holiday.* New York: Doubleday, 1946.

———. *Times and Places.* New York: Thomas Y. Crowell, 1970.

Hyland, Judy. *In the Shadow of the Rising Sun.* Minneapolis: Augsburg Publishing House, 1984.

Jacobs, Abby R. *We Did Not Surrender.* Manila: Privately printed, 1986.

Janson, Dorothy. "Prisoners of War and the YMCA." *American Historical Collection* (n.d.).

Keith, Agnes Newton. *Three Came Home.* New York: MacFadden-Bartell, 1965.

Kelly, Alice M. "The Bua School—A Few Personal Notes." In *Tales of American Teachers in the Philippines*, ed. Geronima T. Pecson and Maria Racelis, 77–82. Manila: Carmelo and Bauerman, 1959.

Lindholm, Paul R. *Shadows from the Rising Sun: An American Family's Saga During the Japanese Occupation of the Philippines.* Quezon City, PI: New Day, 1978.

Magnuson, Frieda. *Out in '45, If We're Still Alive.* Sisters, OR: The One-Book Company, 1984.

Miles, Fern Harrington. *Captive Community: Life in a Japanese Internment Camp, 1941–1945.* Jefferson City, TN: Mossy Creek Press, 1987.

Mills, Scott A. *Stranded in the Philippines: Missionary Professor Organizes Resistance to Japanese.* Quezon City, PI: New Day, 1994.

Nash, Grace C. *That We Might Live.* Scottsdale, AZ: Shano Publishers, 1984.

Panlilio, Yay. *The Crucible: An Autobiography by "Colonel Yay."* New York: MacMillan, 1950.

Phillips, Claire. "I Was an American Spy." *American Mercury,* May 1945, 592–98.

Phillips, Claire, and Myron B. Goldsmith. *Manila Espionage.* Portland, OR: Binfords and Mort, 1947.

Rose, Darlene Deibler. *Evidence Not Seen: A Woman's Miraculous Faith in the Jungles of World War II.* New York: HarperSanFrancisco, 1988.

Sams, Margaret. *Forbidden Family: A Wartime Memoir of the Philippines, 1941–1945.* Edited and with an introduction by Lynn Z. Bloom. Madison: University of Wisconsin Press, 1989.

Savary, Gladys. *Outside the Walls.* New York: Vantage Press, 1954.

Shunk, Caroline S. *An Army Woman in the Philippines.* Kansas City, MO: Franklin Hudson Publishing, 1914.

Utinsky, Margaret. *"Miss U."* San Antonio, TX: Naylor, 1948.

Van Sickle, Emily. *The Iron Gates of Santo Tomas: The Firsthand Account of an American Couple Interned by the Japanese in Manila, 1942–1945.* Chicago: Academy Chicago Publishers, 1992.

Vaughan, Elizabeth. *The Ordeal of Elizabeth Vaughan: A Wartime Diary of the Philippines.* Edited and with an introduction by Carol M. Petillo. Athens: University of Georgia Press, 1985.

Williams, Denny. *To The Angels.* San Francisco: Denson Press, 1985.

Winn, Viola S. *The Escape.* Wheaton, IL: Tyndale House Publishers, 1975.

Yates, Margaret Tayler. *"Via Government Transport."* Manila: Philippine Education Co., 1926.

TRANSCRIPTS, INTERVIEWS, AND UNPUBLISHED PAPERS

Brantley, Hattie R. Interview by Judith R. Petsetki, 9 April 1983, transcript, United States Army Nurse Corps Oral History Program, U.S. Army Center of Military History, Washington, D.C.

Brush, Helen N., to author, 19 December 1995.

Brussolo, Charlotte, to author, telephone interview, 24 October 1996.

Dolphin, Ida Rowe, to author, 7 May 1996.

Dowlen, Dorothy Dore. Unpublished manuscript in possession of the author.

Farmer, Sallie Durrett. Interview by Mary B. Knight, 25 May 1984, transcript, United States Army Nurse Corps Oral History Program, U.S. Army Center of Military History, Washington, D.C.

Foley, Betty. "Jap Jail Birds," 1945–1946. Unpublished paper in possession of the author.

Foley, Betty, to author, 8 February 1996.

Giles, Gladys Ann Mealer. Interview by Maj. Dena A. Norton, 9 April 1983, transcript, United States Army Nurse Corps Oral History Program, U.S. Army Center of Military History, Washington, D.C.

Hanning, Josephine B. "Years to Remember: The Diaries of Josephine B. Hanning, Santo Tomas Internment Camp, Manila, Philippines, January 1942–November 1943." Compiled by Mike Hanning. Unpublished diary in the possession of the author, c. 1989.

Harding, Earlyn Black. Interview by Col. Marilee Tollefson, 9 April 1982, transcript, United States Army Nurse Corps Oral History Program, U.S. Army Center of Military History, Washington, D.C.

Haynes, Edith Shacklette. Interview by Maj. Susan McMarlin, 9 April 1983, transcript, United States Army Nurse Corps Oral History Program, U.S. Army Center of Military History, Washington, D.C.

Heimke, Betsy Herold, to author, 31 January 1996.

Herold, Ethel Thomas. "World War II Diary, December 7, 1941 to May 9, 1945." Unpublished manuscript in possession of the author.

Jenkins, Geneva. Interview by Lt. Col. Joyce Johnson Bowles and Lt. Col. Karen Sollinberger-Vinson, 3 April 1983, transcript, United States Army Nurse Corps Oral History Program, U.S. Army Center of Military History, Washington, D.C.

Manning, Mildred Dalton. Interview by Lt. Col. Ruth Mobley, 11 April 1984, transcript, United States Army Nurse Corps Oral History Program, U.S. Army Center of Military History, Washington, D.C.

Meier, Rose Rieper. Interview by Maj. Margaret Lauer, 12 March 1984, transcript, United States Army Nurse Corps Oral History Program, U.S. Army Center of Military History, Washington, D.C.

Millet, Ethel Blaine. Interview by Maj. Patricia Rikli, 9 April 1983, transcript, United States Army Nurse Corps Oral History Program, U.S. Army Center of Military History, Washington, D.C.

Moore, Inez. Interview by Col. Connie Slewitzke, April [?] 1986, transcript, United States Army Nurse Corps Oral History Program, U.S. Army Center of Military History, Washington, D.C.

Nelson, Mary Rose Harrington. Interview by Maj. Donna Owen, 23 April 1983, transcript, United States Army Nurse Corps Oral History Program, U.S. Army Center of Military History, Washington, D.C.

Nestor, Helen M. Interview by Maj. Thomas Beeman, 9 April 1983, transcript, United States Army Nurse Corps Oral History Program, U.S. Army Center of Military History, Washington, D.C.

Sams, Margaret, to author, telephone interview, 18 January 1996.

Stubbs, Minnie Breese. Interview by Peg Baskerfield, 9 April 1983, transcript, United States Army Nurse Corps Oral History Program, U.S. Army Center of Military History, Washington, D.C.

Transcript of interview with Betsy McCreary by Rita Cumming Knox, in possession of author, March 1, 1992, 4.

Ullom, Madeline M. "The Philippines Assignment: Some Aspects of the Army Nurse Corps in the Philippine Islands, 1940–45." Unpublished manuscript, U.S. Army Center of Military History, Army Nurse Corps, Washington, D.C.

Untitled song by anonymous author, Navy Nurse POW File, Navy Bureau of Medicine and Surgery, Washington, D.C.

Wygle, Peter R. "References Regarding Actions Which Affected American Civilians in the Far East at the Approach of WWII." Unpublished paper, n.d.

SECONDARY SOURCES

Aldecoa-Rodriguez, Caridad. *Negros Oriental from American Rule to the Present: A History.* Vol. 2. Tokyo and Dumaguete City, PI: Toyota Foundation and the Provincial Government of Negros Oriental, 1989.

Anderson, Karen. *Wartime Women.* Westport, CT: Greenwood Press, 1981.

Apple, Rima D. "Constructing Mothers: Scientific Motherhood in the Nineteenth and Twentieth Centuries." In *Mothers and Motherhood: Readings in American History,* ed. Rima D. Apple and Janet Golden, 90–110. Columbus: Ohio State University Press, 1997.

Atchinson, Joan R. "The U.S. Navy Nurse Corps Involvement in Military Conflicts: Past and Present." M.S. thesis, University of Maryland, 1991.

Banner, Lois W. *American Beauty.* Chicago: University of Chicago Press, 1983.

Bederman, Gail. *Manliness and Civilization: A Cultural History of Gender and Race in the United States, 1880–1917.* Chicago: University of Chicago Press, 1995.

Bloom, Lynn Z. "Escaping Voices: Women's South Pacific Internment Diaries and Memoirs." *Mosaic* 23 (Summer 1990): 101–12.

———. "Reunion and Reinterpretation: Group Biography in Process." *Biography* 13 (Summer 1990): 222–34.

———. "Women's War Stories: The Legacy of South Pacific Internment." In *Visions of War: World War II in Popular Literature and Culture,* ed. M. Paul Holsinger and Mary Ann Schofield, 66–77. Bowling Green, OH: Bowling Green State University Popular Press, 1992.

Bodnar, John E. *Remaking America: Public Memory, Commemoration, and Patriotism in the Twentieth Century.* Princeton: Princeton University Press, 1992.

Brands, H. W. *Bound to Empire: The United States and the Philippines.* New York: Oxford University Press, 1992.

Bureau of Publicity, Department of General Affairs, Japanese Military Administration. *The Official Journal of the Japanese Military Administration.* Vols. 1 and 3. Manila: Nichi Nichi Shimbun Sha, Inc., n.d.

Calica, Dan P., and Nelia Sancho, eds. *War Crimes on Asian Women; Military Sexual Slavery by Japan During World War II: The Case of the Filipino Comfort Women.* [Manila?]: Task Force on Filipina Victims of Military Sexual Slavery by Japan; Asian Women Human Rights Council–Philippine Section, 1993.

Cannon, M. Hamlin. *Leyte: The Return to the Philippines.* Washington, DC: Office of the Chief of Military History, 1954.

Castelnuovo, Shirley. "Internment and the Rules of War." *Oral History Review* 19 (Spring/Fall 1991): 115–20.

Clymer, Kenton J. *Protestant Missionaries in the Philippines, 1898–1916: An Inquiry into the American Colonial Mentality.* Urbana: University of Illinois Press, 1986.

Corbett, P. Scott. *Quiet Passages: The Exchanges of Civilians Between the United States and Japan During the Second World War.* Kent, OH: Kent State University Press, 1987.

Cott, Nancy F. *The Bonds of Womanhood:"Woman's Sphere" in New England, 1780–1835.* New Haven: Yale University Press, 1977.

Dower, John W. *War Without Mercy: Race and Power in the Pacific War.* New York: Pantheon Books, 1986.

Flanagan, Edward M., Jr. *The Los Banos Raid: The 11th Airborne Jumps at Dawn.* Novato, CA: Presidio, 1986.

Flexner, Eleanor. *Century of Struggle: The Woman's Rights Movement in the United States.* New York: Atheneum, 1971.

Gleeck, Lewis E., Jr. *The Manila Americans, 1901–1964.* Manila: Carmelo and Bauermann, 1977.

Hartendorp, A. V. H. *The Santo Tomas Story.* Ed. Frank H. Golay. New York: McGraw-Hill, 1964.

Hartmann, Susan M. *The Homefront and Beyond.* Boston: Twayne Publishers, 1982.

Hays, Sharon. *The Cultural Contradictions of Motherhood.* New Haven: Yale University Press, 1996.

Hicks, George. *The Comfort Women: Japan's Brutal Regime of Enforced Prostitution in the Second World War.* New York: W. W. Norton, 1995.

Horn, Florence. *Orphans of the Pacific: The Philippines.* New York: Reynal and Hitchcock, 1941.

Hunter, Jane. *The Gospel of Gentility: American Women Missionaries in Turn-of-the-Century China.* New Haven: Yale University Press, 1984.

Introduction. In *Behind the Lines: Gender and the Two World Wars,* ed. Margaret Randolph Higonnet et al., 1–17. New Haven: Yale University Press, 1987.

Karnow, Stanley. *In Our Image: America's Empire in the Philippines.* New York: Random House, 1989.

Kenny, Catherine. *Captives: Australian Army Nurses in Japanese Prison Camps.* St. Lucia, AUS: University of Queensland Press, 1986.

Kerber, Linda K. *Women of the Republic: Intellect and Ideology in Revolutionary America.* New York: W. W. Norton, 1980.

Kerr, E. Bartlett. *Surrender and Survival: The Experience of American POWs in the Pacific, 1941–1945.* New York: William Morrow, 1985.

Kwantes, Anne C. *Presbyterian Missionaries in the Philippines: Conduits of Social Change, 1899–1910.* Quezon City, PI: New Day, 1989.

Ladd-Taylor, Molly, and Lauri Umansky. Introduction. In *"Bad" Mothers: The Politics of Blame in Twentieth-Century America,* ed. Molly Ladd-Taylor and Lauri Umansky, 1–28. New York: New York University Press, 1998.

Lake, Marilyn. "Female Desires: The Meaning of World War II." In *Feminism and History,* ed. Joan Wallach Scott, 429–49. New York: Oxford University Press, 1996.

Leonard, Elizabeth D. *Yankee Women: Gender Battles in the Civil War.* New York: W. W. Norton, 1994.

Manchester, William. *American Ceasar: Douglas MacArthur, 1880–1964.* Boston: Little Brown, 1978.

Matsumoto, Valerie. "Japanese American Women During World War II." In *Unequal Sisters: A Multi-Cultural Reader in U.S. Women's History,* 2d ed., ed. Vicki L. Ruiz and Ellen Carol DuBois, 436–49. New York: Routledge, 1994.

Meyerowitz, Joanne, ed. *Not June Cleaver: Women and Gender in Postwar America, 1945–1960.* Philadelphia: Temple University Press, 1994.

Norman, Elizabeth M., and Sharon Eifried. "How Did They All Survive? An Analysis of American Nurses' Experiences in Japanese Prisoner-of-War Camps." *Nursing History Review* 3 (1995): 108.

Norton, Mary Beth. *Liberty's Daughters: The Revolutionary Experience of American Women, 1750–1800.* Boston: Little, Brown, 1980.

"Nurses As Prisoners." *The Oak Leaf* [Oakland, CA], 9 April 1943, photocopy of article in Navy Nurse POW File, Navy Bureau of Medicine and Surgery, Washington, D.C.

Rafael, Vincente L. "White Love: Surveillance and Nationalist Resistance in the U.S. Colonization of the Philippines." In *Cultures of United States Imperialism*, ed. Amy Kaplan and Donald E. Pease, 185–217. Durham: Duke University Press, 1993.

Rittner, Carol, and John K. Roth, eds. *Different Voices: Women and the Holocaust*. New York: Paragon House, 1993.

Scott, Joan Wallach. "Gender: A Useful Category of Historical Analysis." In *Feminism and History*, ed. Joan Wallach Scott, 152–80. New York: Oxford University Press, 1996.

Smith, Sidonie. *A Poetics of Women's Autobiography: Marginality and the Fictions of Self-Representation*. Bloomington: Indiana University Press, 1987.

Spector, Ronald H. *Eagle Against the Sun: The American War with Japan*. New York: Free Press, 1985.

Stevens, Frederic H. *Santo Tomas Internment Camp, 1942–1945*. Limited private edition: Frederic H. Stevens, 1946.

Tomblin, Barbara Brooks. *G.I. Nightingales: The Army Nurse Corps in World War II*. Lexington: University Press of Kentucky, 1996.

Wygle, Peter R. *Surviving a Japanese P.O.W. Camp: Father and Son Endure Internment in Manila During World War II*. Ventura, CA: Pathfinder Publishing, 1991.

INDEX

The names in this index, like those in the book, reflect the ones used by the women in their autobiographies. Therefore, some are incomplete and/or pseudonymous.